Circling the Earth

United States Plans for a Postwar Overseas Military Base System, 1942–1948

ELLIOTT V. CONVERSE III

Air University Press
Maxwell Air Force Base, Alabama

August 2005

Disclaimer

Opinions, conclusions, and recommendations expressed or implied within are solely those of the author and do not necessarily represent the views of Air University, the United States Air Force, the Department of Defense, or any other US government agency. Cleared for public release: distribution unlimited.

Air University Press
131 West Shumacher Avenue
Maxwell AFB AL 36112–6615

Published by Books Express Publishing
Copyright © Books Express, 2011
ISBN 978-1-78039-971-3

Books Express publications are available from all good retail and online booksellers. For publishing proposals and direct ordering please contact us at: info@books-express.com

Contents

Foreword

Much has been written about the collapse of World War II's Grand Alliance into a sharply divided postwar world, the onset of the Cold War, and the somewhat reluctant assumption of Western leadership by the United States. Plans for an extensive postwar overseas military basing structure and the nexus of political, military, and commercial interests which drove that planning are important parts of the story that have gone largely unexplored.

In many ways, the evolution of planning for overseas bases from 1942 through 1948 reflected the growing sophistication and political maturation of American foreign and military policy. In spite of the dismal failure of the League of Nations, early planning focused on basing requirements for an envisioned postwar international police force. The unabashed idealism expressed in this notion and the breathtaking assumptions required to make it feasible appear exceptionally naive to the contemporary observer, but only in the crisp focus of hindsight. Many believed that a sweeping victory by the Grand Alliance could make all things possible, even a successful international police force to keep the peace and bring order out of postwar chaos.

Meanwhile, national security concepts based on hemispheric defense continued to dominate much of the thinking about postwar basing requirements well into 1945. These were very traditional ideas with roots reaching back over 100 years to the Monroe Doctrine. In the two decades just before World War II, these traditional concepts had taken on physical substance in hemispheric defense plans, exercises, and operations, with many centered on the protection of the Panama Canal and the shipping lanes leading to and from the canal. Other prewar plans expanded the hemispheric defense idea across the Pacific to the US territories such as the Hawaiian and Philippine Islands. In sum, the notion of hemispheric defense, with its expansion across the Pacific, was deeply rooted in the American psyche, which otherwise had strong isolationist tendencies. However, the idea of an expanded hemispheric defense would be dwarfed by the demands of the postwar world.

As World War II entered its final phases, friction with the Soviet Union grew, and it became quite clear that American national security had to be considered from a global perspective. The perceived threat of a hostile Soviet Union (determined to spread its control and influence) was the principal driver behind the globalization basing plans. A second was the obvious truth that for the foreseeable future, only the United States had the wherewithal to effectively oppose the Soviets. Great Britain was virtually bankrupt, and its people were exhausted from the strain of the war. France was in tatters both physically and politically. Germany was prostrate in its own rubble and divided between East and West. Moreover, to a great many victims of German aggression, the thought of a rearmed West Germany, even as a bulwark against the Soviet menace, was anathema.

A third driver of overseas base planning was the rise of so-called *atomic airpower*, widely assumed to be the lead military element used to deter Soviet aggression. Airpower required bases within reasonable range of the Soviet Union, particularly in the age of propeller-driven B-29 and B-50 bombers. Only the controversial B-36 bomber, which would not begin entering the active inventory of the US Air Force until the summer of 1948, had true intercontinental range while carrying a nuclear payload. The day of the all-jet heavy-bomber and a range-extending aerial tanker force was even further in the future. As a result, bases and basing rights around the periphery of the Soviet Union became a critically important objective.

At least two other factors also shaped the overseas base planning process. One was the desire on the part of civilian interests to further the development of American commercial aviation, the disparate requirements of which did not always mesh well with perceived military necessities. Interservice rivalries, now exacerbated by the addition of the newly independent US Air Force to the fray and sharp reductions in postwar defense budgets, also shaped the planning process. Bitter squabbles erupted over postwar service roles and missions as each service attempted to carve out or protect its niche in a nuclear world they only vaguely understood. These internecine struggles had deleterious effects on the planning process.

The overseas base planning process reflected the evolution and growing sophistication of American strategic thinking during the tumultuous period from 1942 through 1948. The results of the planning shaped, in many ways, the East-West struggle for much of the second half of the twentieth century. Elliott Converse has performed a great and remarkable service by capturing the often confusing and chaotic essence of the base planning effort during this turbulent period. His exhaustive research brings the issues, attitudes, and personalities involved into clear focus. This is a seminal work.

DENNIS M. DREW
Colonel, USAF, Retired
Professor and Associate Dean
School of Advanced Air and Space Studies

About the Author

Elliott V. Converse III is a retired Air Force colonel with a doctorate in history from Princeton University. His career included assignments as a faculty member at the US Air Force Academy and the Air War College, as an air intelligence officer in Southeast Asia, as a strategic planner with the Joint Chiefs of Staff, and as commander of the Air Force Historical Research Agency, Maxwell AFB. After retiring from the Air Force, Dr. Converse taught history at Reinhardt College, Waleska, Georgia, and again at the Air Force Academy. He is currently the lead historian on a project sponsored by the Office of the Secretary of Defense and the military services to write a history of the acquisition of major weapon systems by the armed forces since World War II. His volume in the series will cover the years 1945–1958. Dr. Converse is also the principal author of *The Exclusion of Black Soldiers from the Medal of Honor in World War II* (1997) and editor of *Forging the Sword: Selecting, Educating, and Training Cadets and Junior Officers in the Modern World* (1998).

Preface

My interest in post–World War II overseas military base planning began in a research seminar on the History of American Foreign Relations at the University of Wisconsin in 1971. I resumed my study of the subject at Princeton University in 1975 and completed my dissertation, "United States Plans for a Postwar Overseas Military Base System, 1942–1948," in 1984. This book is an adaptation of that dissertation. I found the topic both interesting and significant because of the conjuncture between force and diplomacy that overseas base selection represented and because of its ties to the study of strategic planning, the nature of American civil-military relationships, the controversial questions of the origins of the Cold War, and the character of American foreign policy. I was, as were many students during these years, much influenced by "New Left" or "revisionist" historiography. My research and conclusions did not, in the end, reinforce that general interpretation, but the interpretation substantially enlarged my understanding of history.

Many people contributed to my graduate education and to the preparation of the dissertation. Among them are the teachers who introduced me to the serious study of history: Professors Pierce C. Mullen, Alton B. Oviatt, and Richard B. Roeder of Montana State University; University of Wisconsin professors Edward M. Coffman and John A. DeNovo, who began my graduate education in military and diplomatic history; and Princeton University professors Cyril E. Black, Richard D. Challener, Robert Darnton, Arno J. Mayer, and Carl E. Schorske, each of whom played an important role in my doctoral program. A special thank you goes to Dr. John M. Thompson who, during the year he served as a distinguished visiting professor at the United States Air Force Academy (USAFA), provided suggestions and assistance at a critical stage.

Numerous skilled archivists cheerfully assisted my research. I especially want to mention Mrs. Priscilla Sutcliffe of the Special Collections Division of the Robert Muldrow Cooper Library, Clemson University; Mr. Edward J. Boone Jr. of the MacArthur Memorial Archives; Mr. William H. Cunliffe and Mr. Charles A. Shaughnessy of the Modern Military Branch staff at the National

Archives; Dr. Dean C. Allard, Mr. Bernard Cavalcante, Mrs. Gerri Judkins, and Mrs. Nina Statum of the Operational Archives Branch of the United States Naval Historical Center; Mrs. Nancy Bressler of the Seeley G. Mudd Manuscript Library, Princeton University; Mr. James N. Eastman Jr., Mrs. Judy Endicott, Ms. Kathy Nichols, and Mr. Wayne Robinson of the United States Air Force (USAF) Albert F. Simpson Historical Research Center (now renamed the Air Force Historical Research Agency); Mr. Dennis Bilger, Mr. Harry Clark, Mr. Philip Lagerquist, and Mr. Warren Ohrvall of the Harry S. Truman Library; and Mr. Duane Reed of the USAFA Library's Special Collections Branch.

Mr. Charles B. Gary and Vice Adm E. R. McLean Jr., USN, retired, who participated in some of the planning this study describes, were particularly generous in offering detailed first-hand information about the postwar base planning process. Their help, however, does not represent an endorsement of the historical interpretations contained in this work. I alone am responsible for those.

During most of the period I worked on this dissertation, I was privileged to be assigned to the faculty of the Department of History at the USAFA, and I am indebted to Brig Gen Alfred F. Hurley, USAF, retired, former head of the department, and to the United States Air Force for giving me the opportunity to pursue doctoral training. My former colleagues in the department, Lt Col Harry R. Borowski, USAF, retired; Col Thomas A. Keaney, USAF, retired; Brig Gen Carl W. Reddel, USAF, retired; and Col John F. Shiner, USAF, retired, each an accomplished historian, gave the kind of support and encouragement only friends can give.

I was pleased that the Air University Press decided to publish the dissertation. In this respect, I am grateful to Col Dennis M. Drew, USAF, retired, and associate dean of the Air University School of Advanced Air and Space Studies; Mr. Robert B. Lane, former director of the Air University Library; Dr. Richard R. Muller, former dean of education at the Air Command and Staff College; and Dr. James R. W. Titus, former dean of research at the Air University Center (now College) for Aerospace Doctrine, Research and Education.

Introduction

Before World War II the United States possessed only a handful of overseas military installations. These included bases in the Philippine Islands, Guam in the Mariana Islands, Wake Island, Midway Island, and the Hawaiian Islands, all in the Pacific; and bases in the Panama Canal Zone, Cuba, Puerto Rico, and the Virgin Islands in the Caribbean. By the end of the war, the United States had established military installations of one kind or another at more than 3,000 locations around the world.[1] The American military sought to retain only a small percentage of them following the war; even so, one scholar has called the number of postwar bases the Army Air Forces (AAF) alone planned to maintain "an imperial system of overseas bases encircling the earth."[2] Another has suggested that postwar basing plans reflected the military's acceptance, as early as 1945, of a "global peacemaking" role for American military forces.[3] Whether the postwar base network was "imperial" or the military saw a responsibility to police the world can be debated. Nevertheless, there was a dramatic expansion from the prewar period in the number of overseas bases the military believed would be necessary, demonstrating by 1945 an appreciably enlarged conception of national defense requirements.

This book examines the American military establishment's planning between 1942 and 1948 for a system of postwar overseas bases. Certainly, bases were but one aspect of military planning and that, in turn, only one feature of the US government's overall postwar policies. But connections do exist between base planning and larger issues such as the nature of military planning, the effects of institutional or interservice rivalry, the state of civil-military relationships, and the character of postwar American foreign policy.

A detailed analysis of postwar base planning is useful for several reasons. Most important to the military professional, it reveals the inner workings and complexities of military planning. Who in the military services actually drew up plans for the postwar base system? How did they formulate their recommendations for bases? What factors had a bearing upon those recommendations? Some may be surprised to learn that traditional military considerations such as the threat posed by a potential enemy or new developments in weapons technology were only one element—and often not the most important element—in the selection of overseas bases. Other factors were the pressures of interservice rivalry, the concerns and active involvement of civilian officials in the defense establishment and in other parts of the government, anticipated reductions in postwar defense budgets, and the largely negative reaction of foreign governments and peoples to the presence of US military forces and bases.

Examination of the factors bearing on base planning illuminates, in turn, the military's role in and impact on national security policy formulation. Choosing the location for a military base is a highly political decision; moreover, it is political in several dimensions. In terms of international politics, the planned location of a base or series of bases reflects the nation's perception of its role in the international state system, particularly with respect to the application of force. Domestically, recommendations for bases, especially in terms of how many bases or the extent of their development, indicated military and civilian leaders' assessment of the degree of popular support for a strong defense establishment. In addition, base planning, as it became entangled in interservice and interagency rivalries, reflected the pressures of bureaucratic politics. American military planners, as this book shows, did not divorce themselves from the political dimension of overseas base selection. Civilian government officials, notably in the War and Navy Departments, sometimes resented what they viewed as military intrusion into the civilian policy-making arena and sought to assert their authority. Thus, a close look at military base planning provides insight into the condition of American civil-military relations during and immediately following World War II.

Analysis of postwar base planning is also useful for understanding the roots of postwar American foreign policy. Some scholars, usually labeled as "New Left" or simply "revisionist," argued during the 1960s and 1970s that pressure for postwar economic expansion and not fear for physical security was the primary driving force in US foreign policy after 1945. This book will assess this thesis by examining the role of commercial aviation in base planning and in the expansion of US military activity abroad.

Commercial aviation promised to be a vital element in postwar American economic prosperity. Indeed, some maintained that American commercial aviation was on the verge of the same sort of tremendous growth that the railroads had experienced in the 1840s.[4] Many hoped American air carriers would be able to penetrate every corner of the globe in search of investment opportunities, markets, and raw materials for American business and industry. Shortly after the death of President Franklin D. Roosevelt, President Harry S. Truman told Secretary of Commerce Henry A. Wallace that, along with reparations, the future of international aviation was "the most important postwar international problem."[5] In the 1940s little difference existed between an airfield used for military purposes and one used for commercial aviation. Civil aviation leaders, top military officers, and other government officials recognized the potential in linking the two. From the beginning of the postwar planning process, they hoped to integrate military and civil airfields into a vast network, assuring both physical and economic security for the United States. How much weight these expectations carried in decisions concerning postwar military base planning is considered in the hope of contributing new evidence to the question of whether economic expansion or physical security was the predominant motive in American foreign policy after 1945.

US government records are the principal documentary sources used in this book. The most important official military records were those of the Joint Chiefs of Staff, followed in significance by the records of the individual services. For explaining the Army's viewpoint, the files of the Operations Division of the War Department General Staff and the files of the chief of staff were vital. The Navy's key records included CNO-COMINCH (chief of naval operations-commander in chief US fleet), the Strategic Plans Division, the Political-Military Division, and the files of the secretary of the Navy. Air Force records are scattered hither and yon and are not well organized. Those most useful for this book were the records of the assistant secretary of war for air and the large and heterogeneous collection of documents located at the US Air Force Historical Research Agency. In addition to military records, the official records and personal papers in the Truman Library were essential. Other government records that proved valuable were National Security Council papers, the records of the State Department's Office of European Affairs, the Minutes of the Committee of Three, the files of the State-War-Navy Coordinating Committee, the records of the Air Coordinating Committee, and published documents in the *Foreign Relations of the United States* series. Individual manuscript collections were also an important source of information, namely the papers of Gen Henry H. Arnold, Adm Richard E. Byrd, James F. Byrnes, James V. Forrestal, Adm William D. Leahy, Adm Chester W. Nimitz, Robert P. Patterson, and Gen Carl Spaatz.

Anyone who has served in government knows that the work is largely anonymous; the final draft of a plan or program staffed through layers of the bureaucracy very rarely credits its original author. Sometimes the work is altered radically; sometimes it remains essentially unchanged. Some effort has been made here to identify those who wrote postwar base studies or prepared base plans, not so much to make the story more human but more to reveal some of the individual intellectual perspectives that went into base planning.

The author knows well this book's limits. The book is the US government's and largely the American military's story of postwar base planning. There are other stories worth telling. How, for example, did Americans outside the government react to the prospect of far-flung military bases? In fact, an extensive public debate roughly coinciding with the years covered by this book took place. What happened as American officials sought to obtain military base rights in foreign countries? As many stories exist in this respect as there are nations the United States approached for postwar base privileges. To tell one of these stories properly requires investigation of the archives of each nation involved. Finally, perhaps the most dramatic story of all: How did the Soviet Union view the postwar world? What did its military planning look like? The complete story of the Cold War's origins can be written only when scholars with unrestricted access to the Soviet Union's documentary records explain that nation's part in it.

Notes

1. United Press, "U. S. Spent 13 Billion Abroad in 5 Years On Service Pay, Bases, Materials, Loans," *New York Times*, 26 November 1945, 12.

2. Daniel Yergin, *Shattered Peace: The Origins of the Cold War and the National Security State* (Boston: Houghton Mifflin Company, 1977), 202.

3. Michael S. Sherry, *Preparing for the Next War: American Plans for Postwar Defense, 1941–1945* (New Haven: Yale University Press, 1977), 238.

4. L. Welch Pogue, chairman, Civil Aeronautics Board, address to the National Aviation Clinic, Oklahoma City, Okla., 20 November 1945, in folder 657 (1945–August 1946), box 1520, Official File, Papers of Harry S. Truman, Truman Library, Independence, Mo.

5. Diary entry, 27 April 1945, in John Morton Blum, ed., *The Price of Vision: The Diary of Henry A. Wallace, 1942–1946* (Boston: Houghton Mifflin Company, 1973), 437.

THIS PAGE INTENTIONALLY LEFT BLANK

Chapter 1

The First Plans, 1942–1943

Military planning for the postwar period began before the Japanese attacked Pearl Harbor. In November 1941 Army chief of staff general George C. Marshall, in order to avoid the disarray and weakening of American military strength that had accompanied the Army's demobilization after World War I, called Brig Gen John McAuley Palmer out of retirement to serve as his special adviser for postwar plans.[1] But formal groups whose sole job was drawing up postwar military plans—the War Department's Special Planning Division, the Navy's Special Planning Section, and the Army Air Forces' (AAF) Post War Division—were not established until mid-1943.[2] Consideration of postwar issues, however, did not wait upon the creation of specialized structures, and officers assigned to the Joint Chiefs of Staff (JCS) organization first dealt with the complex problems raised by the proposal for a system of postwar overseas military bases in late 1942.[3]

The intensity of American military interservice rivalry is legendary. Not even a total war silenced it, as evidenced by the clash in the first half of 1943 between the Army and the AAF on one side and the Navy on the other over the control of land-based aircraft in antisubmarine warfare operations. This particular difference of opinion was but one facet of the larger and longer struggle between the proponents of the primacy of airpower in warfare—and organizational autonomy for the nation's air arm—and those fiercely resisting any diminution of the older services' influences. Until the war ended and the Navy and AAF emerged as the principal combatants (the Army having made its peace with the aviators during the war), the battle was mostly sub rosa. One of its features was the tendency for all the services (though most pronounced in the Navy) to hold their postwar plans, particularly those indicating force levels, closely to their institutional vests. Only the Army and the AAF coordinated their postwar programs to any appreciable extent.[4] The location of postwar bases abroad proved, however, to be one part of the postwar planning process that saw a significant measure of interservice coordination. This was true for several reasons. First, President Franklin D. Roosevelt (FDR) initially threw the bases issue to the JCS. Second, the acquisition of base rights in foreign countries meant involvement by the State Department and attendant pressure from that quarter for the military to consolidate base requirements. Finally, as historian Michael Sherry convincingly argues, American military men, whatever their differences, "found they had the same goals and worked together to secure them. They shared a similar past and believed they faced a common future of international uncertainty, explosive technology and public neglect."[5]

The sum of common assumptions about postwar defense making up the military's worldview was what Sherry calls an "ideology of national preparedness."[6] American military leaders almost unanimously believed (and their civilian superiors shared their perceptions) that war would come again, that it would be a total war, similar to the conflict then raging, and that it would be provoked by a modern, industrial, totalitarian-type state. Since it was assumed the attack would be sudden and carried out with the most advanced long-range weapons, the oceans would no longer offer the protection and the time for preparation as they had in the past. For these reasons, the United States must maintain a military establishment much larger than that of the prewar period, capable of rapid mobilization, and able to deter aggression or, better yet, to stamp out danger at its first appearance.[7]

In late December 1942, amidst this atmosphere of a developing "preparedness" worldview, FDR asked the JCS to prepare a study of locations for air facilities for an "International Police Force."[8] Recently, Vice President Henry A. Wallace had spoken publicly of his vision of an international air force to keep the peace after the war.[9] But the catalyst for the president's interest on this occasion appears to have been a memorandum from the Australian legation urging development of an alternate air route across the Pacific to reduce the danger that a Japanese thrust in the southwest Pacific might cut off communication from North America. The proposed new route was Washington, D.C., to Miami, Florida, to a point on the west coast of North

America (perhaps Acapulco, Mexico), across the island stepping-stones of French Oceania (Clipperton Island, the Marquesas Islands, and the Society Islands), to Aitutaki in the Cook Islands, and thence to Auckland, New Zealand, and Sydney, Australia. The route would require the construction of airfields in both the Marquesas and on Clipperton.[10] The Australians suggested that any necessary preparatory work "be shared between the governments concerned."[11] In 1943 FDR dispatched an expedition to survey the French South Sea island sites for postwar military bases and commercial airports. Toward the end of 1944, a British effort to develop such a route unilaterally prompted the landing of an armed US Navy observation party on Clipperton Island and a sharp letter from FDR to Prime Minister Winston Churchill.[12] All of this indicates that FDR may have been less concerned with an international police force in 1942 than he was in preventing any non-Western hemispheric power from establishing a military presence on Clipperton Island, or in the role that an air route through France's South Central Pacific possessions might play in the growth of postwar commercial aviation.

Whatever the president's motives in asking for the base study, the military had difficulty fulfilling his request. The JCS first referred it to their top planning group, the Joint Planning Staff (JPS), who in turn directed that a special subcommittee of officers from the three services prepare the report.[13] The JPS subcommittee met twice in January 1943 and considered several models for global systems of air bases as background material in their own deliberations. One of these, a proposal known to Vice President Wallace and drawn up by Col George F. Schulgen, a War Department General Staff officer, provided for the creation of a "World Security Force" composed primarily of heavy bombers stationed at approximately 50 mutually supporting bases determined by the location of the world's energy resources.[14] A second scheme, authored in September 1942 by another General Staff officer, was a plan for defeating the Axis powers by using airpower operating from forward bases in advance of seven major base areas in Siberia, China, Africa, India, and South America.[15] A third plan was contained in an October 1942 memorandum to General Marshall from Maj

Gen Thomas T. Handy, chief of the General Staff's Operations Division (OPD). This plan assumed the United States would be on the offensive in the Pacific, on the strategic defensive in the European theater, and conducting air attacks against the Nazis in northern Europe from bases on the "Arctic shores of North America, Greenland, Iceland, and Spitzbergen."[16] The three plans had several common features: each relied on air bombardment for its execution; each was a proposal for use in the war then in progress (though Schulgen's plan was also designed for the postwar world); finally, each used a polar projection of the earth's surface to illustrate the strategic importance of the Northern Hemisphere.

The JPS subcommittee, however, never got far in selecting air bases for an international police force. At a conference on 25 January 1943, the subcommittee chairman (an Army officer) and two other members (AAF and Navy officers) acknowledged the impossibility of identifying specific bases without the guidance of "certain basic assumptions" stemming from an in-depth analysis of the "overall political and international implications of an International Police Force." In short, before determining the location of facilities through or from which military force was to be applied, the officers needed to know the probable condition of the postwar world. To ensure that there would be no delay in answering the JCS directive, the committee agreed to make its own assumptions. In its view, an international police force was to be "essentially an Air Force" with facilities located along "the Strategic Air Routes of the World" employed to "eliminate subversive or dangerous focal points before they can develop to the point where they become a danger to the security of the world."[17] At this juncture, however, the committee's senior naval member, Capt M. B. Gardner, informed the chairman that he had been directed by the Navy Department to request a recess in the group's activities because, insofar as assumptions about the general implications of an international police force were concerned, there was "no factual data to guide us in these matters and, so far as we can determine, no sufficiently coherent authoritative ideas on the subject to form the framework, composition and coloring of the picture, a part of which we have been directed to paint."[18]

No direct evidence exists, but it is possible, as one scholar has implied, that the Navy's real motive for bringing a halt to the committee's work was a hostile reaction to the dominant role envisioned for airpower in the international police force. A letter from Adm Ernest J. King, chief of naval operations, to the secretary of the Navy on 9 February 1943, requesting that the Navy's General Board independently examine the postwar employment of an international police force and possible uses of air bases, seems to support this interpretation.[19] In any event the JCS, agreeing that they must come up with a common policy relative to an international police force, transferred the entire matter to the Joint Strategic Survey Committee (JSSC)—a group of three senior officers who advised the JCS "on broad questions of national policy and world strategy."[20]

* * *

While the JPS subcommittee struggled through its largely futile motions, civilian government officials also approached the postwar international air base problem, but in the context of postwar commercial aviation. In September 1942 Assistant Secretary of State A. A. Berle, premier analyst of the modern corporation, member of FDR's original "Brains Trust," expert on Latin American affairs, and a vigorous proponent of international civil aviation expansion, had written Secretary of State Cordell Hull of his belief that aviation would have a greater influence on American foreign interests and American foreign policy than any other nonpolitical consideration. Arguing that aviation's effect on future American defense and commerce would be comparable to the effect that sea power had had in the past, Berle declared, "We cannot remain unconcerned as to the location of airports, present and postwar, control of those airports, and arrangements by which they are controlled and maintained."[21] Early in January 1943, Berle, apparently responding to initiatives undertaken by the British in the field of postwar civil air transport, obtained permission from Hull to set up an informal departmental working group, later known officially as the Interdepartmental Committee on International Aviation.[22]

5

The working group held its first meeting in Berle's office on 7 January 1943. The meeting's chief purpose, as reported by Assistant Secretary of War for Air Robert A. Lovett in a lengthy memorandum to Gen Henry H. Arnold, AAF commander, "was to consider ways and means of obtaining some unity of approach and planning in connection with the postwar problem of international aviation." Lovett summarized his own remarks before the committee, indicating that his emphasis was on the need for the United States to ensure that the heavy American investment in the development of air routes (including the construction of airfields and installation of communications, navigation, and weather facilities) throughout the world for use during the war should be put to good advantage in obtaining both postwar military base rights and commercial aviation privileges. Additionally, Lovett said he told the committee that in the Caribbean and South America, "we [the AAF] feel strongly both from the point of view of military defense as well as from the point of view of peacetime commercial operations [that] treaties and agreements should provide that no foreign owned or operated line other than a United States line shall be permitted to operate in this territory."[23]

Lovett also told those assembled in Berle's office of the importance of protecting American rights to airway facilities in Canada "since on a proper air map representing the globe, the four most likely airline operations with modern equipment all pass over Canadian territory or require landing privileges therein."[24] He went on to point out that in the next war the greatest danger to the United States would most probably be an unannounced air attack on the nation's industrial centers via one of the four northern routes.[25]

Lovett's letter to General Arnold highlighted a distinctive characteristic of the postwar overseas base issue: a network of military air bases for national defense or an international police force was seen as intimately related to any system of facilities supporting commercial aviation. Military and civil aircraft were likely to use many of the same routes (Lovett had mentioned those to Europe via Canada). Moreover, since routes determined the location of airfields, electronic aids to navigation, and weather stations, military and civil aircraft could share these as well.

The pressure to link postwar military base needs and commercial aviation requirements originating both from within and without the military establishment elicited considerable cooperation among the various government departments. At the same time, such pressure also generated friction between the uniformed military and civilians—tensions caused mostly by the former's contention that *military* considerations must take precedence.

* * *

In February 1943, as directed by the JCS, the three senior officers of the JSSC, Army Lt Gen Stanley D. Embick, Vice Adm Russell Willson, and Maj Gen Muir S. Fairchild of the AAF met to fashion the military's policy toward an international police force.[26] Their first task was to define the scope of the problem under study.[27] Significantly, in their instructions to the JSSC, the JCS had already subtly enlarged the field of inquiry by describing the president's directive as covering "postwar use of airbases, *including their use for international police forces*" [emphasis added].[28] The JSSC cited this wording change, the broad scope of the General Board review, and the investigation being conducted by the Interdepartmental Committee on International Aviation as justification for declaring that their job was "to make a study of a post-war worldwide system of air bases, including their use for International Military Forces—the subject to be examined primarily from the military point of view—in order to recommend a policy to be followed by the Joint Chiefs of Staff."[29] The JSSC, in sum, intended to analyze air bases from three angles: national defense, an international military force, and, to some degree, commercial aviation.

The JCS debated the study's broadening scope during their meetings on 9 and 23 March 1943. There was no objection to considering postwar overseas air bases in relation to national defense or an international police force; but a difference of opinion surfaced over whether the JCS should make any recommendations concerning commercial air transportation. Adm William D.

Leahy, military chief of staff to the president, stood alone in maintaining that the JCS should refrain from commenting on anything that was not of strictly military significance. The other officers, including Admiral King and General Arnold, argued that military use could not be divorced from commercial use. Lt Gen Joseph T. McNarney, the Army's deputy chief of staff, reminded everyone present that "the commercial bases originally set up in South America had been designed primarily for future military use." General Arnold thought that while it might be desirable to avoid entanglement in the subject of commercial aviation, he doubted such restraint was possible and believed that the British were linking postwar commercial with military aviation—no matter what the United States did. The JCS finally agreed that in the policy guidance then being prepared by the JSSC there should be no specific reference to commercial aviation but a general statement recognizing the close relationship between postwar military and commercial interests.[30]

The JSSC papers of March 1943 represented the first high-level formal expression not only of the military's idea of postwar base needs but also their view of the likely pattern of postwar international relations.[31] The JSSC analysis closely approximated Roosevelt's "Four Policemen" concept, which assumed the principal Allies would be able to maintain their "solidarity" beyond the war's end.[32]

After the defeat of Japan, the United States, Great Britain, and Russia (assisted by China) would keep the peace in various zones until particular areas were ready to be turned over to the supervision of a yet to be determined international organization. During this immediate postwar period (albeit one of indeterminate length) the United States would be responsible for an "American Zone," Great Britain and Russia for a "Europe, Africa, and Middle East Zone," and the three major powers (plus China) for a "Far Eastern Zone."[33] Once the world peacekeeping organization was in full operation, Generals Embick and Fairchild and Admiral Willson felt it would retain a strong regional flavor since, "viewed realistically," it was difficult to imagine any international military forces "as being multi-national in composition and worldwide in responsibilities."[34] The JSSC officers thought it more probable there would be a police body for each of the three zones, with the major power or powers contributing the lion's share of its region's armed forces. The JSSC cautioned that an international organization might never be established or, once created, might not last. Therefore, the United States must look first to its own defense, Western Hemisphere security, and maintenance of the American position in the Far East. Military bases were necessary to achieve these goals, and, for this reason, the acquisition and development of "adequate" bases must be among the United States's "primary war aims." Such a policy would not be inconsistent with "ultimate collective security," however, because "the bases acquired and developed with the primary aim of assuring our own security will be available under adequate safeguards for international military forces, when established."[35]

Initially, the JSSC specified the bases for both national defense and an international military force in a general way. The location of bases, more properly base areas, indicated what the JSSC meant by the "American Zone." In the Atlantic the United States should retain for "national security" purposes rights to bases in all areas leased from Great Britain in 1941, bases elsewhere in the Caribbean, and on the northeastern Brazilian coast. An international military force might require air bases in other parts of Latin America, although the United States would not. As for the Pacific, the United States should fortify a chain of bases west from Hawaii to and including the Philippine Islands and the Bonin Islands.[36] The bases would be "essential to the defense of our position in the Far East, and valuable for international military purposes." The United States should also control or "neutralize" all other islands south of the 30th parallel but north of the equator. Bases along air routes to the southwest Pacific, most south of the equator, might belong to an international force.[37]

While the JSSC bowed to the JCS's insistence that any policy guidance not refer specifically to the tie between military bases and commercial aviation facilities, the longer paper of 15 March frequently linked the two. The JSSC declared that the American investment in overseas bases would be a valuable bargaining chip in obtaining postwar commercial air privileges throughout Europe, Asia, and Africa. Moreover, routes across the north, central, and south Atlantic and southwest Pacific should be developed and maintained for both "international military and commercial purposes." Specific places mentioned in the military-commercial context were the Azores, Galapagos Islands, and Clipperton Island.[38]

The JCS received the JSSC papers coolly. Although evidently satisfied with national defense coverage in the Pacific, all (but especially Admirals Leahy and King) thought the United States must have many more bases in the Atlantic to provide sufficiently for national security. The service chiefs and their deputies noted Greenland, Iceland, the Azores, West Africa (Dakar in Senegal), and Ascension Island as key omissions in the JSSC study. Admiral Willson, apparently the only officer from the JSSC attending the meeting, defended the committee's work, arguing that ambitious American demands for airfields "would conflict with the interests of other countries." A postwar peace conference would require give-and-take, and the United States should not be "overreaching." These points failed to sway the JCS, however. Admiral King, for one, "felt that to limit the location of bases for national defense puts ammunition in the hands of the isolationists," something he was loath to do. Consequently, the JSSC was told to go back to the drawing board and present a paper with separate listings of bases for national defense and an international police force.[39]

The revision, however, still failed to satisfy the JCS. The JSSC strategists, to the annoyance of their superiors, had not designated any international-military-force air bases in continental areas. Their explanation for the omission was that in order to select continental bases, one must know to what extent individual nations would cooperate in a collective security system. Furthermore, the JSSC officers had declined to add to the list of bases for national defense a single one of the strategic sites brought up by the JCS at the 30 March meeting. Instead, all were placed in the category of bases suitable for an international police force. General Arnold, who had previously expressed the opinion that all islands in the Atlantic were necessary for national defense, remarked that the JSSC's choices "both for the international police force and the needs of national defense seem to leave out some rather important bases, without adequate explanation as to why they were omitted." Admiral King noted that a fruitful approach to the complex problem of identifying international-force bases might be to locate them in places where they could protect the well-established trade routes. Again, the study was rejected—Embick, Willson, and Fairchild were told to redo it but made no further progress.[40] Finally, in September 1943 the JCS order initiating the study was withdrawn.[41]

The only indication of postwar air base requirements to come out of the JCS before November 1943 was a letter sent to Berle dated 16 March 1943. Prepared by the JSSC, the letter gave a brief summary of the base areas the JCS believed to be in "the interests of the national security of the United States and of the other nations in the Western Hemisphere." These included base rights in the areas leased from Great Britain in March 1941, the remainder of the Caribbean, the Galapagos Islands, the northeastern Brazilian coast, and Clipperton Island. The letter also suggested that after the war, control of the Japanese Mandated Islands (former German possessions transferred to Japanese supervision by the League of Nations following World War I) should pass to the United States. Base rights along three transatlantic air routes: (1) a route across Africa, (2) a route across the Middle East extending to the Far East, and (3) a route through the southwest Pacific would be required to support the US air component of an international military force.[42]

Both the JCS and the officers on the JSSC were aware of the many uncertainties surrounding postwar bases. Perhaps, for this reason the former chose not to press the air base project to completion. None of these top military leaders had manifested much enthusiasm for the idea of international peacekeeping in the first place. They preferred a division of the world into spheres of influence, with their primary concern providing bases for national defense. The nub of the disagreement between them was over the size of the American Zone. The JCS argued for a greatly expanded American sphere in the Atlantic, but the JSSC, apparently not perceiving the effect of the war on England's ability to wield military power abroad, clung to

the traditional view of the eastern Atlantic as a British responsibility.[43]

* * *

In the first half of 1943, the admirals on the Navy's General
Board, in obedience to Secretary of the Navy Frank Knox's directives, also investigated the topic of postwar bases.[44] Since
the beginning of the century, the voice of the General Board
had been heard in the realm of high-level naval policy and
strategy. By 1939 its influence on strategy formulation had
markedly diminished, although it still served as a "deliberative
body that considered any sort of problem assigned to it by the
Secretary."[45] The historian of the Navy's postwar planning contends that it made little imprint on that activity.[46] Nevertheless,
in early 1943 no group had yet been formally assigned to postwar planning in the Navy. So Admiral King's request to Secretary Knox for the General Board to examine the matter of postwar air bases and an international police force was quite
natural.[47]

The fundamental premises on which the General Board
built its analysis are similar to the assumptions made by the
JSSC. An American commitment to a worldwide pact intended
to keep the peace immediately after the war was unwise. The
best guarantee of good order around the globe was an effective
combination of the four great powers, the United States, Great
Britain, Russia, and China. Only on this firm foundation (and
after an unspecified though obviously lengthy time) could a
workable international peacekeeping organization be built.
The General Board officers, like their JSSC counterparts, stayed
away from fixing continental air base locations for an international police force and considered only the oceans. Since the
seas were the focus of attention, it was determined that naval
as well as air facilities should be included (the JSSC recognized this fact also). However, at this point, the General Board
steered a course quite different from that of the JCS staff officers. Since they named no continental bases, the admirals
saw the problem as essentially one of "policing the high seas,"
and (either shrewdly or opaquely) defined this largely as a task

for naval forces. Only the United States and Great Britain, however, would have strong navies; therefore, "the policing of the sea areas will necessarily devolve upon them." But how were the oceans to be divided? In the Pacific, the General Board recommended that the American sphere take in everything to "the shores of China" except the areas contiguous to British Dominion or Dutch territory. The General Board, as we shall see, had banished the French from the Pacific. In the Atlantic, the admirals proposed a kind of twentieth-century, papal line of demarcation by dividing the American and British spheres, at 25° west longitude. On the west lay Greenland and the Azores, while to the east were Iceland, the Cape Verde Islands, the West African bulge, and Ascension Island. The board listed 50 places that were to function for both national defense and international policing (commerce, they claimed, had been a slight factor in the selections). Some were outside the American Zone (e.g., Iceland, Dakar, Liberia, Ascension Island, and Shanghai, China), but the General Board tagged these as joint projects from which the United States might better "enforce law and order in its own spheres" or help others do so in theirs. All of these arrangements were to be confirmed by early negotiations with the British.[48]

Two additional General Board papers, nothing if not detailed briefs for American aggrandizement in the Pacific, quickly followed and supplemented the basic study. In "Post War Sovereignty over Certain Islands of the North Pacific," the admirals called for the United States to acquire the Marshall, Caroline, and Mariana Islands (former German possessions mandated to Japan after World War I), Marcus Island, and the Volcano and Bonin groups (small Japanese-owned islands lying between Japan and the mandates). The board cited the preservation of American security and a probable commitment for postwar defense of an independent Philippines as reasons justifying these transfers. According to the board, this would not constitute "territorial aggrandizement" because the Japanese themselves had referred to the islands as "unsinkable aircraft carriers." Taking them out of Japan's hands would simply be "part of her disarmament."[49]

13

In its analysis of the Central and South Pacific regions, the General Board suggested some rather startling changes, supporting them with the flimsiest of arguments. Pointing to the jumble of sovereignties south of the equator (the United States, Great Britain, New Zealand, and France all owned territory there), and the fact that the board expected the United States to "extend its policing responsibility" almost to New Zealand and Australia, the admirals urged that the "political situation in the area be simplified in order to facilitate the military task at hand." What the General Board meant by "simplification of the political and administrative situation" was for the United States to acquire sovereignty over: (1) British claims in the Gilbert, Ellice, Phoenix, and Line Islands; (2) the New Zealand mandate of Western Samoa; and (3) *all* French territory in the South Pacific (except the French half of the New Hebrides, which should pass to British control) from the large island of New Caledonia in the extreme southwest Pacific near the Australian coast, east several thousand miles to the Marquesas Islands. None of these changes added up to "territorial aggrandizement," asserted the General Board, because they would not occur "at the expense of a defeated enemy," thus conforming to the Atlantic Charter's "spirit" (surely a novel interpretation of that document). Obviously, as far as the General Board was concerned, all was indeed fair in both love and war. While suggesting no specific course of action, board members concluded that all "current and future planning" should be directed toward attaining the stated political objectives.[50]

What makes the General Board's air and naval base studies so noteworthy is that, unlike the JSSC papers, these reached the president.[51] In a June 1943 letter to Knox, Roosevelt recalled that the two had previously discussed postwar air routes west from the Panama Canal and South America, and he was now interested in finding out what progress the Navy had made in its air bases inquiry. Roosevelt's letter to the Navy secretary, just as his December communication to the JCS, revealed the president's special attraction for the South Pacific. "I have particularly in mind," he wrote, "the islands of the Tuamotu Archipelago and the Marquesas."[52] Roosevelt suggested "air transport experts should visit these islands on whatever craft can be made available without interfering with the war effort."[53] Knox then forwarded the three General Board base papers to the president, who replied that he had read the studies with interest but "the sweeping changes in sovereignty recommended by the Board may not be attainable, and, from an economic point of view, all of the acquisitions recommended may not be desirable." For this reason, Roosevelt thought it necessary to decide "now" what islands "promise to be of value as commercial airports in the future." He wanted another study of the area based on "charts and distances" to be followed by an expedition of "commercial aviation experts," preferably headed by Adm Richard E. Byrd, the polar explorer.[54]

At the end of July, the General Board submitted a letter covering postwar air routes from the Panama Canal and South America to New Zealand and Australia. Declaring this time that no military considerations had intruded upon their analysis, the admirals selected a northern route (Canal Zone to Clipperton to the Marquesas to Samoa) and an extreme southern route (Valparaiso, Chile, to Easter Island to the Marquesas), named seven airport sites, and attached detailed information on Clipperton Island.[55] Roosevelt was not happy with the General Board's report. He disagreed with the board's assumption that 2,100 miles was the longest stretch that could be flown with any significant payload and reminded the naval officers of the tremendous advances likely for aviation in the foreseeable future. He did not want the planned expedition's civilian experts to be hampered by such unrealistic restrictions, nor did he desire that much effort be spent in surveying the route far to the south. Additionally, Roosevelt felt that the northern route, rather than being based on a flight from the Canal Zone to Clipperton Island, should entail "a flight across Mexico to some place on the west coast of Mexico, and thence to Clipperton Island." (This, of course, was the precise route the Australians had outlined in their memorandum of December.) The president viewed the Canal Zone as a commercial air "crossroads" between Australia and South America.[56] Certainly, it was not on the most direct route from Australia to North America.

In response to FDR's request, the Navy moved rapidly to comply with the expedition's needs. Admiral King released a cutter from North Atlantic escort duty, and Knox invited representatives from the civilian airlines to go along. The expedition, commanded by Admiral Byrd, set out for the South Pacific on 5 September 1943 and remained at sea until December.[57]

* * *

For some reason President Roosevelt, after approaching the JCS in December 1942, had next sought advice on postwar military air bases and on civil airports from the Navy's General Board rather than the AAF (seemingly the logical source for such information). Perhaps FDR, who had been assistant secretary of the Navy from 1913 to 1921, had turned to the General Board almost instinctively or because the Pacific, especially this early in the war, was preeminently the Navy's theater. Perhaps he had simply given up on getting anything out of the JCS. In any case, the president should have gone first to the youthful and ambitious AAF, particularly its Air Transport Command (ATC). There he would have found a wealth of information and expertise about overseas air facilities. Commanded by Maj Gen Harold "Hal" George, ATC was carrying passengers and cargo to American and Allied bases around the world. The scope of its activities was enormous, employing more than 300,000 military and civilian personnel by 1945. The daring "Hump" missions, flown from India over the Himalayan Mountains into western China, were probably its best known operations.[58]

When the war broke out, General Arnold knew that leading figures in the airline industry had pioneered the growth of American civil aviation and were among the most qualified to plan and direct a vast air-transport network, and he tapped this resource liberally. In April 1942 he wrote the board of directors of American Airlines, asking for the loan of C. R. Smith, the company's president. Arnold made him ATC's deputy commander.[59] Other former airline officials found a home in ATC's Plans Division. A gathering of its officers might easily have been mistaken for a corporate board meeting. Harold R. Harris had been vice president of Pan American, Grace Airways. As an AAF lieutenant colonel, assigned to ATC Plans in 1943, he was a member of the JPS subcommittee studying air bases for an international police force and represented the War Department on the working subcommittee set up by the Interdepartmental Committee on International Aviation. G. Grant Mason, who served as head of ATC Plans for most of the war, was employed by Pan American Airways in Cuba from 1927 to 1938, and was a member of the Civil Aeronautics Board (CAB) after mid-1940. Other ATC Plans officers were William B. Harding, an investment banker and vice president of the Airlines Credit Bank and Samuel E. Gates, a lawyer and the CAB's international counsel from 1938 to 1942, and, in late 1944, a member of the American delegation to the International Civil Aviation Conference in Chicago. The ATC Plans officer having the most impact on postwar air base planning was 1st Lt and later Capt Oliver J. Lissitzyn, a lawyer. His book *International Air Transport and National Policy* had been published in 1942.[60]

Although the attention of these men focused on gaining victory in war, they also devoted time and effort to winning the peace to follow. As a member of the so-called Glassford mission to French West Africa late in 1942, C. R. Smith wrote Pierre Boisson, French governor-general, that "it is our understanding that postwar use of the facilities which may be constructed . . . is a subject which you would prefer not to discuss at this time but . . . [it] will be discussed by the appropriate authorities at a later date."[61] ATC's Plans Division compiled 133 research and other special reports from mid-1942 until the end of 1944. Most dealt with current operations, but many concerned postwar air routes, military base rights, and commercial air facilities. ATC Plans Report no. 33, 10 January 1943, for example, dismissed the Australian proposal for an alternate South Pacific route (the area could be better policed after the war from mid–Pacific islands, its author claimed). ATC Plans Report no. 39, 1 March 1943, was an investigation of the United States's postwar air transportation potential illustrated with a map of polar air routes. ATC Plans Report no. 61, 24 July 1943, entitled "U.S. Interest in Air Bases on Foreign Soil," discussed the need for early negotiations for postwar air rights.[62] The AAF's commanding general had authorized this postwar planning in October 1942 when he wrote ATC's commander:

It is necessary in all of our air transport operations, that we consider the effect of our current and projected activities on the air transport operations, both military and civil, after the war. Whenever practicable, consistent with our war effort, we should take action to insure that our military air transport routes and facilities are establishing and furthering our postwar position in the air transport field.[63]

To ensure that postwar air transport would receive appropriate attention, Arnold directed a committee be formed to keep the matter under continuous study.[64] Lovett later said he told the other civilian members of the Interdepartmental Committee on International Aviation that ATC "in laying out its planning . . . had very definitely in mind the establishment of routes which would benefit the United States in time of peace."[65]

ATC Plans, however, was well below the apex of planning activity in the AAF. The top position was the office of assistant chief of the Air Staff, Plans (AC/AS-5), one of five major staff agencies at AAF Headquarters. AC/AS-5's primary function was drawing up the AAF's long-range wartime campaign plans.[66] By the time Brig Gen Laurence S. Kuter took over Air Staff Plans on 8 July 1943, the staff unit was also responsible for most of the AAF's postwar planning. Shortly after his arrival from a combat post in North Africa, Kuter organized the Post War Division (PWD) within his office to handle the increasing flow of postwar subjects.[67]

One of the first problems Kuter faced in his new job was Secretary Lovett's attempt to shift the work currently done in ATC Plans in the field of postwar commercial aviation to Air Staff Plans. In a memorandum to General Arnold, Lovett offered several reasons to justify the transfer. The first was that the subject involved the whole AAF, not just ATC. Second, he wanted to "disassociate" ATC from postwar planning: "The idea is becoming widespread that we are going to use the Air Transport Command after the war as a sort of gigantic commercial airline. To have the Air Transport Command participating to an increasing extent in the postwar planning field might give a misleading impression." Third, Lovett claimed a desire to escape "criticism that might come from having the Air Force's postwar commercial planning done in a command in which there are several very able officers, who were former officials of some of . . . the airlines." Finally, the secretary pointed out that a unit established in AC/AS-5 could more readily assist his own work on the Interdepartmental Committee on International Aviation.[68] Lovett, to be sure, was not opposed to involvement of former airline officials in postwar military planning. As a matter of fact, he held out the possibility that along with a transfer of responsibility, ATC officers on the committee that had been appointed following Arnold's directive the preceding October, might also move to Air Staff Plans.[69] By this maneuver, in other words, Lovett was suggesting a method of avoiding the appearance— though not the fact—of conflict of interest.

Here, then, was a delicate question for the officers at AAF Headquarters to resolve. Kuter recommended that Arnold accept Lovett's proposal to transfer responsibility for postwar military and civil air transport planning from ATC to the Air Staff; but, so as not to detract from the ATC's wartime operations, the AAF's commanding general should agree to move only one of the officers from ATC Plans.[70] In a letter to Lovett, Arnold expressed confidence that this arrangement would "work out all right because Plans Division can always call upon the Air Transport Command for such information as they may need."[71]

But wherever the responsibility for planning (or even the planners, themselves) resided, the important point is that the career military men, the uniformed civilians in ATC, and the civilian secretary *all* recognized the interdependence of economic and military factors in planning for commercial aviation facilities and military air bases overseas. In early August 1943, Arnold again demonstrated his awareness of the need to link the two when he directed that Kuter, in coordination with the commanding general, ATC, prepare a staff study containing recommendations for ultimate referral to the JCS covering

1. the bases, facilities and rights for operation of U.S. military aircraft which should be acquired by the U.S. in and over territory not now under exclusive U.S. sovereignty; in order to meet present U.S. requirements, as far as such requirements can now be foreseen, [and]
2. method or methods by which those bases, facilities and rights should be acquired.[72]

But, what had prompted Arnold to ask for a projection of US postwar air base requirements in the first place? The answer probably is that Arnold's interest that August had been stimulated, at least in part, by the general dissatisfaction of the military, but especially of the AAF, with what had been coming out of the subcommittee of the Interdepartmental Committee on International Aviation.

* * *

Chaired by L. Welch Pogue, head of the Civil Aeronautics Board, the subcommittee was the Interdepartmental Committee on International Aviation's working group. The JCS had first responded to its efforts in March 1943.[73] At that time Assistant Secretary of State Berle, in advance of upcoming talks with the British, asked the JCS to comment from the point of view of "national security" on a preliminary report of Pogue's group.[74] This study suggested certain policies to be followed in securing postwar commercial and military rights (particularly where facilities had been constructed with US funds) and in liberalizing the flow of worldwide air commerce, generally.[75] The JCS reaction to this document was quite favorable. They approved the subcommittee's recommendation that any postwar international agreement should provide for the exclusion of civil aircraft from certain areas of military interest and urged that any negotiations should include the acquisition of long-term rights for the operation of US military aircraft.[76]

After this promising start the subcommittee's ideas quite often ran into military resistance. In July 1943, the JCS rejected a subcommittee proposal to create a "United Nations Airport Authority," which was clearly a scheme to protect American interests in air facilities built or financed by the United States abroad for war purposes. The United Nations Airport Authority was to be run by the Combined (American and British) Chiefs of Staff for the rest of the war and then be turned over to civilian administrators once the war ended. The international agency would control airports in territory seized from the enemy, those located in countries whose allegiance was doubtful, those of strategic value that were situated in nations financially unable to maintain them, and those constructed by any United Nations member outside its own territory.[77]

While the military was no less desirous of safeguarding the US investment in air bases abroad, the JCS threw cold water on the plan to associate the airport authority with the Combined Chiefs of Staff. They thought it might endanger wartime cooperation between American and British military leaders "as it would inject into their strictly military responsibilities the national rivalries and controversies that inevitably arise in connection with international-commercial aviation."[78]

The fear that the British would take advantage of the changed circumstances wrought by the war to carve out new air routes or capture those pioneered by others lay behind the formation of the Interdepartmental Committee on International Aviation and guided the work of Pogue's subcommittee. Hopefully, the two aviation giants could reach amicable accord, thereby avoiding a costly postwar struggle. The United States, however, had first to determine a national policy respecting postwar international aviation, and there were many issues of great complexity to decide. Would the United States, for example, continue to permit Pan American Airways to dominate American international routes as before the war when Juan Trippe's airline had, in effect, been a "chosen instrument"? Or would the government yield to the demands of more than 15 domestic carriers and throw the field open to all, thereby putting an end to Pan American's virtual monopoly? None of this would make any difference, however, if other nations closed their airports to US commercial aircraft or made access so restrictive as to discourage the entry of American carriers. There were several positions on this complicated question. Some, who believed the United States was strong enough simply to bull its way into overseas aviation markets, took a bellicose stance. Some, such as Pogue, wanted to obtain the liberalization of air commerce with bilateral agreements (negotiated first with Great Britain and its dominions). Finally, some, like Berle, leaned heavily toward multilateral pacts as the best means to effect an open door policy in global air commerce.[79]

The reports of Pogue's subcommittee were the results of the first steps taken by the civilian Interdepartmental Committee on International Aviation to arrive at a national policy. The plan for a United Nations Airport Authority was part of a larger report entitled "Proposals for Consideration by the Principal Committee," completed by Pogue's working group in late June 1943. The document stressed that air commerce must flow more freely around the world.[80] In a lengthy critique drafted on 12 August, Air Staff Plans officers pointed out that many of the subcommittee plans (e.g., the Airport Authority) relied for their execution on postwar international cooperation, including substantial Anglo-American agreement along with a structure of international organizations.[81] On this basis, Air Staff Plans judged the subcommittee proposals as lacking "a sufficiently firm foundation of realism and certainty to warrant general approval of them by the War Department as being consistent with sound military policy."[82] The planners asked that before any decision was made on a national policy on international aviation, the War Department have sufficient time to examine the subject and make its own recommendations.[83] In the meantime, they suggested the subcommittee adhere to the following "principles":

1. That any American policy of international cooperation may fail to bring about cooperation on the part of other nations,
2. That the military interests of the United States must not be subordinated to the business interests of international air carriers,
3. That the United States not delegate powers to any international agency which would have authority to determine routes and facilities without reference to the national security or rely on any such agency for the acquisition of rights for air bases and facilities to meet future strategic requirements, and
4. That proposals affecting national sovereignty of air space take into consideration the desirability of the United States obtaining exclusive rights in the Western Hemisphere as part of a hemisphere defense plan.[84]

Clearly, there was great potential for conflict between the military and the proponents of liberalized international air commerce. The subcommittee had previously conceded the necessity of excluding civil aircraft from certain areas. Whether the United States chose bilateral or multilateral agreements, however, it had to *give* in order to *get* commercial air privileges abroad. Just how much incompatibility would exist between a program of commercial air expansion and a demand for exclusive rights in the name of national security no doubt depended

on the extent of exclusivity desired. Since the relationship between overseas military air bases and civil air facilities was so
close and the tide appeared to be drifting in the direction of sub-
ordinating the former to the latter (as evidenced by the nature
of the proposals coming from Pogue's subcommittee), Arnold
may have called on his staff for a postwar air base study to ensure there would be no question about what the military, particularly the AAF, wanted. That Arnold, in requesting the study,
referred to the JCS's omission in their letter to Berle in March
1943 of "areas in which the U.S. should have *exclusive* rights"
(emphasis in original) indicates this was, in fact, probably his
motive.[85]

* * *

Both Air Staff Plans and the ATC Plans Division prepared
lengthy reports in response to Arnold's request.[86] Evidently, the
two offices coordinated their work to some degree because each
document contained an identical listing of military air bases
required by the United States after the war.[87] Moreover, Col
George A. Brownell, Lovett's military assistant, reported to his
chief that there was "complete coordination between the ATC
and Air Staff, or at least complete willingness to cooperate,"
though there was not much evidence yet of "dirt flying."[88] Both
studies were finished by mid-October 1943, and while containing significant similarities, there were also important differences between them.

Only the Air Staff paper went forward to the JCS; it therefore stands as the best representation of AAF opinion. The Air
Staff planners justified a "far-flung chain of bases" by arguing
that only from such platforms well beyond American shores
could the nation's armed forces (but preeminently an "adequate" air force) counter an enemy employing such advanced
weapons as "long-range, super-heavy bombers, radar control,
glider and rocket bombs" in time to prevent the nation from
suffering "a sudden devastation beyond any 'Pearl Harbor' experience or our present power of imagination to conceive." But,
how far away was far enough? Rejecting "air domination of the
world" as "not compatible with our national policy, present or

future," the AAF assumed that the United States, Great Britain, Russia, and China would divide the world into spheres of influence after the war to keep the peace.[89]

In the AAF blueprint, the enormous sphere of responsibility of the United States included all of the Western Hemisphere and nearly the entire Pacific. The bases "essential" for the defense of the United States, its territories, and the Western Hemisphere defined a giant perimeter. It ran southwest from extreme northwestern Alaska, through Attu in the Aleutian Islands, Paramushiru in the Kuriles, the Bonin Islands, to the Philippines, thence eastward through the South Pacific (via New Britain, the Solomon Islands, Suva, Viti Levu Island, Samoa, Tahiti, the Marquesas Islands, Clipperton Island, and the Galapagos Islands) to the west coast of South America, and around the northern rim of that continent to the northeast Brazilian coast. From there, the US eastern defense line ran to Ascension Island in the South Atlantic, and north along the west coast of Africa through the Azores and Iceland. The northern boundary extended from Iceland through Greenland and across Canada to Alaska. Within the sphere (but exclusive of the continental United States), the Air Staff paper identified a number of bases as secondary outposts and intermediate points along internal lines of communication, particularly in the Pacific, the Caribbean, and Canada. The airmen also believed serious thought should be given to acquiring base rights on a route across North Africa and South Asia that would connect the eastern and western edges of the defense perimeter.[90]

Although no effort was made to classify the bases by priority of military importance, more than a third were along or near the defense perimeter's northern rim. "Reference to a globe or polar projection chart," stated the Air Staff planners, "clearly indicates that the shortest approach from either Europe or Asia is via the extreme north." Furthermore, advances in aircraft range and capabilities would make "sub-Arctic flight" even more feasible in the future. Thus, the AAF sought to expand (though not erase) the "customary conception" of the Atlantic and Pacific defense boundaries.[91]

The attitude the Air Staff planners displayed toward an international police force was openly skeptical. The world might someday achieve the "millennium" of goodwill among nations, but until that time, the United States must stand ready to throw back its enemies. No world police force could safely be "a complete substitute for a purely nationalistic plan of defense." Furthermore, for a world police force's bases to be at all effective they would have to be placed near centers of potential disruption. Yet, so located, the more likely would they "constitute a potential threat against the purely nationalistic security of adjacent boundaries." Thus, an international police force and national self-defense might be "mutually exclusive" concepts. The best way to keep the peace in a world of nation-states was for each great power to police its own sphere.[92]

If the bases of a supranational body would arouse nationalism in countries near to them, then why should any nation accede to an American request for base rights? The first reason offered by the planners for the probable acceptance of US military bases nicely mirrors the image Americans have had of themselves and their country from the time the Reverend John Winthrop told prospective Massachusetts Bay Colony settlers in the seventeenth century that their experiment was to be as a city upon a hill. According to the Air Staff officers, other countries would grant base rights to the United States due to "our reputation for integrity of international agreement and traditional lack of imperialistic ambition."[93]

The Air Staff Plans paper drew a sharp line between bases for national defense and those for an international police force. The United States might on occasion be forced to exclude all foreign aircraft from the former. As a matter of fact, staff officers foresaw no likely centers of unrest in the American sphere after the war and, consequently, not much of a role for an international police force. The potential trouble areas were in Central Europe, the Near East, and the India-China region. But, pending the establishment of a world security force, the United States would probably be invited by the other three major powers to "participate in the policing" of those areas. Therefore, the acquisition of base rights in Central Europe should be "kept constantly in mind." Furthermore, the "immediate present" appeared to be the most opportune time for negotiations for rights in China and to indicate to the Chinese a "possible requirement" for bases in Indochina (to support a route linking the eastern and western borders of the defense perimeter).[94]

Like the Air Staff planners, the authors of the ATC Plans study forecasting US postwar base needs took the position that in view of the uncertainty surrounding the nature of the postwar world, national concerns must come first.[95] In this and many other respects, the massive ATC document (40 pages of analysis, more than 20 appendices, and five maps, totaling 182 pages) found common ground with the Air Staff product. Both used the same list of bases required to be operated by the United States in foreign territory, and both adopted the idea of a national defense perimeter. Each stressed the importance of quick action by the State Department to obtain postwar rights for US military aircraft. Despite these and other similarities between the two planning documents, there were also obvious differences. First, ATC planners had a much broader conception of the role of US bases in foreign territory. They noted that the JCS, in their letter of 16 March 1943, had defined the function of overseas bases as the "national security" of the United States and the other Western Hemisphere nations. However, in their study, ATC analysts described the primary purpose of overseas air bases more broadly as the protection of US "national interests."[96] Second, the officers in ATC Plans were far less sanguine about the prospects for postwar cooperation among the four great powers (particularly between the United States and the Asiatic nations, Russia, and China). The future was just too cloudy to forecast—"whether policing will be on a regional basis or a world-wide basis for all participants or, in fact on any precise basis of international cooperation which can now be foreseen." Therefore, the ATC planners felt compelled to "consider the worldwide use of American aviation combat forces."[97] Finally, emphasis throughout the ATC Plans study was on the close relationship between military and commercial aviation. The Air Staff Plans officers, while recognizing that the two subjects were interwoven, had asserted that their approach to the postwar bases subject had been "from the premise of its fundamental importance to the National Security and with every effort to exclude consideration of anything but the purely military aspects of postwar aviation."[98] In contrast, the former airline officials in ATC Plans did not restrict their study in this way and sought to view postwar air bases, facilities, and rights in the total civil and military context.

To buttress the case for the importance of commercial aviation in national defense, the ATC planners drew liberally on examples from the recent past. They recalled the apparent threat posed to American security by the network of German-dominated civil airlines (and the Italian-operated transatlantic service [LATI]) prior to the war.[99] First Lieutenant Lissitzyn, in tracing the history of the ties between civil and military aviation, stressed the contribution made to the American war effort by Pan American Airways in its development of airways in the South Pacific, Caribbean, and South America. As Lissitzyn put it, "Regular commercial operations along air routes have the effect both of increasing the effectiveness of the routes and bases for the purpose of military operations, and of rendering the proper maintenance of the routes and bases less expensive, since they are included in a running commercial organization with part of the cost covered by commercial receipts."[100] After the war, civil aviation would once again play this role because, as the ATC analysts pointed out, "It seems obvious that the people of the United States would be unwilling during peacetime to support a military force capable of fighting a major war. Rather it must maintain a framework in which the military organization required to fight such a war can be built." American commercial airlines, by operating and maintaining air routes and bases, would provide such a "framework."[101] The world's other major powers might also join American taxpayers in rebelling against a ring of bases involving "military control of nearly two-thirds of the earth's surface." Such opposition, argued the ATC planners, might force the United States to modify its program or share air police facilities in its traditional sphere of influence, Latin America, with other nations.[102]

The degree of exclusivity sought for the American sphere was a friction point between the ATC Plans officers on the one hand and the Air Staff planners and the assistant secretary of war for air on the other (as indeed it was between commercial aviation expansionists and the professional military, generally).

The ATC paper recalled Lovett's letter of the preceding January, in which the assistant secretary had asserted an American right to exclusive use of air facilities built by US funds in Latin America, and a similar, if less sweeping, position, taken in the critique of the report of Pogue's subcommittee. While granting the necessity for exclusive US military base rights in the Pacific islands or the Western Hemisphere and even the prudence of excluding foreign civil aircraft from the Canal Zone, the ATC planners contended that an airtight Western Hemisphere (one denying access to both foreign military and civil aircraft) would conflict with the Good Neighbor Policy, also raising the possibility that such action "would be met with retaliatory action in Europe and Asia."[103]

The ATC study went beyond its Air Staff counterpart in identifying routes for the US component of an international police force. Proceeding on the simple assumption that "trouble is most likely to occur where there are people to make trouble," the ATC planners laid out routes within the American defense ring and from the United States over the North Pole, North Atlantic, and North Pacific to points (usually the principal cities) throughout Europe, the Soviet Union, and China.[104] The military routes, whether solely within the US defense perimeter or those for an international police force, were in many cases identical to the routes displayed on another polar projection labeled "Principal International Routes of the World Likely to be Operated or Sought by U.S. Air Carriers." However, there were some differences between the military and commercial routes. For example, the preferred military route connecting the eastern and western edges of the American defense perimeter depended on bases in North Africa (e.g., Telergma, Algeria, and Benghazi, Libya), while the more attractive, if less militarily efficient, commercial route used the European capitals as stepping-stones. From Cairo, Egypt, the military and commercial routes were the same (i.e., Cairo to Abadan Island at the head of the Persian Gulf to Karachi and Calcutta in India), but took divergent paths to Manila in the Philippines (the commercial route ran from Calcutta to Chungking, China, to Canton, China, to Manila, while the military route went directly to Manila through Hanoi, French Indochina). There were, additionally, several more planned transpacific military routes (supporting Pacific out-posts) than preferred commercial routes across that ocean. In short, military requirements, even when confined to the American sphere, did not always coincide with the path promising the greatest profit.[105]

One final and visually arresting difference between the two postwar base investigations is that the ATC planners displayed route and base information on a polar projection, but the Air Staff Plans chart was a standard Mercator-projection map (one, moreover, lacking coverage of most of Eurasia, Africa, and the Indian Ocean). The Air Staff Plans use of the Mercator as opposed to the polar chart is difficult to understand. In August 1943 at a meeting attended by Air Staff Plans officers (including Col P. M. Hamilton, head of the newly created Post War Division and probable author of the Air Staff's base paper), at which the subject was the AAF's postwar planning in general, the presiding officer had declared:

> In studying the strategic aspects of the postwar Air Force, I strongly recommend using this Polar projection of the world as your basic map rather than anything else. . . . The areas of power of the world are relatively few. . . . One is the United States—the other is Central and Eastern Europe—and the other is the China-India area. On a Polar projection these areas form a triangle and in the world of the future I believe that a great deal of air commerce will be directed between the corners of this triangle. That will have to be considered with the access of bases in the vicinity of those areas.[106]

Why, then, did the Air Staff planners not use a polar projection? Unfortunately, the documentary record does not reveal the reason. The officers attending the meeting were also told to assume that the United States, Great Britain, and the Soviet Union would enforce peace in their own "strategic spheres."[107] Perhaps use of the Mercator projection was due to the regional, spheres of influence orientation that so dominated military thinking about the postwar world in 1943. Certainly, absence of a polar projection did not stem from a lack of appreciation of the strategic significance of the northern approach to the United States because the AAF recommended 23 bases in the defense perimeter's northern reaches, more than one-third of the total installations.

The AAF submitted the postwar base study prepared by Air Staff Plans to the JCS on 9 October 1943.[108] Thereupon occurred a minor incident offering a glimpse into the state of civil-military relationships. At Arnold's request, almost immediately after sending the document to the JCS's secretariat, General Kuter withdrew it without explanation.[109] The next day it was sent to the office of the assistant secretary of war for air for comment as a study the commanding general, AAF, "proposes" to forward to the JCS.[110] The General Board had routed its base recommendations through the secretary of the Navy, but Air Staff Plans had completely bypassed Lovett, the AAF's nominal civilian chief.

Secretary Lovett approved the paper for submission "as written" but sounded one cautionary note: "[The list of air bases] is so extensive in scope as to raise in my mind the question of the possibility of realistic attainment." What bothered Lovett was that many of the proposed bases were in Canada and parts of the British Empire, "where the problem of national sovereignty and national pride pose questions which can only be settled by the most adroit negotiations." He thought that an undifferentiated list of demands might upset the whole base applecart, and that distinction ought to be made between those areas required merely for transit and limited use (e.g., refueling) and those where the installation of permanent facilities (hangars and barracks) was contemplated.[111]

Lovett, like the Air Staff and ATC planners, was grappling with the sensitive problem of how best to secure postwar base rights overseas. In 1943 the only postwar military operating privileges possessed by the United States were in the 99-year-lease bases obtained in the famous "destroyer-base" deal of March 1941 and on Canton and Enderbury Islands (located in the central Pacific just south of the equator) by virtue of a 50-year joint United States–Great Britain agreement signed in 1939. The Air Staff Plans officers had recommended "purchase, lease or any other intergovernmental agreement" as methods of acquiring long-term postwar military base rights.[112] Since many wartime rights were the result of informal agreements between local military commanders or civilian officials, there was also a need to clarify and to establish firmly rights for wartime use as well as for postwar purposes.[113] The ATC planners pointed out, in fact, that ironclad wartime agreements were a foot in the door to postwar rights. "If U.S. rights to operate military aircraft for the war-period were definitely established in all of the countries in which American aircraft now operate," stated the ATC report, "the United States delegates to the Peace Conference could delay the signing of the peace until such time as satisfactory postwar agreements were reached with the knowledge that U.S. operations could continue in the interim."[114] For the high-priority postwar locations, argued Lovett, the United States should simply "dig in and retain them at all costs" while leaving the less important to ceremonial diplomatic negotiations.[115] Everyone in the AAF seems to have agreed on this point; the hoary phrase "possession is nine points of the law" appears in Lovett's memorandum and in the Air Staff Plans and the ATC base papers.[116]

During the fall of 1943, the State, War, and Navy Departments agreed on a procedure to employ what might be called the "see if you are big enough to do anything about it" tactic of securing postwar military and commercial holdings before American military forces abandoned airfields constructed abroad at US expense.[117] The Senate Special Committee to Investigate the National Defense Program, popularly known as the Truman Committee and watchdog over military expenditures during the war, was particularly enthusiastic about plans for such a skillful blending of military power and diplomacy. (The procedure had been first tentatively agreed to by the State, War, and Navy Departments at a Truman Committee hearing on 19 October 1943.) A committee member keenly interested in seeing that the United States got its money's worth from airfields built at public expense overseas was Sen. James Mead (D-N.Y.).[118] In mid-1944 he raised the issue of airfields constructed in Canada but wrongly claimed that the airfield at Goose Bay, Labrador, had been built by the United States. John D. Hickerson, then chief of the State Department's Division of British Commonwealth Affairs, asked Berle to "straighten" Mead out on the subject. Hickerson deemed it "dangerous" to "start talking about our postwar rights merely because we happen to feel a construction job was necessary for military purposes to help win the war." Hickerson concluded "the step from such talk to rank imperialism troubles me."[119] Whether Hickerson knew it or not, "such talk" had been a virtual lingua franca in various parts of the government, most prominently the office of assistant secretary of war for air and elsewhere in the AAF, for many months. In practice, after the war the United States routinely held troops in place as a lever to assist American diplomats in their bargaining for postwar military and commercial rights.

* * *

In October 1943, while the AAF was formulating its postwar base recommendations, FDR demonstrated his own interest in the subject for the third time in less than a year. Once again, the president channeled his message to Admiral Leahy and the JCS through his naval aide. The catalyst this time was a letter from Vice Adm William A. Glassford, evaluating the economic potential of West Africa. The naval aide reported the president "was not so much interested in the financial aspect of the Dakar Mission as with the all-important question of making up our minds now what areas in West Africa we should seek to control as air and naval bases after the war." The president wanted to know, the aide said, how the JCS were coming with their base studies.[120]

The JCS, of course, had long since buried the project; but, for a second time, they passed the assignment along to the JSSC. Embick, Willson, and Fairchild drew on their own previous plans and the AAF's and General Board's recommendations, completing their work by the first week in November.[121] The JCS reviewed the document while on board the USS *Iowa* en route to the conferences at Cairo, Egypt, and Tehran, Iran.[122] General Arnold, probably using the Air Staff Plans study as reference, proposed a paragraph requesting the president to direct the State Department to begin negotiations for specific base rights as soon as possible.[123] On 15 November, the JCS approved the paper as amended, and Admiral Leahy handed it to Roosevelt the same day.[124]

The JCS base plan, eventually designated JCS 570/2, was a blueprint for military air bases in two periods. The first covered the interval between the defeat of Germany and the surrender of Japan, and the second identified bases for a period of "worldwide peace enforced under the Four Power Agreement pending establishment of a worldwide organization for collective security." The JCS, however, declined to recommend bases for a third period during which peace was to be enforced by worldwide machinery since those base requirements "cannot be solved on a realistic basis at this time."[125]

Several assumptions underpinned the base network outlined by the JCS for the period following the end of the war in Europe and Asia:

1. The major United Nations have maintained their solidarity.
2. [They] have established some preliminary United Nations machinery for enforcing the peace—as represented by the Four Powers' Pact.
3. Peace enforcement is accomplished by major powers exercising responsibility on a combined or a regional basis.
4. U.S. interests will be primarily the Western Hemisphere, and the central Pacific to the Far East.[126]

Although the area of American responsibility drawn up by the JSSC and approved by the JCS did not exactly correspond to any of the previous formal expressions of high-level military opinion on the subject, it had much in common with them, as it did with FDR's "Four Policemen" concept.

The JCS marked an area, bordered in blue on a Mercator projection map, in which the United States was to have exclusive military rights. The region, closely resembling the JSSC's proposals of the preceding March, included bases "for direct defense of the U.S. leased areas, and possessions, including the Philippines." It enclosed Alaska, the Philippines, the Japanese Mandated Islands, the American possessions in the Pacific (most of the Pacific south of the equator was omitted), the Galapagos Islands, Central America, and the Caribbean (excluding Mexico), and the 99-year-lease bases from Trinidad north to Newfoundland. A green-bordered region showed bases, in addition to those in the blue area, that would be required for the defense of the Western Hemisphere, most of Canada, Greenland, Iceland, the Azores, West Africa, Ascension Island, northern

South America, and Clipperton Island. American rights in this area were to be on a participating or reciprocal basis. The combination of the blue and green perimeters was a near twin to the proposals made by the AAF. What had been done in effect was to separate those places where an American claim to exclusive rights would go unchallenged from those demanding respect for the sovereignty of another nation. The blue and green separation seems to signify the military's awareness of the sensitive problem pointed out by Lovett and its response to the rebuke given the General Board by Roosevelt. Finally, a black border surrounding bases in the far southwest Pacific, Indochina, and the eastern half of China, Korea, and Japan represented the sphere of American responsibility "as one of the Great Powers enforcing peace." Here also, the United States was to have participating rights.[127]

On 19 November, still on board ship, FDR responded favorably to the JCS's base paper, asking for only one modification. In a partial reversal of the attitude he had demonstrated when the General Board argued for sweeping changes of sovereignty in the South Pacific, Roosevelt now told the JCS that he wanted the blue border (the area of exclusive US military rights) extended south and east of Samoa. This was done so the American sphere would take in the Society and Marquesas island groups.[128] FDR held the French, whom he believed had not resisted the Germans very strongly in 1940, in very low esteem. On the way to the Tehran conference, he told the JCS that he doubted France would regain the first rank of nations for a quarter century, and at the conference he appeared to join with Soviet leader Joseph Stalin against Churchill in a "determination to treat France almost as an enemy country."[129] At the shipboard meeting, the president also observed that the French-owned Marquesas and Society Islands were relatively close to Mexico, the Panama Canal, and South America. He believed that "with the development of aircraft, planes could base in the Society Islands 10 years from now and make things uncomfortable on the West Coast of the Americas." Arnold chimed in that indeed B-29s might reach those areas from the Marquesas; but FDR had something else in mind. The president also said that in addition to bases, he wanted "the commercial traffic open to the world in all these islands."[130]

Roosevelt's desire to promote postwar American prosperity through the expansion of commercial aviation, rather than a concern for the possible military significance of the islands of French Oceania, probably stimulated his interest in that far corner of the world. Before the war, commercial aircraft transiting the Pacific had to pass through Hawaii, but the United States had denied foreign aircraft access to the islands. This prevented the Canadians and Australians from establishing a connecting air route, prompting retaliation by Australia against the United States.[131] The Americans were certainly aware that with Hawaii and Alaska they would again control the air routes to the Far East and be able to exclude whomever they chose. However, liberalization, not restriction, of air commerce was the US objective. American carriers were especially eager to take advantage of routes already developed by the British across Europe, the Middle East, and South Asia. If the United States could not agree with the British on postwar rights and thus dampen the already intense rivalry, Great Britain, according to a report of the Interdepartmental Committee on International Aviation, would be able "to negotiate agreements shutting us out of most of the countries from West Africa to Singapore."[132] Hawaii was fundamental to this accord because Hawaiian transit rights "were major bargaining considerations in any prospective agreement with the British Commonwealth members."[133] Hawaii, then, is quite likely the key to understanding fully FDR's fascination with the south central Pacific. If the British could outflank Hawaii via Clipperton, the Marquesas, and the Society Islands, the United States would lose some of the leverage it hoped to apply toward expanding its international commercial aviation. This was a strong motive for developing the air route before the British.

Along with the French South Pacific islands, Roosevelt also focused on postwar US bases in western Africa. The JCS felt that the United States needed participating rights to airfields, seaplane facilities, and naval bases at Casablanca and/or Marrakech and Port Lyautey, Morocco; in the Canary Islands; at Dakar; and at Roberts Field in Liberia.[134] But FDR thought these were not sufficient. After returning from the Cairo and Tehran conferences, he directed that base rights in the Cape Verde Islands (located several hundred miles west of Dakar and the African bulge and within the green-bordered portion of the American sphere) be included in the JCS plan.[135] FDR evidently saw Dakar as a kind of "police station." In a January 1944 conversation with Isaias Medina, president of Venezuela, FDR talked about joint postwar defense of the hemisphere, and his hope for US and Brazilian occupation and use of this strategic site.[136] The American republics, he asserted, could not allow the British or the French to fortify either Dakar or Trinidad (Roosevelt intimated the latter might come under an arrangement similar to the proposed US-Brazilian venture in Dakar).[137]

After the changes pertaining to French Oceania and western Africa had been made, the president signed a letter prepared for him by the JCS containing instructions to the secretary of state for putting the base plan, JCS 570/2, into effect "at the earliest possible moment." The State Department, after receiving information from the War and Navy Departments regarding the relative importance of each air facility, maximum rights desired, and the minimum acceptable in each, was to determine the timing and plan of negotiations for obtaining them. Never were commercial aviation matters to supersede military requirements for air bases.[138] Another letter drafted by the JCS directed the State, War, and Navy Departments and the JCS to examine also the subject of "adequate base facilities for naval and ground forces," though air base rights were to have first priority. The second letter is particularly significant because it established the JCS as the "coordinating" body to furnish military guidance to the State Department in connection with the negotiations. The military chiefs, before supplying their advice, were required to consult their civilian superiors in the War and Navy Departments only in the somewhat hazy instance of "matters involving departmental policy." FDR quite likely recognized the threat this arrangement posed to the traditional pattern of relationships within the nation's military establishment since he added in his own hand, the otherwise superfluous comment that "all the above [i.e., the second letter's contents but especially the selection of bases] is subject to the approval of the President."[139]

The president's letters, sent in January and February 1944, prompted the usual burst of bureaucratic activity. Representatives of the State, War, and Navy Departments met quickly and agreed to ask the JCS to provide a priority listing of bases by and within each foreign country and identification of exact facilities required.[140] Following the president's cue, all concurred in seeking the JCS's view of the possibility of military occupation of the Society and Marquesas Islands, Aitutaki in the Cook Islands, and Tongareva (or Penrhyn) Island.[141]

The JCS had some difficulty in determining just which of its several committees was to furnish the base data to the State Department. Up to that time, the postwar base issue had been handled by the JSSC. Arguing their province was "policy rather than details," the JSSC passed the more mundane work to the Joint War Plans Committee (JWPC), which operated directly under the three senior officers who constituted the Joint Staff Planners.[142] Almost immediately, however, the Joint Staff Planners decided to set up a "Special Team" of the JWPC to deal exclusively with postwar base matters.[143] This team of four officers was to coordinate with the JSSC in the realm of broad policy and strategy and to prepare detailed base studies for the State Department.[144] That the special team was made up of officers who did not initially belong to the elite JCS staff is indicative of the relative status of postwar subjects at the highest military planning level. In other words, it appears that the "best" plans officers worked on tasks directly related to prosecution of the war.

* * *

By early 1944, more than a year after the president first raised the general subject of overseas air bases, the United States had a postwar base plan and intragovernmental machinery for implementing it. In drafting the plan, the JSSC had considered the views of each of the services; and until its revision in the fall of 1945, JCS 570/2 served as the benchmark for postwar military base planning. Even the doggedly independent Navy acknowledged its overarching authority. Capt A. D. Douglas, the Navy's postwar base expert, termed JCS 570/2 "our base bible."[145]

The base bible and the long planning process it emerged from revealed much about the military's attitudes toward the application of force in international affairs by the United States after the war. The military planners selected bases not with any particular enemy in mind but saw them rather as defining a protective ring or perimeter around the country. Sherry points out that in 1943 they were most concerned with "the nature of war itself" rather than any identifiable enemy.[146]

The next war was sure to be a total war with national survival at stake, and consequently the planners emphasized "national security" in their analyses. Still, the military did not ignore the use of force on behalf of US "interests." The Air Staff Plans study, for example, treated the Philippines "as an area from which our Pacific interests may be defended rather than United States territory against which attacks from any direction . . . can be interdicted."[147]

Regionalism most characterized the military planning that culminated in JCS 570/2. The American sphere was to spread over a vast area of the Pacific and the Western Hemisphere. The sharpest clash of opinion occurred over the extent to which the American Zone should expand into the eastern Atlantic, a region traditionally dominated by Great Britain. The JSSC initially opposed, and the service chiefs (including Admiral Leahy) and the AAF advocated an extension through Greenland, Iceland, the Azores, and West Africa. (The General Board kept more or less to the middle of the stream.) JCS 570/2, by drawing a line in the Western Hemisphere generally between those areas in which the United States could easily claim exclusive rights and those in which rights would have to be negotiated thus papered over any disagreement that might have remained over the size of the American Zone. None of the military planners proposed permanent postwar bases in Europe, the Middle East, or South Asia, but the AAF believed thought should be given to obtaining base rights in those areas to prepare for the "highly probable" contingency that American forces would be "invited to participate in their policing." Not only did the military distrust a universal collective security organization, but also the planners (especially those in the AAF) hoped "international peacekeeping" would be on a regional basis. In sum, in 1943 American military planners were not inclined to assume global postwar responsibilities for US forces. In an attachment to the base paper given to the president in November, the JCS urged that "in both the immediate and the ultimate phases of the international organization, U.S. military commitments should be limited insofar as possible to the Western Hemisphere and the Far East."[148]

The direct line of communication set up between the JCS and the State Department by the president's letters further enhanced the JCS's overall power and influence. The arrangement effectively eliminated the War and Navy Departments from an arena in which the political and military were undeniably mixed. Toward the end of the war, as the civilian secretaries sought to reinsert themselves between the JCS and the president, overseas bases became an area of contention.

In late 1943 to early 1944, there was more harmony than disagreement within the government about postwar bases abroad. Everyone appreciated the value that the hundreds of US-built airfields ought to have in securing postwar military and commercial air rights, and the wish to press this apparent advantage spread quickly. Lovett summed up the feelings of many in a letter to General George, the ATC commander. Recalling the experience with the beneficiaries of American aid after World War I, the assistant secretary of war for air wrote, "I feel . . . we must make the trades while we still have something to trade with and not rely on the good faith and gratitude of the recipients of American help." Winning the war was most important, he said, but the United States should direct its "planning and activities" so as to be able, at the end of the war, "to hand the torch on to the next runner with precision and a head start."[149]

The military, eager to acquire long-term base rights in foreign countries, shared Lovett's sentiment completely. Military leaders also acknowledged the symbiotic nature of the relationship between military air bases and commercial air routes and facilities. Given the results of Pan American's prewar activities in Latin America and the Pacific, nothing was more natural for the military than to accept close ties between civil and military aviation in places like French Oceania (and later Alaska).

Yet, the promise of mutual facilities did not always mean harmony of purpose between military and commercial aviation; each suspected that the other might foul the common nest. The ATC planners, in suggesting that well-developed overseas air transport facilities could serve as the framework around which to erect a military base structure in wartime, were trying to avoid the chill that extensive military demands for overseas base rights would likely bring upon negotiations for commercial aviation privileges in the same country. Most international aviation promoters realized the United States would have to make concessions to other nations regarding air transit rights in order to expand its own overseas airline operations. Thus, assertions by the professional military and civilians like Lovett of a need for far-reaching exclusive rights or the superiority of strictly military to business concerns were as much red flags to commercial aviation expansionists as a United Nations Airport Authority or allegedly excessive liberalization of the doctrine of air sovereignty was to the military.

Notes

1. Michael S. Sherry, *Preparing for the Next War: American Plans for Postwar Defense* (New Haven, Conn.: Yale University Press, 1977), 1–5.

2. See ibid., 8–15, for an account of the organization and makeup of the Special Planning Division. For the Navy's Postwar Planning Section, see Vincent Davis, *Postwar Defense Policy and the U.S. Navy, 1943–1946* (Chapel Hill: University of North Carolina Press, 1966), 12–14; and for the Army Air Forces (AAF) Post War Division, see Perry McCoy Smith, *The Air Force Plans for Peace: 1943–1945* (Baltimore: Johns Hopkins University Press, 1970), chap. 1.

3. The four Joint Chiefs of Staff (JCS), the top US military leaders, remained the same throughout the war. In addition to General Marshall, who led the Army, Adm Ernest J. King held both the post of chief of naval operations (CNO) and that of commander in chief, United States Fleet (COMINCH); Gen Henry H. Arnold commanded the AAF; and Adm William D. Leahy served as military chief of staff to the president and nominal chairman of the JCS. The JCS was supported by a staff of officers assigned to a series of committees.

4. Sherry, *Preparing for the Next War,* 20–21.

5. Ibid., 26.

6. Ibid., ix.

7. Ibid., 52–57.

8. Capt John L. McCrea, naval aide to the president, correspondence, to Adm William D. Leahy, 28 December 1942, JCS 183, sec. 1, file CCS 360 (12-9-42), Combined Chiefs of Staff (CCS) Decimal Files, 1942–1945, Record Group (RG) 218 (Records of the US Joint Chiefs of Staff), National Archives (NA), Washington, D.C.

9. Robert A. Divine, *Second Chance: The Triumph of Internationalism in America during World War II* (New York: Atheneum, 1967), 80–81.

10. Clipperton is a small, uninhabited island, almost barren of vegetation, located at approximately 10° N by 110° W in the eastern Pacific Ocean southwest of Mexico and due west of the Panama Canal.

11. Australian Legation, memorandum concerning air routes across the Pacific, 9 December 1942, JPS 101/D, sec. 1, file CCS 360 (12-9-42), RG 218.

12. See p. 15–16 this chapter and chap. 2, 77–82.

13. Memorandum for Brig Gen E. E. Partridge, 8 January 1943, file 145.86-15, USAF Historical Research Agency (AFHRA), Maxwell AFB, Ala.

14. Ibid., minutes, meetings of JPS subcommittee, 11 and 18 January 1943. For a copy of Col George F. Schulgen's plan, see file 145.86-33B, vol. 1, 1943–1946.

15. Ibid., Brig Gen E. E. Partridge, memorandum for the Sub-Committee on International Air Bases (Plan for Defeat of Axis Powers), n.d., file 145.86-15.

16. Ibid., enclosed in Brig Gen E. E. Partridge, memorandum for the Joint Staff Planners Sub-Committee (Arctic Bases), 19 January 1943.

17. Ibid., Notes on Conference, 25 January 1943.

18. Ibid., Capt M. B. Gardner, memorandum for Col Willard R. Wolfinbarger, Operations Division (OPD) staff officer, 29 January 1943.

19. Smith, *Air Force Plans*, 45; Col Joseph Halvorsen, memorandum for General Anderson, 17 February 1943, file 145.86-15, AFHRA; Admiral King to secretary of the Navy, letter, 9 February 1943, sec. 1, file CCS 360 (12-9-42), RG 218.

20. Extract of minutes of JCS 61st meeting, 9 February 1943. For the quotation and additional background on the Joint Strategic Survey Committee (JSSC), see Maurice Matloff, *Strategic Planning for Coalition Warfare, 1943–1944* (Washington, D.C.: Office of the Chief of Military History, Department of the Army, 1959), 108.

21. Assistant Secretary of State Adolph A. Berle to Secretary of State Cordell Hull, letter, 9 September 1942, in Adolph A. Berle, *Navigating the Rapids, 1918–1971*, ed. Beatrice Bishop Berle and Travis Beal Jacobs (New York: Harcourt Brace Jovanovich, Inc., 1973), 481.

22. Ibid., 481, Berle diary entry, 2 January 1943. The members of the committee were Berle; Wayne C. Taylor, undersecretary of commerce; Robert A. Lovett, assistant secretary of war for air; Artemus L. Gates, assistant secretary of the Navy for air; L. Welch Pogue, chairman of the Civil Aeronautics Board; and Wayne Coy, deputy director of the Bureau of the Budget.

23. Lovett, memorandum for the commanding general, AAF, 7 January 1943, file SAS 580, ATC [Air Transport Command] case 54-197, box 142,

41

Papers of Henry Harley Arnold (hereafter Arnold Papers), Library of Congress (LOC), Washington, D.C.

24. Ibid. These routes were the "Northwest Operation to Alaska, the Northern Route over the Pole to Northern Europe, the Central Route Northeast to Northern Europe and England, and the more easterly route via Newfoundland to Europe."

25. Ibid.

26. Lt Gen Stanley D. Embick and Vice Adm Russell Willson had come out of retirement to serve on the JSSC.

27. Brig Gen John R. Deane, memorandum for Lt Gen Stanley D. Embick, 13 February 1943; and Deane, memorandum for the Joint Strategic Survey Committee, 17 February 1943, both in sec. 1, file CCS 360 (12-9-42), RG 218.

28. Extract of minutes of the JCS 61st meeting, 9 February 1943, found in sec. 1, file CCS 360 (12-9-42), RG 218. The 28 December 1942 directive did not quote the president directly, but was a paraphrase by the naval aide who wrote Admiral Leahy that "the President stated that we must keep in mind the peace negotiations and that he visualizes some sort of international police force will come out of the war. Pursuing this thought further, the President stated he wished you to have a study made by the Joint Chiefs of Staff to the end that when the peace negotiations are upon us we will be decided in our own minds where it is desired that 'International Police Force' air facilities be located throughout the world; this plan to be without regard to current sovereignty."

29. Ibid., JSSC to JCS, 5 March 1943.

30. Ibid., minutes of JCS 65th meeting, 9 March 1943, and JCS 69th meeting, 25 March 1943.

31. Ibid., JCS 183/5 (revised), 25 March 1943. A policy statement, "Post War Military Problems with Particular Reference to Air Bases," (pp. A22320-23) is dated 25 March 1943, while a longer paper (pp. A22324-36) with the same title (the policy statement was a summary of this paper) is dated 15 March 1943.

32. Ibid., A22321. For a discussion of Roosevelt's concept of the Four Policemen and his attitude toward collective security in general, see Robert A. Divine, *Roosevelt and World War II* (Baltimore: Johns Hopkins University Press, 1969), 49–71.

33. JCS 183/5 (revised), A22321-22, sec. 1, file CCS 360 (12-9-42), RG 218.

34. Ibid., A22336.

35. Ibid., A22333.

36. Iwo Jima is in the Bonin Islands which lie between the Japanese home islands and the island of Guam in the Mariana Islands.

37. JCS 183/5 (revised), A22322, A22334-35, sec. 1, file CCS 360 (12-9-42), RG 218.

38. Ibid., A22334-36.

39. Ibid., supplementary minutes, JCS 71st meeting, 30 March 1943.

40. Ibid., for the revision, see JSSC 9/4, 8 April 1943, and JCS comments, minutes, JCS 74th meeting, 13 April 1943, both in sec. 2.

41. Ibid., unsigned memorandum for record, 7 September 1943.

42. Ibid., Adm William D. Leahy to A. A. Berle, letter, 16 March 1943, sec. 1.

43. See Sherry, *Preparing for the Next War*, p. 54, note 63, for evidence that by mid-1943 some War Department analysts were aware of the implications for US defense of declining British fortunes.

44. For the documents that brought the General Board (G. B.) into the postwar air base question, see Adm Ernest J. King's letter to secretary of the Navy, 9 February 1943, sec. 1, file CCS 360 (12-9-42), RG 218; and Frank Knox to G. B., 10 and 17 February 1943, both in file Naval Bases December 1942–December 1946, series 14 (Records of the Postwar Naval Planning and Sea Frontiers Section, Office of the Commander-in-Chief, U.S. Fleet), Records of the Strategic Plans Division, CNO, Navy Operational Archives (hereafter cited as NOA) Branch, United States Naval Historical Center, Washington Navy Yard, Washington, D.C.

45. Ernest J. King and Walter Muir Whitehill, *Fleet Admiral King: A Naval Record* (New York: W. W. Norton & Company, Inc., 1952), 295–96.

46. Davis, *Postwar Defense Policy*, 10.

47. King and Whitehill, *Fleet Admiral King*, 294–98. Admiral King sat on the G. B. in 1939–1940 and, during that period, he and other board members thoroughly examined the need for additional overseas bases.

48. Chairman, G. B. to secretary of the Navy, letter (General Board no. 450, serial no. 236), 20 March 1943, file Naval Bases December 1942–December 1946, series 14, Records of the Strategic Plans Division, NOA.

49. Ibid., chairman, General Board to secretary of the Navy (G. B. no. 450, serial no. 240, Postwar Sovereignty over Certain Islands of the North Pacific, 27 March 1943, file Naval Bases March 1943–May 1946.

50. Ibid., G. B. no. 450, serial no. 240-A, Islands in the South Pacific, change in status of, 5 April 1943.

51. Not until November 1943 did Roosevelt see a completed JCS postwar base study.

52. The Tuamotu Archipelago is between the Marquesas Islands and the Society Islands though somewhat south of both.

53. President Roosevelt to secretary of the Navy, 12 June 1943, file Air Routes June 1943–November 1944, series 14, Records of the Strategic Plans Division, NOA.

54. Ibid., President Roosevelt to secretary of the Navy, 12 June 1943.

55. Ibid., Frank Knox to president, letter, 26 July 1943, enclosing chairman, G. B., to secretary of the Navy (G. B. no. 450, serial no. 246), Postwar Air Routes from the Panama Canal and South America to New Zealand and Australia, 21 July 1943. The seven airport sites were Clipperton Island; Nukahiva Island, Marquesas; Hiva Oa Island, Marquesas; Makatea, Tuamotu; Fakarava, Tuamotu; Easter Island; and Juan Fernandez, Henderson Group.

56. Ibid., President Roosevelt, memorandum for secretary of the Navy, 29 July 1943.

57. Admiral King, memorandum for secretary of the Navy, subject: Detail of Coast Guard Cutter for Exploration of Postwar Air Routes, and 29 July 1943, Knox to chairman, G. B., 29 July 1943, both in file Demobilization July 1943–July 1945, series 14, Records of the Strategic Plans Division, NOA; and Report of Investigation by Special Mission of Certain Pacific Islands in Connection with National Defense (primarily) and Commercial Air Bases and Routes, 6 vols., box 2, Papers of Rear Adm Richard E. Byrd, NOA. The airline representatives on the voyage were the vice president of Northeast Airlines; the superintendent of airways and airport engineering, Transcontinental and Western Airlines; the assistant vice president and Pacific operations manager, United Air Lines; the chief airport engineer, Pan American Airways; the director of communications and radio, American Airlines; and the chief of dispatching and meteorology, American Export Airlines.

58. Statistical History of the Air Transport Command, 29 May 1941–31 May 1948, 1–7, 28–29, file 300.197, AFHRA.

59. Gen Henry H. Arnold to board of directors, American Airlines, Inc., letter, 4 April 1942, file Commercial Airline Facilities, box 42, Arnold Papers; and H. H. Arnold, *Global Mission* (New York: Harper & Brothers, 1949), 294–95.

60. Biographical data on Harris, Mason, and Harding was drawn from *Who's Who in Aviation: A Directory of Living Men and Women Who Have Contributed to the Growth of Aviation in the United States, 1942–1943* (New York: Ziff-Davis, 1942); and the information on Samuel E. Gates and Capt Oliver J. Lissitzyn was taken from *Who's Who in America*, 39th ed., 1976–1977 (Chicago: Marquis Who's Who, 1976).

61. C. R. Smith to Governor General Pierre Boisson, letter, 15 December 1942, sec. 1, and bulky package, file CCS 334, Glassford Mission (12-9-42), RG 218, NA. The mission, headed by Rear Adm William Glassford, was sent by the JCS to secure base rights at strategic Dakar in Senegal to support both Allied forces then battling Germans and Italians in North Africa and antisubmarine-warfare operations in the Atlantic.

62. The document, "Bibliography of Plans Reports (with Abstracts)," is a summary of the reports submitted by ATC's Plans Division from 23 June 1942 to 31 December 1944. A copy is in box 495 (Bulky Decimal File), Army Air Forces Air Adjutant General, Classified Decimal File, 1946–1947, RG 18 (Records of the Army Air Forces), NA. Document is now declassified.

63. General Arnold to AFATC [Air Force Air Transportation Command], letter, subject: Study of Future Air Transport Possibilities, 10 October 1942, file Post War Civil Airlines, box 44, Arnold Papers.

64. Ibid.; and Arnold, *Global Mission*, 437. The ATC Plans officers appointed to the committee were Harris, Mason, and Gates.

65. Robert A. Lovett to Gen Henry H. Arnold, correspondence, 7 January 1943, file SAS 580, ATC case 54-197, box 142, Arnold Papers.

66. The other four were Assistant Chief/Air Staff (AC/AS)-1, Personnel; AC/AS-2, Intelligence; AC/AS-3, Operations, Commitments, and Requirements; and AC/AS-4, Materiel, Maintenance, and Distribution.

67. Smith, *Air Force Plans*, 5–6. The Special Projects Office, a special staff section reporting directly to General Arnold, was also involved in postwar planning, but it mostly coordinated the AAF's postwar plans with the War Department's Special Planning Division, which itself operated as the coordinating body for all Army and AAF postwar planning.

68. Robert A. Lovett, memorandum for General Arnold, 10 July 1943, file Post War Civil Airlines, box 44, Arnold Papers.

69. Ibid.

70. Ibid., Brig Gen Laurence S. Kuter, memorandum for General Arnold, 17 July 1943.

71. Ibid., General Arnold to Robert A. Lovett, letter, 20 July 1943.

72. General Arnold to assistant chief of the Air Staff (Plans), US Military Requirements for Air Bases, Facilities and Operating Rights in Foreign Territories, 5 August 1943, box 199, file Plans, Policies and Agreements, Office, Assistant Secretary of War for Air, RG 107 (Records, Office of the Secretary of War), NA.

73. See p. 11 this chapter.

74. A. A. Berle to Adm William D. Leahy, n.d., enclosing Preliminary Report of the Interdepartmental Subcommittee on International Aviation, sec. 1, file CCS 360 (12-9-42), RG 218.

75. Ibid.

76. Ibid., Adm William D. Leahy to A. A. Berle, correspondence, 16 March 1943.

77. A. A. Berle to Adm William D. Leahy, correspondence, 30 June 1943, enclosing Preliminary Report of the Interdepartmental Subcommittee on a United Nations Airport Authority, file CCS 686 (6-30-43), RG 218.

78. Ibid., memorandum by the Joint Strategic Survey Committee, 10 July 1943.

79. For examinations of the development of United States international aviation policy and Anglo-American commercial aviation rivalry during World War II, see John Andrew Miller, "Air Diplomacy: The Chicago Civil Aviation Conference of 1944 in Anglo-American Wartime Relations and Postwar Planning" (PhD diss., Yale University, 1971); and Henry Ladd Smith, *Airways Abroad: The Story of American World Air Routes* (Madison: University of Wisconsin Press, 1950), 92–181.

80. L. Welch Pogue to A. A. Berle, correspondence, 25 June 1943, enclosing Proposals for Consideration by the Principal Committee (19 June 1943), file Aviation, box 11, Hickerson-Matthews Files, Records of the Office of European Affairs, 1934–1947, RG 59 (General Records of the State Department), National Archives (NA).

81. Brig Gen J. E. Hull, acting assistant chief of staff, OPD, to JCS Secretariat, correspondence, 20 August 1943, enclosing Draft of Proposed Reply by the War Department, and Air Staff (Plans) Comments on Report of Interdepartmental Subcommittee on International Aviation, all attached as tab I

to ATC Plans Division Report no. 76 (hereafter ATC Plans Division Report no. 76), U.S. Military Requirements for Air Bases, Facilities and Operating Rights in Foreign Territories, 16 October 1943, file 300.04-20, AFHRA.

82. Ibid., Comments on Report of Interdepartmental Subcommittee on International Aviation, 8.

83. Ibid., 9.

84. Ibid., Draft of Proposed Reply by the War Department, 1–2.

85. Arnold to assistant chief of staff (plans), U.S. Military Requirements for Air Bases, Facilities and Operating Rights in Foreign Territories, 5 August 1943, box 199, file Plans, Policies and Agreements, Office of Assistant Secretary of War for Air, RG 107.

86. The Air Staff Plans report appears as a memorandum from the commanding general, AAF, for the JCS, United States Military Requirements for Air Bases, Facilities and Operating Rights in Foreign Territories (hereafter Air Staff Plans report, Air Bases), n.d., sec. 2, file CCS 360 (12-9-42), RG 218, 15, 19; and tab R of the ATC Plans Division Report no. 76.

87. See Air Staff Plans report, Air Bases 15–19, and ATC Plans Division Report no. 76.

88. G. A. B. [George A. Brownell], memorandum for Robert A. Lovett, 1 September 1943, box 199, Plans, Policies and Agreements, Office of Assistant Secretary of War for Air, RG 107. A lawyer from New York City, Brownell was commissioned a lieutenant colonel in the AAF in 1942. He had previous military experience in World War I but was not a career officer. He eventually rose to the rank of brigadier general and, in 1946, was appointed personal representative of the president with the rank of minister to negotiate in the Middle East and in India bilateral air transport agreements and other air matters for the United States.

89. Air Staff Plans report, Air Bases, 2, 5–6, and 8.

90. Ibid., 9–10. Rights to the bases connecting the eastern and western edges of the defense perimeter (Telergma, Algeria; Benghazi, Libya; Cairo, Egypt; Abadan, Iran; Karachi, India; Akyab, Burma; and Hanoi, French Indochina) apparently were not viewed as required for national defense because they were omitted from the Air Staff Plans base listing. Moreover, the map illustrating the base locations did not picture most of Africa and Eurasia. However, the connecting bases were included on the ATC Plans Division list.

91. Ibid., 7.

92. Ibid., 5 and 7–8.

93. Ibid., 11.

94. Ibid., 8–9.

95. ATC Plans Division Report no. 76, p. 10.

96. Ibid., 10–11.

97. Ibid., 10.

98. Air Staff Plans report, Air Bases, 20.

99. ATC Plans Division Report no. 76, p. 32; and tab T, The Axis Influence in South American Air Transport, Its Military Implications, and Its Elimination, file 300.04-20, AFHRA.

100. Ibid., tab U, Capt Oliver J. Lissitzyn, The Military Importance of Commercial Air Routes.

101. Ibid., 11 (quotation), 17, 28–29, 31–32, 38, and 41.

102. Ibid., 38.

103. Ibid., 24–26.

104. Ibid., 12; map 1 of the ATC Plans report, a polar projection titled Projected Post-war U.S. Military Air Routes and Bases; map 5 of the report is a polar chart of population density overlaid with the probable commercial air routes.

105. Pakistan was a part of India until 1947.

106. Quoted in Smith, *Air Force Plans,* 56–57.

107. Ibid.

108. Brig Gen Laurence Kuter, memorandum for Col A. J. McFarland, secretary, JCS, 9 October 1943, sec. 2, file CCS 360 (12-9-42), RG 218.

109. Ibid., memorandum for record, 12 October 1943.

110. Brig Gen Laurence Kuter, memorandum for Office of Assistant Secretary of War for Air (Attn: Col George A. Brownell), 13 October 1943, box 199, file Plans, Policies and Agreements, Office of Assistant Secretary of War for Air, RG 107.

111. Ibid., Robert A. Lovett, memorandum for assistant chief of Air Staff (Plans), 19 October 1943.

112. Air Staff Plans report, Air Bases, 12.

113. See ATC Plans Division Report no. 76, tab O, which is a letter from Berle to Lovett, dated 26 July 1943. In the letter, Lovett asked for clarification of US air operating rights in Brazil, Palestine, Iraq, Iran, Egypt, and India, referring to the JCS letter of 16 March 1943 to Berle as the "basis for our special interest in this area."

114. ATC Plans Division Report no. 76, p. 21. The ATC planners also suggested the substitution of a commercial transport system as a way to provide the "framework" for wartime expansion in cases where either the American people would not support maintenance of military facilities or where foreign governments were unreceptive to the permanent presence or even the transit of American military aircraft.

115. Lovett, memorandum for assistant chief of Air Staff (Plans), 19 October 1943, box 199, file Plans, Policies and Agreements, Office of Assistant Secretary of War for Air, RG 107.

116. Air Staff Plans report, Air Bases, 3, and ATC Plans Division Report no. 76, p. 21.

117. E. R. Stettinius Jr., acting secretary of state, to secretary of the Navy, 27 October 1943; and Knox to Berle, 12 November 1943, both in file Policies July 1940–October 1946, series 14, Records of the Strategic Plans Division, NOA.

118. After Truman became vice president, Mead took over the committee and immediately began to pressure the JCS regarding military base requirements.

119. John D. Hickerson to A. A. Berle, correspondence, 30 August 1944, file Postwar Disposition of Defense Projects, box 12, Hickerson-Matthews Files, RG 59, NA.

120. Rear Adm Wilson Brown to Adm William Leahy, correspondence, 7 October 1943, sec. 2, file CCS 360 (12-9-42), RG 218.

121. Ibid., JCS 570, U.S. Requirements for Post War Air Bases, 6 November 1943.

122. Sherry, *Preparing for the Next War*, 46–47.

123. Minutes, JCS 123d meeting, 15 November 1943, sec. 2, file CCS 360 (12-9-42), RG 218. See Plans, Policies and Agreements file, Lovett, memorandum for the chief of the Air Staff, 17 November 1943, box 199, Office of Assistant Secretary of War for Air, RG 107, for evidence that General Arnold probably took the Air Staff Plans paper with him on board the ship.

124. Minutes, JCS 123d meeting, 15 November 1943, sec. 2, file CCS 360 (12-9-42), RG 218.

125. Ibid., JCS, memorandum for the president, US Requirements for Postwar Air Bases, 15 November 1943.

126. Ibid., map of Military Air Base Requirements, Period II, attached to the 15 November 1943 JCS memorandum for the president. The assumptions are printed on the map.

127. Ibid., quotations are taken from the map Military Air Base Requirements, Period II.

128. Ibid., minutes, JCS meeting, 19 November 1943.

129. Gaddis Smith, *American Diplomacy during the Second World War, 1941–1945* (New York: John Wiley and Sons, Inc., 1965), 76–77.

130. Minutes, JCS meeting, 19 November 1943, sec. 2, file CCS 360 (12-9-42), RG 218.

131. Smith, *Airways Abroad*, 128.

132. Report of the Interdepartmental Committee on International Aviation, 31 August 1943, 4, file 145.86-343, AFHRA.

133. Ibid., 7.

134. JCS, memorandum for the president, 15 November 1943, sec. 2, file CCS 360 (12-9-42), RG 218.

135. Ibid., HCJ to records, 30 December 1943.

136. The island of Trinidad, one of the 99-year-lease bases, lies just off the Venezuelan coast.

137. Philip W. Bonsal to Duggan and E. R. Stettinius, 20 January 1944, file Venezuela, box 17, Hickerson-Matthews Files, RG 59. Bonsal, of the State Department's American Republic Affairs Division, acted as interpreter during the conversation with Venezuelan president Medina.

138. President Roosevelt to Cordell Hull, 7 January 1944, appendix to JCS 570/2, U.S. Requirements for Post War Air Bases, 10 January 1944, sec. 2, file CCS 360 (12-9-42), RG 218.

139. Ibid., JCS 570/7, 5 February 1944, enclosing President Roosevelt's letters to Cordell Hull, 1 February 1944.

140. Brig Gen J. E. Upston, memorandum for General Handy, Negotiations for Postwar Military Air Bases, 19 January 1944, file 580.82TS, sec. 2, cases 7-, box 101TS, Operations Division Classified Decimal File, 1942–1944, RG 165 (Records of the War Department General and Special Staffs), NA. Those attending the meeting were Berle; James C. Dunn (chief of the Division of European Affairs); Hickerson, and Green Hackworth (the secretary of state's legal adviser) from the State Department; Capt 0. J. Colclough from the Navy Department; Brig Gen J. E. Upston and Col Briggs, Operations Division, War Department General Staff; Col G. A. Brownell, Office of the Assistant Secretary of War for Air; and Col P. M. Hamilton, AC/AS-5. Document is now declassified.

141. Ibid. Bora Bora in the Society Islands had been occupied by the US Navy since 1942. After the war passed it by, the base on Bora Bora was placed in reduced status in April 1944 but was not disestablished until June 1946 (see United States Bureau of Yards and Docks, *Building the Navy's Bases in World War II*, vol. 2 [Washington, D.C.: Government Printing Office, 1947], 191, 202). The Cook Islands belonged to New Zealand. Sovereignty over Tongareva (Penrhyn) was disputed between the United States and Great Britain.

142. JCS 570/3, 10 January 1944, sec. 2, file CCS 360 (12-9-42), RG 218. The Joint War Plans Committee (JWPC), approximately 20 officers, were divided into color-coded "teams" made up of an officer from each service. One of the criteria for selection for the JWPC was recent and distinguished performance in a combat assignment.

143. Ibid., JWPC 185/D, 3 February 1944.

144. Early in June 1944, the "Special Team" became the Joint Post War Committee (JPWC), with additional officers assigned and its functions enlarged to include all postwar military problems of interest to the JCS (except those concerning postwar internal organization or occupation of enemy countries). From then on, the JPWC operated directly under the JSSC.

145. Capt A. D. Douglas, memorandum for F-1, 29 August 1945, file Naval Bases December 1942–December 1946, series 14, Records of the Strategic Plans Division, NOA.

146. Sherry, *Preparing for the Next War*, 53.

147. Air Staff (Plans), United States Military Requirements for Air Bases, Facilities and Operating Rights in Foreign Territories, n.d., sec. 2, file CCS 360 (12-9-42), RG 218, 9.

148. Ibid., JCS 570, 6 November 1943, appendix B, Recommended Policy on Postwar-Military Problems.

149. Robert A. Lovett, memorandum for Maj Gen Harold George, 8 January 1943, file SAS 580, ATC case 54-197, box 142, Arnold Papers.

THIS PAGE INTENTIONALLY LEFT BLANK

Chapter 2

Base Planning, 1943–1945

Between the preparation of JCS 570/2 in the autumn of 1943 and the beginning of efforts to have that plan revised in the spring of 1945, the American military moved toward creating the presidentially approved regional base network. Although the services did not coordinate with each other in drawing up their overall plans for the size, composition, and deployment of postwar military forces, JCS 570/2 nonetheless constituted a common framework for selecting postwar overseas bases.[1] While each service's postwar planning group was at work, the Joint Post War Committee (JPWC) (the name eventually assumed by the "Special Team" organized at the beginning of 1944), in cooperation with the State Department, undertook the job of what Assistant Secretary of State Berle described as "gathering in the military air bases."[2] But civilian War and Navy Department officials who were part of a movement (since the summer of 1944) to reassert the traditional place of the War and Navy Departments in the formation of American policy became dissatisfied with the meager results produced by the JCS and State Department committees on postwar bases. In early 1945, they started to apply pressure on the JCS to update their postwar overseas base requirements.

* * *

The October 1943 Air Staff Plans study of postwar air bases showed where the AAF thought the United States would need air-base rights, but the first indication of what strength was to be deployed to which overseas bases came in a June 1944 supplement to the AAF's *Initial Post-War Air Force* (*IPWAF*) Plan.[3] The mid-1944 document deployed air units to bases located "in an area extending eastward from the Philippine Islands to the west coast of Africa within the limits shown in the Blue and Green areas on the map entitled 'Period II (Peace Enforced by the Major Powers).'"[4] In other words, JCS 570/2 was as much a base bible for the AAF as it was for the Navy.

In contrast to JCS 570/2, the June 1944 deployment plan was not founded on the assumptions of the JCS's Period II during which peace would be enforced by the major powers, but rather for the postwar environment of Period III during which formally established worldwide machinery would keep the peace. In the latter phase, the United States would have accepted certain peacekeeping obligations growing out of its membership in the international organization. The AAF planners assumed that Great Britain and the USSR would "enforce peace in Europe and in most of Africa," while the United States would keep peace in the Pacific and, along with China, police Japan. In short, the PWD forecasted no long-term US role in Europe. The plan called for one very heavy bombardment group (30 aircraft) and one fighter group each to be stationed in Iceland, Dakar, and Casablanca—the closest any of the 105 AAF units would come to Europe and the Middle East under the supplement to the *IPWAF* Plan. This left the bulk (over 90 percent) of American airpower standing ready at Pacific, Alaskan, Caribbean, and continental US bases.[5] Despite the tranquil nature of Period III, the AAF planners still cautioned that the United States must be prepared to ward off attacks at all times, since international political relations could deteriorate at any time. They felt the most serious threats would come from Europe or Asia, most likely through the northern latitudes—the shortest routes to vital areas in the Western Hemisphere. Yet, of the 91 groups scheduled for overseas stations only 14 (about 15 percent) would go to bases along North America's northern reaches (and actually half would always be on continental US bases serving as a strategic reserve).[6] What explains this obvious discrepancy?

One historian of the AAF's postwar planning contends that the personnel of the PWD, although recognizing that the Soviet Union might be a long-term threat, thought in Mercator terms. Based on this thinking, they were unable "to grasp the strategic significance of the combination of a spherical planet, the location in the Northern Hemisphere of all the major powers, and the long, but not unlimited range of strategic bombardment aircraft."[7] The June deployment study, with a lineup of postwar air forces concentrated largely at bases in the Pacific, Far East, and Caribbean seems solid evidence that "Mercator projection thinking" did indeed dominate the AAF's PWD. Even when an officer from another Air Staff division suggested that "realistic planning must provide for protection against the real threat" and, consequently, this "might well indicate a greater concentration of force in Alaska and the Aleutians," Col R. C. Moffat, chief of the PWD, defended the June plan vigorously.[8]

Moffat's counterargument, based on some very practical considerations, illustrates the dilemma of the military planner who must somehow deal with past, present, and future. The PWD chief rejected the proposal to focus Pacific deployment on Russia because "the immediate task is to keep Japan in line by holding a big stick over her head." "But," he explained, "the deployment oriented on the former enemy is not primarily designed to fend off a blow from that quarter but to prevent Japan's rearming."[9] In mid-1944 Japan was not yet defeated, and a concern that she not be allowed to get back on her feet militarily was quite natural, just as would be a lessening of the intensity of those feelings as the war's end drew closer. Then, why were the planners not equally concerned about a resurgent Germany? The answer is that President Roosevelt, in approving JCS 570/2, had in effect indicated to the military that Europe would be outside the American sphere. The wartime policy of cooperation with the Soviet Union also probably restrained the AAF planners from programming a large postwar deployment against that country. "Our outposts in the Aleutians and Alaska, in the Atlantic bases and west coast of Africa," wrote Moffat, "are purposely not strong enough to constitute a dagger pointed at the Soviet heart or at Europe, but do provide routes for reinforcement to these countries and also, in our hands constitute a deterrent to offensive action aimed against the western hemisphere." In the event of war with Russia (or Great Britain), the strategic reserve would be used "to delay a decision until all our military might can be mobilized and brought to bear. Nothing short of an all-out full-scale effort would conceivably bring victory to the United States in the event of such a war."[10]

Other factors militated against an increased postwar deployment to Alaska. For one thing, Moffat thought that "the expense of maintaining additional groups" in Alaska was "not justified by the situation."[11] Alaska, with a climate as hard on machines as on people, was still a frontier in every sense.[12] For another thing, if one wanted to reach the USSR via the northern latitudes, then Alaska was not the best launching platform. "Alaska is close to the eastern extremity of Siberia," said Moffat, "but the latter is far distant from the sources of Soviet power."[13] (The shortest northern route to the urban and industrial regions of the Soviet Union, even if one proceeded directly over the pole, was not via Alaska but along a Great Circle route using bases in the northeastern United States, Newfoundland, or Iceland—all listed in the *IPWAF* Plan.) Later, in 1946 the AAF made much of a program to develop bases in the "arctic frontier." But, by then, relations with Russia had soured. The AAF had not suddenly discovered the strategic significance of transpolar attack routes. What the airmen found out was that by waving a polar-projection map around, one might impress an audience with the vital importance of airpower.

Rather than a blueprint drawn by geopolitical incompetents, the June 1944 overseas deployment plan was a document written by men who assumed, given the guidance of JCS 570/2, that the United States would have a regional, not a worldwide, postwar base network from which air forces would perform a number of tasks. Among these tasks would be (1) to defend the nation, its possessions, and the Western Hemisphere; (2) to police the Pacific, including Japan; and (3) to maintain US "economic well-being by ensuring access to essential raw materials, safeguarding our unhampered use of sea routes; and by providing for the military protection of our global air commerce."[14] The plan, in sum, distributed the available force so that it might be applied for a variety of purposes.

The AAF's postwar plans had to be integrated with those of the ground forces, but the War Department's overall plan for the size, composition, and deployment of the postwar military establishment remained unfinished at the war's end—primarily because the AAF rejected what it viewed as the ludicrously small number of groups (16) allotted for the postwar Air Force by the War Department's Special Planning Division.[15] In the summer of 1945, the AAF produced, in conjunction with the revision of JCS 570/2, a detailed study of postwar air-base requirements, but the War Department did not come out with an approved postwar overseas base plan that included the type and number of forces deployed to each base until 1946.

* * *

In the meantime, and in contrast to their War Department counterparts, the Navy's postwar planners, goaded by Secretary of the Navy James Forrestal (who had become secretary of the Navy in May 1944 after Frank Knox's death), completed their work in May 1945, and submitted their plan to the president and Congress in June. *Basic Post War Plan No. 1*, dated 7 May 1945, was the first Navy planning document to indicate both naval and air bases desired for postwar use, and the relative size and mission of each.[16] The Navy's postwar programmers, as had the AAF planners, proposed to maintain bases within the regional boundaries delineated by JCS 570/2. Analysis of the Navy's planning reveals not only the factors bearing on the selection of postwar bases, but also the nature and extent of Forrestal's influence.

At the beginning of 1944, Admiral King assigned a section of his staff (a group of about 100 officers and men through whom King planned and directed the Navy's combat operations during the war) to work full-time on postwar planning.[17] The following explanation of the Navy Department's wartime organization reveals the full significance of this change.

During the war, Admiral King was the COMINCH and CNO, spending nearly all of his time on the operational matters stemming from his COMINCH role and his position as one of the JCS, and leaving the tasks normally performed by the CNO (largely related to logistics) to Adm Frederick J. Horne, vice chief of Naval Operations (VCNO). In the COMINCH organization, King's chief of staff for much of the war was Adm R. S. Edwards. In September 1944, Edwards assumed the newly created post of deputy COMINCH–deputy CNO, becoming in effect the Navy's second most powerful officer. Admiral Horne stayed as VCNO, and his activities were confined to the Navy's logistical side.[18]

Postwar planning was completely under Horne's cognizance until the fall of 1944. In August 1943, Secretary Knox and Admirals King and Horne had agreed that a special planning section should be established in the CNO organization to handle postwar planning activities. At first, this was a one-man operation consisting of retired Adm H. E. Yarnell Jr. Later Yarnell's involvement ended, and the work was done by a handful of more or less anonymous CNO staff officers.[19]

The first plan to come out of the office of the CNO was *Navy Basic Demobilization Plan No. 1*, 17 November 1943.[20] Admiral Edwards, then King's chief of staff, forwarded a copy to Rear Adm D. B. Duncan, COMINCH's assistant chief of staff (plans), noting that "the idea is that VCN0 will in general make a tentative exploration of demobilization matters without reference to COMINCH, in view of the fact that the U.S. Fleet is too deeply engaged in prosecuting the war to give attention to post war problems at the present time." Edwards also remarked that sooner or later the planners on the COMINCH staff would themselves have to get involved in problems associated with the postwar Navy (e.g., fleet and task force composition and number of bases), but until then might, "if they have any spare time," give the subject some preliminary consideration. "Admiral King," Edwards concluded, "knows nothing about this as yet." King knew that postwar planning was being done under Horne but there is no evidence that he reviewed this plan, or knew that Edwards told Duncan's division to encourage some of his subordinates to think about postwar planning. Admiral King at this point was totally dedicated to running the Navy's war effort and almost had to be dragged into the business of postwar planning. In 1943 King would probably have looked askance at any of his COMINCH staff officers spending their time, spare or otherwise, on postwar planning. Edwards's memorandum does show, however, that postwar planning would someday come under the purview of the strategic planning experts on the COMINCH staff.[21]

The time came early in October 1944, when King directed Edwards to assume supervision of all of the Navy's postwar planning. A section, F-14 in Duncan's division, was assigned to assist in the overall postwar planning effort. Headed by Capt A. D. Douglas, the Postwar Naval Planning Section, as F-14 was eventually designated, went to work the first week in October 1944. Postwar planning also continued in the Office of CNO. In fact, Capt Charles J. Moore was brought back from the Pacific (where he had been Adm Raymond A. Spruance's chief of staff) to head a Postwar Planning Section (the absence of the word "naval" distinguished it from Douglas's section) in the CNO organization. Moore was to be (in theory) the actual chief of the work done in both sections, reporting directly to Edwards.[22]

What had motivated the restructuring and upgrading of the Navy's postwar planning? One of the officers in Douglas's section recalled after the war that he believed Forrestal was behind the move.[23] Indeed, on 21 September 1944 R. Keith Kane, one of Forrestal's civilian assistants, had sent the Navy secretary a memorandum sharply criticizing the Navy's postwar planning as understaffed, poorly coordinated, and lacking in direction. In fact, it was so bad that it endangered the Navy's prospects for securing congressional approval of its postwar program.[24] But Vincent Davis, author of the most authoritative study of the Navy's postwar planning, felt the Navy's standing with Congress was only a part of the reason for Forrestal's intervention. It was also due to "the failure of the Navy's postwar planners to see for themselves that Russia was the new enemy and their consequent failure to plan on this basis which prompted him to precipitate a major shakeup in the planning, the methods, and the staff personnel in October 1944."[25]

Forrestal had been harboring doubts about the Soviet Union for months. In May 1944, he reportedly exclaimed to George Earle, former governor of Pennsylvania, "My God, George, you and I and Bill Bullitt [US ambassador to the Soviet Union from 1933 to 1936] are the only ones around the President who know the Russian leaders for what they are."[26] Still, it is doubtful that Forrestal sought to influence the strategic aspects of the Navy's postwar planning in the fall of 1944 or even to communicate his suspicions of the USSR to the Navy planners.

Actually, Forrestal's first inquiry into postwar planning had occurred not in late September, but in May 1944. Shortly after

Knox's death, he asked Horne to bring him up-to-date on the Navy's postwar program, and the admiral dutifully forwarded the most recently completed plan.[27] With regard to possible enemies, the plan stated only that "the future of Russia as a naval power cannot be foreseen but it is reasonable to assume that this arm of her military forces will be considerably increased." The document also declared "Great Britain will be a strong commercial rival with the attendant possibility of future differences."[28] Though these statements reveal that the plan's authors labored under the long-held belief that the purpose of a navy was to fight another navy, they also show no particular focus on Russia as the next enemy of the United States.

Yet, Forrestal, who was then voicing great alarm about the intentions of Soviet leaders, apparently raised no objection to the plan sent to him by Horne. Forrestal undoubtedly shared with the Navy's top admirals the firm conviction that the United States must have a strong postwar fleet. He had also gained their gratitude for aggressively promoting (by means of a vigorous public relations effort) the Navy's position in the unification struggle then getting under way in Washington.[29] But this does not mean that men like King, Edwards, or Willson welcomed him into the arena of military strategy. On the contrary, they often held Forrestal at arm's length.[30] Part of this was a reflection of the general exclusion of the civilian leaders of the War and Navy Departments (and the secretary of state) from matters of high policy and strategy that were a consequence of the close relationship FDR had with the JCS.[31] Yet, Forrestal's isolation went beyond this. Secretary of War Henry L. Stimson, for example, described an attempt by Forrestal in the summer of 1944 to find out what strategy was to be followed in the Pacific. "This is a question," Stimson recorded in his diary, "which is now being thrashed out in the Combined Chiefs of Staff and I trod my way warily."[32] Obviously, Forrestal had not felt confident enough to approach King for the information—no doubt because, in contrast to the warm relationship between Stimson and Marshall, that between Forrestal and King was ice-cold. Some of this was due to differences in temperament between the two men, and some was the result of King's resentment of

Forrestal's campaign, even as undersecretary of the Navy, to separate the posts of COMINCH and CNO.[33]

Along with the clash over bureaucratic territory, the personality conflict between King and Forrestal, and the overall tendency for the civilian secretaries to be excluded from high military councils, an additional reason for the sharp limits to Forrestal's influence during this period was that the admirals were wary of the public relations outfit the secretary of the Navy had set up in his office to beat the Navy's drum. The following incident illustrates why. On the same day that he received R. Keith Kane's memorandum deploring the state of the Navy's postwar planning, Forrestal asked Admiral King for information on the progress of efforts to acquire overseas bases for postwar use. King replied on 26 September with a two-page status report and a copy of the president's letter of 1 February 1944 to the secretary of state. He pointedly remarked that, "it is my opinion that the subject of post war strategic bases may be said to be well in hand and will be followed closely by the Joint Chiefs of Staff and their agencies."[34] Little did King know that the public relations hustlers in the secretary of the Navy's office had prepared an article on the military's postwar base plans for publication in *American Magazine*. A copy of the article reached John Hickerson in the State Department on 27 September. Astonished, he called Admiral Willson to tell him what was going on. The next day, Willson told Hickerson that there had been a "heated session in Secretary Forrestal's office" and that someone—Willson thought it had been Eugene S. Duffield, Forrestal's assistant for public relations—had released the article for the Navy Department. "Willson and the Chiefs of Staff," reported Hickerson, "persuaded the Secretary of the Navy to withdraw the clearance and *American Magazine* was asked not to publish the article even though it had been set up in type."[35] Revelation of the military's postwar base plans in the midst of a war not yet won would have been a monumental indiscretion with immense potential for stirring up trouble both at home and abroad. Certainly, this incident must have put some strain on civil-military relationships in the Navy Department, further encouraging the admirals' tendency not to tell Forrestal anything about long-range military planning unless he specifically asked for information.[36]

Forrestal, in sum, may have prodded King to a reorganization of the postwar planning apparatus in the fall of 1944. But there is no evidence to suggest that he also communicated his belief to the Navy's strategic planners that the Soviet Union would emerge as the next US enemy or that he thought blueprints for the postwar Navy should be drawn to meet such a development. He had not, after all, taken the opportunity to change the direction of planning the preceding May. Moreover, in the fall of 1944 the nature of his relationship with King was such as to put him clearly on the outside looking in, when it came to questions of naval operations and strategy.

Actually, the planners in Captain Douglas's F-14 section, without any cues from Forrestal, had no difficulty concluding that Soviet and American interests were likely to collide after the war. Their assessment of the postwar international environment was perhaps the most perceptive and sophisticated analysis of any of the military postwar planning units. On the other hand, *Basic Post War Plan No. 1* of May 1945 gives no indication that Navy planners concentrated exclusively on the Soviet Union in drawing up the postwar program.

When he started work early in October 1944, Douglas surveyed the other services' postwar plans, noting the absence of "common basic estimates and guidance" for postwar planning. Finding this, he urged that the services coordinate their efforts through the Joint Strategic Survey Committee (JSSC) and JPWC (after those groups had consulted with the State Department). He additionally drafted a letter for Admiral King to submit to the JCS recommending this course of action. In his memorandum transmitting the letter written for Admiral King's signature, Douglas pointed out that JCS 570/2 was a step in the right direction. He argued that for Army and Navy postwar planning to be sound, it should be "based upon a broad analysis and determination of the post war position and responsibilities of the armed forces, and that such analysis and determination should, in turn, be based upon an analysis and estimate of the post war international position of the United

States." King, however, never signed the draft letter, nor is it certain that it even got past Edwards.[37]

With the rejection of the attempt to have Navy planning synchronized with the Army's under an umbrella of strategic assumptions provided by the JSSC and the JPWC, the F-14 planners went ahead on their own. One product of their labors was a 30-page document, dated 26 December 1944, that they referred to as the "Determination" or the "Determination of Requirements."[38] (It had no formal title.) While not without flaws, the Determination manifests a depth of analysis not common to most military postwar forecasts and merits a closer look.

Part I of the Determination was a model statement of the "ideology of national preparedness." The officers in F-14, along with almost every sector of the American military establishment, believed that war would come again. If the war involved one or more of the major powers, it would soon become a world war, inevitably drawing in the United States. If force could be applied soon against "aggressor nations," then world wars would not develop and Americans, consequently, would be spared enormous costs.[39]

Winston Churchill's characterization of the Europe of 1946–47 as a "charnel house, a breeding ground of pestilence and hate" describes well what the F-14 planners thought in 1944 about what mankind's second total war would leave in its wake. In contrast to 1914, the world had entered World War II "with its social and economic structures improvised and questioned and with the masses in a ferment of doubt, unrest and tension." The turbulence to come would exceed that following the Great War. In F-14's opinion, the clash of ideology would dominate the postwar landscape.

> The postwar era will be a revolutionary one, not only in respect to many nations internally, but in the sense of a universal contest between the opposing ideologies of capitalism and socialism, each seeking to attain acceptance as the recognized norm of human organization. The world will be acutely sensitive to this cleavage. Furthermore, but secondarily, the defeat of the Axis will by no means entirely eliminate the belief in fascism, or its continuation as an undercurrent among certain peoples. With the possible exception of parts of the Western Hemisphere, the world will move decidedly to the left in its social and

> economic philosophies and practices; this will be reflected in a wide in-
> crease in socialistic governments and governmental measures.

Against this background, every country would, to some extent, experience "economic dislocation and impoverishment," "social unrest leading in some cases to revolution or civil war," and "political uncertainty or instability." Traditional friction points as "trade and markets, national resources, boundaries, and national and ethnic minorities" would generate tensions be-tween nations, as would a continuation of prewar economic nationalism and war-spawned changes in the world balance of power.[40]

The future, thought the authors of the Determination, por-tended "radical shifts" in the global power balance. The United States, dominant in the Western Hemisphere, and a Soviet Union, ascendant in Europe, Asia, and the Near and Middle East, would be far and away the world's most powerful nations. Though occupying a swing position between two giants, Great Britain's power would be greatly diminished, as would that of France and other European nations. Reaching out to recapture their former possessions, all the European colonial powers would find their grips noticeably weakened, particularly in Asia and the Pacific. The ebb of European power would stimulate Latin American nationalism. China, only potentially a great power, would be the focus of Far Eastern turmoil and a pos-sible arena of conflict between the United States and the So-viet Union. A resurgent Germany was to be feared (the Nazis and German General Staff might go underground), though Japan would not be troublesome.[41]

According to the Determination, the world would witness a massive postwar struggle between capitalism and socialism, and since the United States would be the leading practitioner of the former system and the Soviet Union the most powerful (and only) exponent of the latter, the Navy analysts focused on them. American "prestige and moral influence" would be at its height, though her power and wealth (undeniably given a boost by the fortunes of war) would be resented by many. With con-siderable insight, the Navy planners argued that "the United States, practically alone among the larger powers, will be mak-ing an effort to resist the world current toward socialism and state control of economic life; this divergence may place it in political and economic isolation and in ultimate conflict with other nations." Second only in strength to the United States, the Soviet Union was potentially even more powerful because, as the champion of socialism, "her influence will extend far beyond her frontier and will exert a centripetal effect in a Europe and Asia devastated by war, dislocated economically, and unstable socially. This will be particularly true in Asia, where, in the minds and experiences of the masses, the Western nations are associated more directly with imperialism and colonial exploitation."[42]

Where and over what issues were the Soviet Union and the United States likely to have armed confrontation? The F-14 planners thought that in view of the "political and economic vacuum" created by the defeat of Japan, the two countries might well clash over "material interests" on the Asian mainland. The authors of the Determination did not specifically foresee a struggle with the USSR in Europe; that area having apparently been conceded to the Russian sphere of dominance. Still, confrontation was possible anywhere the United States and the USSR came head-to-head because

> the primary risk of armed conflict . . . will be in the fact that these nations will be the protagonists of the social and economic systems which will be competing in the minds of men for exclusive and universal acceptance and each of which, by the very fact of its existence, represents a continuing threat to the other. The post war world will pose no greater question than whether or not these two social philosophies and economic systems can concurrently exist without physical conflict or internal stress that would undermine one or the other.[43]

Thus, in two sentences, the authors of the F-14 paper captured the essence of the Cold War to come. Their analysis, of course, was not perfect. They did not foresee that the bipolar ideological struggle would mask a pluralistic reality underneath, or that the most potent postwar current was, in fact, the explosive combination of nationalism and a sometimes bewildering variety of socialist experiments. Nonetheless, the F-14 study stands as a thoughtful, sometimes brilliant, effort to define the contours of the postwar world.

Following the estimate of the postwar international situation, the F-14 planners went on to develop a "formula" for the size and composition of the postwar Navy that would apply in the immediate- and long-range future.[44] They concluded that the United States must have the minimum number of naval combatants "required to afford effective combat superiority over the active naval forces that any other single Power, or any combination of likely enemies, whichever is the larger, could bring to bear anywhere in the Atlantic or Pacific Oceans." The United States and Great Britain would have the only navies of significance after the war. The planners dismissed the British as a possible enemy; in their mind, the Soviet Union, without any appreciable navy, was the future opponent. Why, then, recommend a postwar fleet large enough to ensure superiority over a concentrated British navy, instead of the negligible Soviet fleet? Their formula for determining the postwar Navy's size seems to confirm Vincent Davis's observation that the ideas of Alfred Thayer Mahan, the late-nineteenth century American naval theorist, died hard in US Naval planning circles. One of Mahan's key concepts was that the purpose of a navy was to engage another navy. Indeed, according to the Determination, the United States should always maintain a fleet large enough to defeat the massed fleet of any potential opponent.[45]

But what of the Soviet Union with its relatively tiny naval force? "All power is relative solely," declared the F-14 planners, and

> the relative effectiveness of two opposed naval forces can no longer be measured solely in terms of naval vessels and naval aircraft. The capabilities of our own naval forces in relation to those of any other Power in the area in which our forces can or should operate against those of that Power can only be evaluated realistically if full account is taken of the support that can be given to one force or the other in that area by the new factors of land based air power and aerial weapons.[46]

Again, navy was to fight navy, but not independently. This reflected absorption of the experience of World War II and was the planners' answer in advance to any assertion that the United States did not need a large postwar fleet because the Soviets would not have one.

Although Mahan's ideas weighed heavily on the F-14 planners, there is evidence in the Determination that they were beginning to break free of his intellectual shackles. Its authors wrote that the postwar Navy must be a force "capable at any time of sustained operations in enemy waters and *over enemy territory* and capable of immediate and offensive amphibious or triphibious operations or *immediate long-range sea-air strikes*" (emphasis added).[47] These statements indicate that the F-14 planners were aware of the concept of sea-airpower and understood that naval force might be applied against a predominant land power such as the Soviet Union. Did the F-14 planners link the concept of sea-airpower with naval action against the Soviet Union? Yes, but apparently only in Asia, where the American and Soviet spheres overlapped. According to the Determination, active naval forces were to be deployed and advance bases selected to support requirements stemming from US obligations as a member of the UN, and from the demands of a revolutionary postwar era dominated by a "universal contest between the opposing ideologies of capitalism and socialism."[48] This implied that although US naval forces were to be used against another navy, they could also be used against the rising tide of a "left" inspired by the Soviet example. Yet, contrary to the prospect of a worldwide ideological contest, the officers in F-14 anticipated only the regional application of American naval power in the postwar years.

The Determination defined the American naval sphere as the western Atlantic, and the Pacific east of the Malay Peninsula, with the following key operational zones:

1. the North Atlantic approaches to North America,
2. the Middle Atlantic between the bulges of South America and Africa,
3. the eastern and southern approaches to the Caribbean,
4. the Pacific approaches to the Panama Canal,
5. the waters contiguous to Japan and to the Philippines, and
6. the arctic and Alaskan air approaches to North America.

The paper named no specific bases, but suggested that they would be generally available in the Japanese Mandated Islands, the Philippines, Japan, the South and Southwest Pacific, South and Central America, the Caribbean, Canada, the eastern Atlantic, and the west coast of Africa (the parameters of JCS 570/2 are recognizable in this geographical grouping). In sum, there was to be very little naval presence close to Europe (none in the Mediterranean). If naval power were applied against the USSR, it would have to be in the Far East.[49]

Confusion over Great Britain's postwar role and the consequential failure to anticipate US involvement in Europe after the war were the major flaws in the F-14 analysis. The Navy planners predicted Great Britain would be flat on its back economically and undergoing intense pressure for the reduction of its military forces, yet still responsible for the naval policing of the eastern Atlantic, Mediterranean, Middle and Near East, and Indian Ocean.[50] Following the war, the British would be unable to assume this heavy burden, a key factor in the dramatic postwar expansion of American military power into Europe and the Mediterranean—a development for which the Navy, having postwar plans oriented on the Pacific and western Atlantic, was largely unprepared.

How widely did the Determination circulate within the Navy Department, and to what extent did it influence the drafting of *Basic Post War Plan No. 1*? Admiral Edwards, deputy COMINCH-deputy CNO, sent it to Adm A. J. Hepburn, chairman of the General Board, who responded with two pages of comments and the judgment that it was an "excellent" paper.[51] There is no indication that the document ever went to King or Forrestal. Furthermore, there is little trace of the Determination's incisive political analysis (no mention of Russia) in the short, three-page statement ("The United States Navy [Postwar] Basis for Preparation of Plans") signed by King and approved by Forrestal in March.[52] Examination of the process by which the planners in Douglas's COMINCH section and Moore's CNO unit prepared the March document shows what happened to the Determination. Shortly after Admiral Edwards received Admiral Hepburn's comments on F-14's long paper, he asked the planners for a statement to be used as a basis for postwar planning. The statement would need to be suitable for submission to Admiral King and eventually the secretary of the Navy.[53] Much of the language in the five-page paper drafted for this purpose in F-14 was taken from the Determination document, especially those concepts constituting what historian Michael Sherry has tagged the "ideology of national preparedness." Douglas, however, omitted the detailed estimate of the postwar international environment (and any mention of the Soviet Union), listing only several "elements to be studied" in evaluating the US position in the postwar world.[54] Captain Moore then edited a shorter draft of this document intended to provide intellectual underpinnings for the Navy's postwar plans. Admirals Edwards, Willson, and Duncan along with Captains Moore and Douglas would exchange drafts of the shortened version for more than a month.[55] Douglas complained that the statement was becoming much too general (Moore had stricken Douglas's "elements to be studied" from the text), and by March all that remained of the Determination were the preparedness tenets and similar broad definitions of the Navy's postwar sphere of activity.[56]

As finally signed by Admiral King, the statement called for the Navy "to maintain command of the sea in the western part of the North and South Atlantic Oceans including the approaches thereto, and in the entire Pacific Ocean including the approaches thereto." It also declared that the Navy's postwar plan should provide for the maintenance of "naval forces in such strength and condition of readiness that they may be moved promptly and in effective force to any part of the world in support of our national policies."[57] Because this sentence suggests that the Navy now envisioned a global role for itself after the war, its origins are a matter of some interest. As first drafted by Admiral Willson, the sentence read an "effective force *in* any part of the world."[58] Douglas objected that "this seems to take the lid completely off. How can we plan for that?"[59] After talking with Willson, Moore altered the sentence to read "*to* any part of the world" and told Edwards that Willson's sentence had been "misunderstood as a requirement that naval forces in superior strength would be available all over the world. . . . The forces organized to control the Atlantic and Pacific are the ones to be moved promptly and in effective strength to support our policies."[60] This dialogue, resulting in the changing of a preposition, reveals what the Navy officers thought would be the extent of their service's postwar mission. The phrase "to every part of the world" indicates that the Navy had abandoned the view expressed in the attachment to JCS 570/2, Policy on Post War Military Problems. The attachment suggested limiting

American postwar military commitments "insofar as possible to the Western Hemisphere and the Far East."[61]

A change of thinking appears to have taken place; the admirals now seemed to accept the idea that American naval forces should be prepared to operate around the world after the war. Since the fall of 1943, the evolving "ideology of national preparedness" consensus and the increasing prospect that an international policekeeping organization would become a reality had expanded the horizons of Admirals King, Edwards, and Willson. Nevertheless, the admirals' focus in the spring of 1945 was still regional, and overwhelmingly so. Naval forces might be sent worldwide to support national policies, but the admirals' foremost concern was to make the Pacific an American lake, while maintaining a tight grip on the Atlantic approaches to the Western Hemisphere. A close examination of the anticipated postwar tasks shows that *regionalism*, not *globalism*, was most characteristic of Navy strategic thinking in 1944–45.

Navy planners began to identify postwar base sites in the fall of 1944. The process involved consultation with combat commanders in the Pacific and was completed in May when *Basic Post War Plan No.1* was promulgated within the Navy Department. Appendices to the plan listed the Pacific and Atlantic bases desired for postwar use and the peacetime operational status and mission of each base.[62] All were within the framework of JCS 570/2, though most emphasis was on bases in the Pacific.

The subject of postwar bases came up at several wartime conferences that Admiral King held with Adm Chester W. Nimitz, American naval commander in the Pacific. Nimitz first raised the topic at a meeting (29 September to 1 October 1944) in San Francisco, California, in the context of a discussion about base use in the Philippines following the country's liberation (the assault on Leyte Gulf in the heart of the Philippine archipelago was then but three weeks away). Nimitz thought that Manus (an Australian mandate northeast of New Guinea but still south of the equator) and islands in the Japanese Mandates would be logical choices for postwar bases.[63] The next conference was also held in San Francisco, 24–26 November 1944. During the conference, Admiral King read from a lengthy paper on postwar bases in the Pacific that had been prepared under Admiral Edwards's direction and requested "early comment" from Nimitz.[64] The document's key assumption was that postwar national policy would require the Navy to control "the entire Pacific." It outlined previous naval opinion on the postwar base issue (including a summary of the General Board's early 1943 recommendations regarding Pacific bases). It also set forth the government's policy and the joint chiefs' opinion on postwar bases in the Philippines and future control of the Japanese Mandates. Last, it summarized the provisions of JCS 570/2 and presented a list of some 35 tentative sites.[65] Nimitz was slow in responding to King's request; even more than King, he was reluctant to spend time on postwar matters while the war was in progress. King was not alone in this; the planners in Washington had trouble getting Nimitz's formal views.[66]

Forrestal, as noted earlier, was particularly interested in the Navy's postwar base plans, asking Admiral Horne in mid-December 1944 and again in January 1945 for information on the Navy's postwar advance bases. Naval planners were told that Forrestal wanted the data so that he might be prepared to answer questions from congressmen and to avoid embarrassment if the subject came up at cabinet meetings. Horne turned the request over to Moore, who passed it to F-14 (the normal, if cumbersome, procedure). The officers in F-14 prepared a summary similar to that given to Nimitz, suitable for use before congressional committees, and in January (twice) forwarded information on potential postwar base sites. Horne emphasized to Forrestal the very tentative nature of the base selections and that final decisions would have to wait on the resolution of many questions. Horne also advised Forrestal of an important attitude toward advance bases held by the Navy's planners:

> I wish to point out that we do not necessarily need to have naval shore bases at *all* of the sites listed. Such a multiplicity of bases would tend to dissipate our strength, require excess personnel and equipment for their maintenance and defense, and cause a disproportionate amount of our funds to be diverted from our main requirements, i.e., a powerful, mobile fleet, and an adequate train. Dependence on bases, per se, in defense of our interests is a dangerous concept. Advance bases be-

come a source of weakness unless we have the mobile fleet strength to back them. The foregoing considerations coupled with the thought that naval bases to be of value or even to justify their existence must be *used*, puts a pretty definite limit on their number. However, for international political and negotiating reasons, we should *ostensibly* plan to establish bases at every island and location that has any real value as a base in our defense concept.

The Navy, then, did not plan to use a long list of bases as justification for a large fleet. What was important, explained Horne, was the Navy would have "exclusive rights to build and control bases wherever we deem essential."[67] The distinction between actually building and fortifying a base and having the right to do so was important, and increasingly critical, as the budgetary squeeze grew tighter and tighter after the war.

Forrestal's inquiries signaled his increasing involvement in the Navy's postwar planning. In mid-January 1945, he arranged a briefing on the Army's postwar plans from the War Department's Special Planning Division to the Navy's top civilian and military leaders. Briefed that the Army had no basic assumptions about what its postwar role was going to be and that the assumptions governing selection of overseas bases were very general, coming either from the JCS (presumably JCS 570/2) or were self-generated, Forrestal and the admirals agreed that the Navy would, to a certain extent, have to make its own assumptions.[68] Moreover, estimates of the Navy's postwar program should not be geared primarily to anticipated budgetary strictures but to the Navy's probable mission. As Forrestal put it, "I don't think we ought to try to interpret what we think Congress will do. I think we ought to tell them what we want them to do."[69]

Forrestal had little to do with formulating strategic assumptions; his chief role was as a whip driving the planners to finish their work. Early in February 1945, the Navy secretary sent a memorandum to Admiral King (then attending the Yalta Conference) stating that he was "disturbed" about the "rather inchoate condition" of studies on the size of both the postwar Navy and postwar overseas and stateside bases. He pointed out that base size related to decisions about the construction of such facilities as berthing areas and dry docks, all of which turned on the size of the fleet. Forrestal thought that, "this study should be prosecuted more vigorously than it has been up to now."[70] Edwards left a note for King saying that in view of the Navy secretary's memorandum, he was going ahead with a "concrete plan" for the size of the fleet, though it would "not [be] easy to make a realistic estimate of what we will have to fight against in the next war, which is the only logical foundation for the plan."[71] Two days later, Edwards sent a formal memorandum to King (now back from Yalta) repeating these thoughts and mentioning that Nimitz had not yet replied to the request for postwar base recommendations. The memorandum went on to state that he expected to come up with a Navy roughly the size estimated in previous plans (i.e., a Navy of 550,000 and a Marine Corps of 100,000 personnel).[72]

Following the King-Nimitz conference in March 1945 and a meeting King had with Forrestal shortly thereafter (at which the latter got a better idea of what bases the Navy believed should be retained), the F-14 planners were told what tentative decisions had been made regarding Pacific bases.[73] On 13 March, King listed without elaboration those Pacific and Atlantic bases he "intended as a basis for consideration within the Navy Department." King specified Pearl Harbor, Hawaii; a base in the Mariana Islands; three in the Philippines; Manus (Nimitz's recommendation) as the Navy's major operating bases in the Pacific; and eight other locations as secondary bases. Significantly, he listed the Atlantic bases last. Roosevelt Roads (located between Puerto Rico and the Virgin Islands) was the only major Atlantic base. Argentia, Newfoundland; Bermuda; Guantanamo, Cuba; and Trinidad, British West Indies, were to be secondary operating bases. Additionally, the Navy would seek "options" or base rights at several other Pacific sites, in the Natal-Recife area of Brazil, and the Dakar-Bathurst area of West Africa. King's memorandum, a bare outline of the Navy's postwar bases, did not distinguish between naval and air bases. On the other hand, the heavy emphasis on the Pacific was quite noticeable.[74]

Forrestal, whose diary entries between the fall of 1944 and spring of 1945 reveal a man increasingly alarmed about the Soviet Union, nevertheless demonstrated no more interest in Atlantic bases than did the Navy's top admirals. When the subject of postwar bases came up at the periodic meetings of the secretaries of state, war, and Navy (Committee of Three) during this period, the focus was on arrangements for bases in the Philippines, following that country's independence, and for US control of the Japanese Mandates. While on a trip to the Pacific in February 1945, Forrestal asked Adm Thomas C. Kinkaid, Seventh Fleet commander, for recommendations regarding the shore establishment he believed should be retained in the Philippines after the war.[75] On the same trip, the Navy secretary also discussed Philippine bases with Gen Douglas MacArthur, the Southwest Pacific commander, who advised against bases in either Subic Bay or Manila Bay, Philippines, so as not to offend Filipino pride.[76] At the end of March, Forrestal dictated a memorandum stating his view that the main categories of the Navy's postwar problems were

1. Pacific Ocean Areas (POA)—what bases are needed for the security of the POA?
2. definition of our requirements for bases in the Philippines
3. size of the postwar Navy. . .
4. examination of industrial establishments. . . and
5. reserve educational policy at the Naval Academy.[77]

Clearly, Forrestal and the Navy's top brass faced west—not east. The only dissent from the Pacific orientation was in F-14, and that, as we shall see, was relatively muted.

The overseas base appendices to *Basic Post War Plan No. 1* contained detailed data on postwar Pacific and Atlantic bases and revealed fully the extent to which the former overshadowed the latter. At first glance, the more than 75 sites for both the Pacific and Atlantic seemed staggering. But of the 53 Pacific locations, only eight were to be regular operating bases, while 10 would be in reduced or maintenance status, and five in caretaker status, available for emergency use.[78] The rest (30 sites) would be dependent on changing circumstances with Navy forces not normally maintained at the locations. This same pattern held true for the two dozen or so Atlantic sites. All regular operating locations were in the western Atlantic, though the Navy planned to seek participating base rights at such eastern Atlantic locations as Iceland; the Azores; Port Lyautey,

Morocco; Liberia; the Cape Verde Islands; the Canary Islands; and Dakar.[79]

Unlike in the Atlantic, where the most important bases were close to home, the pattern of Pacific bases showed the Navy intended to wield a very big stick in the Far East. In addition to the Philippines, the Navy targeted Guam-Saipan (the Mariana Islands), the Bonin-Volcano Islands, and the Ryukyu Islands for regular operating bases—in other words, almost half of the most important Pacific bases. Significantly, the Ryukyu Islands (encompassing Okinawa) were not enclosed by the blue-bordered area of JCS 570/2 ("required for direct defense of the U.S., leased areas, and possessions, including the Philippines"), but fell in the black-bordered area ("required by the U.S. as one of the Great Powers enforcing peace, pending a world wide organization"). Furthermore, the Navy planned to acquire base rights at 20 places in the black-bordered area; about half in the southwest Pacific with the remainder in the Far East (e.g., parts of the Dutch colonial empire; Bangkok, Thailand; Hainan Island; Formosa; Japan proper; Korea; the Kurile Islands; and North China).[80]

Basic Post War Plan No. 1 was the high-water mark of the Navy's planning for overseas bases. Each subsequent plan during the remainder of 1945 and through 1946 programmed a reduction in the number of bases and the degree of activity planned for bases that were to be retained. All of the overseas base selections were within the blue, green, and black-bordered areas of JCS 570/2. The Navy was not acting independently in this respect, having in fact adopted the assumptions about the regional character of the postwar role of the United States implicit in that document. Moreover, Navy officers at headquarters sought the views of the combat commanders (however misdirected those may have been—i.e., Manus) before choosing bases for postwar use. Aside from the sheer number of locations, the most striking aspect of the Navy's overseas base planning was the emphasis on the Pacific, particularly the concentration of bases in the Far East.

In addition to predicting a worldwide ideological clash between the United States and the USSR, the F-14's Determination of Requirements paper also suggested that "a further risk of conflict . . . will be in the possible clash of material interests in Asia." *Basic Post War Plan No. 1* provided for three Pacific and two Atlantic fleets along with a system of bases concentrated in the western end of the Pacific. This structure was not incompatible with F-14's analysis of the postwar international environment. Under those assumptions, Russia would dominate postwar Europe and the Middle East, while an effective British navy would lie between the two superpowers. In this, the F-14 planners were simply following President Roosevelt's apparent intention, confirmed by his approval of JCS 570/2, to put an end to the American military presence in Europe as rapidly as possible after the war. Mahanian thinking probably had something to do with the way the Navy approached its postwar planning (i.e., in determining the size of the fleet), but the chief influence on the planned distribution of American naval power was the regionalism that dominated all the military services' postwar planning until mid-1945.

From the middle of 1944 through May 1945, Forrestal played a somewhat less influential role in the Navy's postwar planning than scholars have previously believed. There is no question that without his constant prodding, the Navy planners might have ended the war, as did the War Department without a completed plan. On the other hand, he appears to have had little, if anything, to do with formulating the assumptions anchoring the Navy's plans. In July 1945, Forrestal became quite insistent that the United States maintain postwar air bases in Iceland, a concern not shared by Admiral King. As we shall see, the two were not as one over the importance to attach to this North Atlantic outpost in the US postwar base structure.[81] Until the summer of 1945, Forrestal followed the admirals in charting a postwar course to the fringes of the Pacific.

* * *

President Roosevelt was evidently figuring on the bare minimum of permanent American military involvement in postwar Europe. This resulted in American military leaders and planners drawing plans with a strong Pacific bias. The president further encouraged this orientation by repeatedly linking postwar Pacific military bases and civil airports, particularly along the Great Circle route to the Orient via Alaska and the Aleutians and along the route through France's South Central Pacific possessions. After a wartime conference with General MacArthur and Admiral Nimitz in Hawaii in July 1944, FDR, aboard the heavy cruiser *Baltimore*, went north to Alaska before returning to the United States. At Adak in the Aleutians, where some 20,000 American soldiers and sailors were stationed, Roosevelt spoke, drawing a parallel between the far northern Pacific coast and that of northern New England. He hoped, he said, that some of the servicemen would return to Alaska as permanent settlers following the war.[82] While no doubt primarily intended to boost the morale of the troops, the president's remarks also reflected his desire to build up an area that constituted both a potential avenue of air attack and a key air route on the path to the Far East. During his visit, the president expressed interest in aviation's future in Alaska. As a result, Lt Gen Delos C. Emmons, commander Alaska Department, designated a joint board of Army and Navy officers to investigate "current and future military and civil aviation requirements to meet the needs of the war effort and of postwar civil and military aviation for air routes and facilities to and through continental Alaska and the Aleutians."[83] Emmons and Assistant Secretary of War for Air Lovett wanted the Air Transport Command (ATC) to send a qualified officer to advise the board.[84] ATC dispatched none other than the prolific and expert Oliver J. Lissitzyn who wrote most of the joint Army-Navy board's report, prepared for submission to the president.[85] Whether Roosevelt ever saw the report is not known, but it eventually made its way to the JCS, and was referred to by them in the planning for the postwar defense of Alaska that began in the spring of 1945.[86] While the report was being written, Emmons told Lissitzyn that he intended to print the latter's draft "after deletion of certain parts dealing with future political and military prospects."[87] Thus, Lissitzyn's copy of the report is the most interesting, as it gives a complete view of the Army-Navy board's deliberations and a good look at the attitude of Lissitzyn, who in the spring of 1945 would receive a special assignment to help the

AAF revise its postwar base plans.[88]

Lissitzyn's theme was straightforward and argued at great length: the potential for postwar American trade and investment in East Asia was enormous, fast air communications would help the United States tap this mine of economic opportunity, and an air route through Alaska and the Aleutians was the shortest way to the Orient. Therefore, the United States should develop air routes and facilities in its far northern territory.[89] Strong Alaskan military bases were necessary "to repel any surprise attack" and should "be so constructed that they could be expanded readily for use by our striking forces against nations in Eurasia."[90] Still, Lissitzyn's emphasis lay much less on physical security than on furthering postwar American economic growth.

The expansion of American trade and influence into East Asia, wrote Lissitzyn, would tend to promote stability and peace in that area, the economic development of the United States, and a strong national defense. Moreover, America would need to spread its economic tentacles into Asia because "the present war has expanded our economic producing ability to the extent that we must depend upon international commerce for proper utilization of our productive capacities." The main chance must not be lost; the nations of Asia would be America's "principal customers."[91]

American penetration of East Asia was a lucrative prospect (indeed mandated by the swollen wartime production capacity of American industry), but Lissitzyn conceded that it might give rise to conflict with the USSR over China. The risk must be taken, however, since the consequences of a US failure to play an active postwar role in the Far East would be even worse because Russia, China, and Japan might form an "economic coalition," shutting out the United States. However, if the United States could develop strong economic ties in Asia and "demonstrate our willingness to protect our interests there, both politically and by use of force, as indicated by the maintenance of strong bases in the Alaska and Aleutians-Kurile areas, we may be able to lessen the possibility of such conflicts." Bases, as Lissitzyn saw them, were akin to Mahan's coaling stations, only this time primarily for safeguarding air commerce. Adak, he declared, "is strategically located to protect commerce along Great Circle routes to the Far East as well as to serve as a major intermediate base for airlines to the Far East."[92]

What Lissitzyn's thinking boiled down to was a panegyric on behalf of capturing the China market—the goddess that had lured Yankee entrepreneurs since the day in the early 1790s when the *Empress of China* set sail from Boston. After World War II, however, the United States would have no need to follow the British wake in the Orient as in the nineteenth century or have to rely on moral sanctions to uphold the policy of the Open Door. The world's most powerful nation could easily bring force to bear in order to maintain peace and stability. Lissitzyn's vision was "Stimsonianism" in full flower. One must not make more of Lissitzyn's study than it merits. Lissitzyn was a civilian in uniform, approaching questions of postwar military planning from the perspective of commercial aviation. Nonetheless, the fact that he wrote the joint Army-Navy board report shows that some career military officers like Emmons believed commercial and military aviation would be close allies, dependent on one another in the future.

The two appear to have been joined in FDR's mind also, not only in Alaska, but in the South Central Pacific as well. Roosevelt's concern for the fate of Clipperton Island resulted in his sending a warning letter to Churchill toward the end of 1944 and the landing of a small, armed, American force on what was but for the sake of geographic accident a valueless protrusion from the ocean floor. The president had wanted Admiral Byrd's expedition to survey Clipperton Island as a site for a postwar military air base or civil airport. Byrd's party returned from French Oceania in December 1943, and in June 1944, Forrestal forwarded the admiral's six-volume report to Roosevelt.[93] The first five volumes covered commercial air bases and routes, while the last was Byrd's personal summary of the mission's accomplishments and his analysis of future defense considerations in the Pacific.[94] Byrd's report cannot be summarized briefly, but he recommended that the air route best serving the needs of postwar commerce and strategy in the South Pacific was through Clipperton Island, Nuku Hiva in the Marquesas Islands, Aitutaki in the Cook Islands, Tongatabu in the Tonga Islands, thence to New Zealand and Australia. After a detailed discussion of the postwar strategic situation in the Pacific (the admiral thought the United States would control the whole ocean after the war), Byrd concluded that the United States would require a large island base in the South Pacific (not necessarily Clipperton) to defend the Panama Canal. This island base would perform the same function for South America that Hawaii did for North America.[95]

Since the Byrd mission was the president's special project, the report circulated widely throughout the government and received considerable attention. The Operations Division (OPD) of the War Department's General Staff briefed it to General Marshall. Although OPD thought the JPWC should study Byrd's recommendations regarding French Oceania, the Army staff officers criticized the admiral for failing to give sufficient attention to airpower's potential and to future technological advances in aerial weapons. OPD also questioned Byrd's assumption that the Pacific Ocean would be entirely in the US postwar peacekeeping sphere. "It is possible," commented OPD, "that the British would challenge this viewpoint, particularly if they regain Singapore and Hong Kong." The War Department analysts felt the British would need to regain their Far Eastern "prestige" and "their postwar trade will lead them to the great market which China will provide." Australia, New Zealand, and Russia were also likely to assert Pacific roles for themselves, concluded the OPD officers.[96]

The AAF's reaction to Byrd's report was predictable, with the admiral receiving a sermon from General Arnold on airpower's policing capability as it might be embodied in a "striking force of long-range, land based, very heavy bombers and long-range fighters." Moreover, Byrd was told that the proper use of air forces would mean savings in the cost of the postwar military establishment, most notably in naval expenses: "With limited means for maintaining the peacetime establishment, great care must be used in apportioning the effort between land, sea, and air forces to obtain the greatest possible economy. With air supremacy assured over vital sea areas, a smaller Navy can suffice, and hence a lesser need for expensive naval bases."

Needless to say, nothing was said about the price tag of overseas air bases. Although Arnold conceded that no power should be permitted to become entrenched in French Oceania, he doubted that a base on the order of Pearl Harbor was needed to prevent this. The AAF's commander thought the major US base west of Hawaii should be in the Philippines and that the air route through the French islands was not one that must be held "at all costs."[97] As time went on, the AAF increasingly dismissed the Pacific, south of the equator, as of little strategic importance. The Navy, however, remained attached to the seas under the Southern Cross (e.g., the plan for a major base on Manus in the Admiralty Islands and the presidentially inspired attachment to French Oceania) well into 1946.

Late in October 1944, Admiral Byrd received the president's personal thanks at a meeting at the White House, and FDR made the polar explorer a delegate to the International Aviation Conference scheduled to open in Chicago, Illinois in December.[98] Soon after Byrd met with the president, a British scheme to build an airfield on Clipperton Island brought some tension not only to Anglo-American but also to Franco-American relations.

The Royal Air Force, hoping to construct a landing field on Clipperton Island (ostensibly in support of the Pacific war effort), sought US Navy backing. The British wanted US Navy help in their approach to the Mexican government for permission to establish an air route from Belize, British Honduras, to Acapulco and thence to Clipperton. The American military recognized that what the British really wanted was to set up a postwar commercial airway (Admiral King labeled the British ploy an "obvious postwar commercial venture"). It would be masked as a wartime military route from Great Britain through the British West Indies, across Mexico and the French South Pacific islands, to New Zealand and Australia.[99] King declined to give the Navy Department's support, but the British evidently remained undaunted, as a British survey party was observed at Acapulco late in November. Consequently, Roosevelt sent a firm note to Churchill, reminding the British prime minister of the Monroe Doctrine, American public opinion, and the fact that an international gathering was at that moment dealing with postwar civil aviation agreements. FDR suggested "any plan of development of military bases on Clipperton or any other territory in or near American waters be discussed by the governments concerned rather than by the armed forces." The American president requested that Churchill "cancel any instructions by your people about a further survey of Clipperton Island until you and I can discuss it."[100] Just to keep the British honest, the Navy reconnoitered the island by air and landed a small (although armed) observation and meteorological unit in early December.[101]

In explaining these actions in a formal letter to the secretary of state, Roosevelt did not mention the connection between Clipperton and postwar international aviation, saying only that the island's fate was "of significance to the United States because of the strategic location with respect to the Panama Canal."[102] But less than two weeks earlier, the president had revealed another and probably the most important reason for his interest in the island in a conversation with George S. Messersmith, American ambassador to Mexico. Roosevelt told the diplomat that he wanted the island put under Mexican sovereignty rather than returned to French control following the war. According to Messersmith, the president believed that after the change in ownership, appropriate arrangements should be made so that the United States, the British, and others could use Clipperton as a base for commercial air operations because "of its real importance in connection with certain air routes."[103] While the president and the military may have spoken about the possible threat a nonhemispheric military power's presence posed to the Panama Canal, it is more likely that Roosevelt's most pressing concern was stopping the development of a flanking commercial air route south of the United States by the British. With such a route, they might be able to blunt an important American tool for fashioning an "Open Door" in postwar commercial aviation—control of the Pacific air routes.

If the British were frustrated by the American "occupation" of Clipperton Island, the French were quite unhappy. Georges Bidault, France's foreign minister, asserted that his country had been humiliated by American high-handedness.[104] The State Department vigorously disagreed with Roosevelt's contention that postwar base rights could be more easily obtained from the Mexicans than from the French. Not until mid-March 1945 did FDR, who preferred to be his own secretary of state, bow to Secretary of State Edward R. Stettinius's repeated urgings that the United States deal with the French alone in the matter of base rights on Clipperton. According to the secretary of state, it was foolish to support the idea of Mexican sovereignty over Clipperton because "it has not been possible for them for political reasons to go so far as even to discuss our having bases in Mexican territory."[105] In April some American officials proposed that France cede Clipperton to the United States as a quid pro quo for lend-lease aid, but the State Department declined to make such an approach to the French government.[106] American personnel were finally withdrawn from the island in the fall of 1945, when the State Department concluded that the presence of American forces was hindering rather than helping the effort to negotiate an overall postwar base agreement with the French.[107]

Roosevelt did not seek to expand US territorial domain in the Pacific, or to close the Pacific to any nation. In July 1944, he told the military, who wanted to annex the Japanese Mandates outright, that he hoped the UN would make the United States a "trustee" of the islands.[108] In a Seattle, Washington, speech upon his return from Alaska, the president referred to the British and French possessions in the Pacific saying, "We have no desire to ask for any possessions of the United Nations." He further stated, "With them and with their help, I am sure that we can agree completely so that Central and South America will be as safe against attack—attack from the South Pacific—as North America is going to be very soon from the North Pacific as well."[109] This oblique reference to the postwar planning he had just initiated in Alaska and the Byrd mission (the report had already been submitted to him, and he may have read or been briefed on it) reveal the president's firm desire to provide for postwar physical security in the Pacific. As we have seen, the president considered military and civil aviation to be inseparably intertwined. Thus, the reverse of the coin of physical security was economic security, possible through the expansion of international commercial aviation. A well-developed

North and South Pacific military air base and civil airport system would promote both.

* * *

The question of postwar base privileges in France's South Pacific possessions was one of the first subjects to come up between the JCS officers and civilian officials charged at the beginning of 1944 with implementing the base network set forth in JCS 570/2. In February 1944, the JCS replied affirmatively to a query from the State Department's John D. Hickerson, about whether military considerations would permit US forces to occupy France's South Pacific islands if such a move would further the chances for postwar rights.[110] Thus, the intragovernmental base-acquisition drive seemed to be off to an aggressive start. Assistant Secretary of State Berle, who anticipated some trouble with the French, nonetheless launched the effort with high hopes, declaring that "with good luck we might have the whole program fairly well implemented by the first of July 1944; after which I would feel that we had gotten out of this war reasonably safe."[111] By war's end, as noted previously, the United States had not acquired postwar base rights anywhere in French territory.

In fact, as late as March 1945 the JPWC had presented statements of maximum and minimum base requirements only for Brazil, Ecuador, New Zealand, Iceland, and Cuba.[112] The State Department, for its part, had completed but one agreement—that with Brazil signed in June 1944.[113] What was behind such an apparently lackluster performance? In a memorandum to his chief, Assistant Secretary of War for Air Lovett, Col George A. Brownell asked rhetorically, "Have negotiations . . . been delayed because the Joint Chiefs of Staff have failed to present to the State Department the maxima and minima, as the President has directed, or is it the State Department's fault because they have told the Joint Chiefs not to bother?" Brownell blamed the paucity of activity on the State Department, telling Lovett that he had heard that the JCS were told the chances for successful negotiation were slight.[114] Normally, the JPWC did not initiate the statements of base requirements; rather, the State Department made informal requests for them. For instance, the impending visit of Iceland's president in the summer of 1944 (shortly after Iceland declared its independence) prompted a query from State to the JCS for a statement of postwar base needs in that country. While a feeler from New Zealand, indicating that British Commonwealth nation's wish to reach an early agreement with the United States regarding postwar use of air and naval facilities in the southwest Pacific, produced another State Department request.[115] On the other hand, the JPWC had not expressed any dissatisfaction with the frequency of State Department inquiries.

The lack of concrete results was a consequence of several convergent factors. For its part, the JPWC found its hands tied by the general lack of coordination among the services in postwar planning. In October 1944, the JPWC submitted a 10-page analysis of the need for integrated postwar strategic planning within the military establishment to its parent body, the JSSC. "Determination of requirements for post war military bases in pursuance of JCS 570/2," said the JPWC, "would be facilitated by the approval of concepts from which will be derived the specific purposes which the several bases are to serve and the characteristics which they should have."[116] In the absence of an approved postwar strategic concept for the employment of US military forces (or for that matter completed, detailed military base plans of any kind), the JPWC could provide the State Department with only the most general declaration of base needs within any country.

But however integrated, detailed, or extensive the base data provided by the JPWC, the State Department worked under several handicaps of its own. The president's tendency to close the door to State Department officials when it came to designing grand strategy ("That place is like a sieve," he said), to postpone making decisions about vital postwar issues, or simply to keep his own counsel left the State Department bereft of any clear idea of what America's postwar role would be.[117] The State Department, consequently, did not know how much diplomatic leverage could (or should) be applied to obtain postwar base rights.

Even if American military force and diplomacy were joined in pursuit of unambiguous foreign policy objectives, the road would still have been blocked by nationalism. The Mexicans, as Stettinius saw it, could not sit still for American bases on their soil. Berle's naive estimate that all would be locked up in six months, and that there would, for example, be "no worries about the Central Americans" over base rights was, as events were to prove, far from the mark.[118] At the end of 1947, the Panamanian National Assembly *unanimously* rejected a post-war base agreement with the United States, and the American program to acquire long-term base rights was in trouble else-where around the world. There had been difficulties with Ecuador and Peru, with Portugal over the Azores, with Den-mark over Greenland, and with Iceland and the Philippines. Most of these problems were not foreseen by the end of the war (Brazil, after all, was a success and New Zealand, and Aus-tralia seemed to want a close relationship); the State Depart-ment only slowly (and some of the military never) discovered just how disruptive and even counterproductive an American military installation in someone else's backyard could be. They were, no doubt, blinded by what they saw as the apparent ur-gency and essential justice of the cause.

Whatever the explanation for the JCS and State Depart-ment's failures to show much for more than a year of "gather-ing in the bases," their leisurely pace disturbed certain sectors of the government, especially the Office of the Assistant Sec-retary of War for Air. The notes of unhappiness emanating from Lovett's office blended into the chorus of displeasure sounded by civilian War and Navy Department officials who, since the summer of 1944, had been trying mightily to reenter the arena of defense policy making.

Actually, the secretaries of state, war, and Navy were all in the same boat when it came to exclusion from consideration of questions of high policy during the war. In May 1943, Secre-tary of State Hull related to Stimson and Knox that he had not been able to get a copy of the minutes of the Casablanca meet-ing (Hull had been told they were "strictly confidential"). "This led to an admission by each one of us," wrote Stimson in his diary, "of the difficulties we were having in keeping in communication with what our chief, the President, was doing in re-gard to international matters, both civil and military."[119] State had an advantage over war and Navy since the JCS committees often had contacts with the State Department on war or post-war-related subjects. Nothing galled Stimson more than to have subordinate State Department officials short-circuit the secre-taries of war and Navy in dealing with the JCS. Stimson called the practice a "growing infringement upon the responsibilities and duties" of the two civilian secretaries and an embarrass-ment to them. In formal letters of protest to Hull in August and again in October 1944, Stimson cited several instances of matters handled directly between the JCS and State Depart-ment that "instead of being purely of a military character have been problems very largely of a political or civil nature into which the military nature entered only partially."[120] Finally, Stettinius, who had just succeeded Hull, proposed at the end of November 1944 to set up a committee of representatives of the three departments, "charged with the duty of formulating recommendations to the secretary of state in questions having both military and political aspects and coordinating the views of the three departments in matters of interdepartmental in-terest."[121] Thus, the State-War-Navy Coordinating Committee (SWNCC) was born. The JCS, with the possible exception of Admiral King, did not resist the initiative; indeed, Leahy, who claimed to eschew involvement in "political" questions, told Stimson he welcomed it.[122] The SWNCC, along with the new life given the Committee of Three (the meetings of the secretaries of state, war and Navy) after Stettinius became secretary of state, brought a measure of coordination to American policy involving "politico-military" affairs that had not existed previously.[123]

The postwar overseas base network was, of course, a subject with obvious military and political implications and one from which the secretaries of war and Navy had been banned by the special Joint Postwar Committee-State Department relation-ship. Some evidence suggests the manner of handling over-seas base questions was one of the joint chiefs'-State "end-runs" that so upset Stimson. In July 1944, Colonel Brownell told Lovett that in view of the very great political significance of these post war base agreements with foreign countries, the question arises in my mind of how far the Secretary of War's office and this office should be kept advised of and participate in the proceedings, and how far they should be left entirely to the Joint Chiefs of Staff organization. You of course remember the circumstances under which all matters pertaining to the postwar bases were turned over to the Joint Chiefs and, in effect, taken away from the War and Navy Departments.

Brownell recommended that some machinery be set up to enable Lovett to keep Stimson up to date on "any important developments in these political discussions." Lovett replied, in a penciled comment that he had "talked to the S/W [secretary of war] who will take matters up with S/S [secretary of state] and Assistant Secretary of War John J. McCloy will follow up with U/S/S [undersecretary of state] Stettinius."[124]

Lovett's military assistant also seemed to have begun the push to have JCS 570/2 revised. In a long memorandum for Lovett in February 1945 (that was also sent to McCloy), Brownell reemphasized the importance of securing postwar military and commercial rights at airfields constructed abroad during the war; described the kinds of rights military and civil aircraft would need; and outlined the steps to be taken to achieve civil and military overseas airfield objectives.[125] Unlike Berle, Brownell thought that obtaining postwar rights abroad would be quite difficult.

In almost all foreign nations there is great public sentiment against the granting of air base rights to the United States or to any other country. The concession of rights that might be regarded as "sovereign" would in many countries become a political issue of major importance. The fact that we have built or improved new fields in those countries for war purposes by no means gives us the right, and in many cases does not even give us an equitable claim, to the occupation and use of such fields for military or commercial purposes in peacetime.

Brownell's main point was that the JCS; State, War, Navy, and Commerce Departments; and the Civil Aeronautics Board (CAB) would soon have to agree on uniform policies for acquiring military and commercial rights "in order that the postwar interests of the United States be fully protected." One of the first actions should be for the JCS to "bring the recommendations contained in JCS 570 down to date and add any additional bases that we need for military purposes."[126] Lovett then suggested to Lt Gen Barney Giles, deputy AAF commander and chief of the Air Staff that, "the best way to initiate such a revision and amplification of the 570 paper would be for the Air Staff to prepare a study covering the entire field. This study can then be presented to the Joint Chiefs of Staff by General Arnold with a request for its approval."[127]

War and Navy Department civilians reentered the postwar base debate in full force in March 1945, when the war and Navy members of the SWNCC, McCloy and Artemus Gates, assistant secretary of the Navy for air, asserted the right of their superiors, Stimson and Forrestal, to be kept fully informed about overseas bases. At the SWNCC meeting of 9 March, Mc-Cloy suggested "that, steps be taken to have a restatement of base requirements approved by the Secretary of War and the Secretary of the Navy, as well as by the Joint Chiefs and forwarded to the President with the request that he revise his directives to the Secretary of State to provide more specifically for War and Navy Department participation in view of the important departmental interest in the overall question of strategic bases."[128] The SWNCC agreed to ask the State Department to submit a report on the status of negotiations for overseas bases.[129] After receipt of this document, all JCS statements of the maximum and minimum requirements for rights at overseas bases thereafter would go first to the war and Navy members of the SWNCC before their transmittal to the secretary of state. In this way, the civilian leaders of the war and Navy Departments put an end to the special joint chiefs–State Department's relationship regarding overseas bases and regained mastery over another part of their domain.

State, war, and Navy cooperation on bases was only one aspect of the complete intragovernmental coordination Brownell believed necessary. There must yet be a mechanism for the Commerce Department and CAB to coordinate postwar commercial air requirements (both domestic and international) with state, war, and Navy. The formation of the Air Coordinating Committee (ACC) on 27 March 1945 solved this problem. Composed of representatives of the state, war, Navy, and Commerce Departments (with the chairman of the CAB invited to attend each meeting, although he was not to be a voting member), the

ACC was to "examine aviation problems and developments, affecting more than one department or agency, to coordinate the activities of the government departments and agencies interested in this field and to recommend integrated policies for and action by the departments represented on the committee, or by the President." First among the subjects in the international field suggested for the ACC's "early attention" were civil and military operating rights abroad and rights to overseas air bases and airway facilities.[130]

The reinvigorated Committee of Three, the SWNCC, and the ACC were clearly means through which civilian war and Navy Department leaders hoped to influence policy, thereby regaining their traditional places in the military establishment. They were also, as Brownell pointed out in an article he wrote after the war, a kind of "stop-gap coordination" designed to provide the high-level cooperation among the executive departments that ideally should have taken place between the president and the cabinet. Finally, in the case of aviation, Brownell argued that its "technical nature" required "coordination in a body of specialists, or at least in a group that had immediate and daily access to those who knew their way around in the air."[131] One suspects that resentment of the JCS' close relationship with the president and a corollary belief that the military would not take the broadest view of the "politico-military" problems that it more and more confronted were the most important reasons for the proliferation of the coordinating committees. In any case, the stage was now set for the revision of JCS 570/2.

* * *

The American military planned a postwar overseas naval and air-base network for a huge region encompassing the Western Hemisphere and the Pacific Ocean. Most bases would be concentrated in areas of traditional US influence—the Caribbean, along the line of communications through the Central Pacific, and the Far East. Beyond this common denominator, the AAF increasingly emphasized bases in the northern reaches of the defense perimeter, while the Navy showed a relatively long-lived attachment to sites south of the equator.

There were some cracks in the regional thinking exemplified in and further stimulated by JCS 570/2. The Navy, for example, explicitly recognized in its planning documents that naval forces might be deployed to any part of the world after the war. Part of this was due, no doubt, to the realization that the United States was, in fact, headed toward membership in a postwar international peacekeeping organization. While the Soviets were foreseen as a likely future enemy, there was yet no inclination by planners in Washington to push for advance positions in Europe or the Middle East. The United States, however, appeared to be ready to confront the Russians in the Far East, if necessary.

Overseas bases were only one aspect of postwar military planning, but they attracted the attention of civilian policy makers. Civilian leaders increasingly accepted the military's contention that far-flung bases were necessary to help assure physical security in the face of the mushrooming technology of swift destruction. Civilians more than (though not apart from) the military, saw bases as furthering other American "interests" or "political" objectives. In June 1945, for example, acting Secretary of State Joseph C. Grew urged President Harry S. Truman to authorize continued construction of an airfield at Dhahran, Saudi Arabia, even though the military thought the field was no longer a "military necessity" for supporting the Pacific war effort (and, as we have seen, had no plans for a permanent postwar installation in the Middle East).[132] Grew and the secretaries of war and Navy agreed: "Immediate construction of this field used initially for military purposes and ultimately for civil aviation would be a strong showing of American interest in Saudi Arabia and thus tend to strengthen the political integrity of that country where vast oil resources now are in American hands."[133]

The future disposition of Middle Eastern oil reserves was a matter of vital national interest because it was part of the problem of providing for postwar American economic prosperity. Many believed that the United States, with its industrial machine bloated by the demands of the war, would more than ever have to ensure access to raw materials and, most importantly, capture overseas markets after the war. Encouraging the expansion of US air commerce abroad through a well-developed system of air routes and facilities was seen as a means to this end.

The studies by Lissitzyn and Byrd show how some military planners related domestic economic needs and national defense requirements in an integrated overseas military base and civil airport network. President Roosevelt may have held a similar view. Neither study, however, was any more typical of the military's postwar views than the men themselves were of the military as a whole. Actually, the AAF's June 1944 deployment plan, with its more or less pro forma bow to the need to protect American economic interests, was probably more characteristic of military thinking on the subject. Nonetheless, armed forces leaders and planners all believed American commercial airlines and the US military would share overseas air facilities to some degree after the war.

In the summer and fall of 1945 the JCS reexamined overseas base requirements. During this review, the JCS would consider the extent to which military base plans should conform to commercial needs, the priority to attach to particular overseas military base areas, and the number of places at which base rights should be sought. This reexamination would not be the same as the preparation of JCS 570/2 in 1943, for the JCS progress would be monitored by civilian policy makers through the interdepartmental committees revitalized or newly established in late 1944 and early 1945.

Notes

1. Michael S. Sherry, *Preparing for the Next War: American Plans for Postwar Defense, 1941–1945*, chap. 1 (New Haven, Conn.: Yale University Press, 1977); Perry McCoy Smith, *The Air Force Plans for Peace, 1943–1945* (Baltimore: Johns Hopkins University Press, 1970), passim.

2. A. A. Berle to Stokeley W. Morgan et al., 15 April 1944, file Aviation, box 11, Hickerson-Matthews Files, Records of the Office of European Affairs, 1934–1947, Record Group (RG) 59 (General Records of the State Department), National Archives (NA).

3. For a discussion of the origin and development of the February 1944 Army Air Forces' (AAF) *Initial Post-War Air Force* (*IPWAF*) Plan and its June 1944 supplement, see Smith, *Air Force Plans*, p. 54–62 and 77–79. The *IPWAF* Plan called for 105 air groups. By comparison, the AAF's wartime strength rose to 243 groups, compared to the 1930s' peak of 30 groups. Although the

AAF planners much preferred 105 groups, the Post War Division (PWD) used several other planning figures at one time or another, including 78, 75, 70, 65, 45, 25, and 16 groups. Finally, in August 1945, the AAF settled on a postwar Air Force of 70-groups, 400,000-personnel, religiously sticking to those figures until 1950.

4. Deployment of the Initial Post-War Air Force: Study by Assistant Chief of Staff, Plans, 14 June 1944, 2–3, file 145.86-67, Air Force Historical Research Agency (AFHRA).

5. Ibid., 1, 4, tab A.

6. Ibid., 4, 5, tab A.

7. Smith, *Air Force Plans*, 82–83. Smith is probably in error on this point. Evidence cited in chapter 1 shows a widespread understanding within the War Department of the strategic significance of far northern advance bases. Their importance was common knowledge in the Operations Division (OPD) of the War Department General Staff, in the Office of the Assistant Secretary of War for Air, in Air Transportation Command (ATC) Plans, and in Air Staff Plans, including the PWD. While "Mercator-projection thinking" may have existed in the PWD, there are many references to northern attack routes in its files. The October 1943 Air Staff Plans overseas base paper (written by Col P. M. Hamilton, first chief of the PWD and later AAF representative on the Joint Post War Committee [JPWC]), and the *IPWAF* deployment study analyzed here are examples. Another is a letter from Col R. C. Moffat to Brig Gen Patrick W. Timberlake, one of the AAF's deputy assistant chiefs of staff, dated 15 February 1945, in which the PWD chief commented on a study of the development of US airfields for B-36 aircraft. He advised selection of Westover, Massachusetts, over Fort Dix, New Jersey, because of its "preferable strategic location," and Moses Lake, Washington, over Mountain Home, Idaho, in part because "It would be farther north and west as a jump off point for transpolar missions as well as long range operations to the westward." See file 145.86-33B, vol. 2, 1943–1946, AFHRA. The best evidence, however, is a major PWD study, "U.S. Requirements for Post War Military Air Bases and Rights in Foreign Territory," 11 July 1945, and revised 14 August 1945. This document was the AAF's contribution to the revision of JCS 570/2; it contains a polar projection prepared by the PWD in June 1945. See chap. 3 in this book for analysis, 105–113.

8. Quoted in Smith, *Air Force Plans*, 79.

9. Col R. C. Moffat, memorandum for Assistant Chief/Air Staff (AC/AS) Plans (hereafter Moffat memorandum, 14 June 1944), 14 June 1944, file 145.86-67, AFHRA.

10. Ibid.

11. Ibid.

12. For a perceptive analysis of AAF deployment to forward bases in Alaska in 1946–1947, which shows quite clearly that the AAF was not able to operate with any effectiveness in the Arctic in the immediate postwar years, see Harry R. Borowski, *A Hollow Threat: Strategic Air Power and Con-*

tainment before Korea (Westport, Conn.: Greenwood Press, 1982), chap. 4, 72–90.

13. Moffat memorandum, 14 June 1944.

14. Deployment of the Initial Post War Air Force, study by assistant chief of Air Staff (Plans), 14 June 1944, 1–2, file 145.86-67, AFHRA.

15. Sherry, 108–19.

16. *Basic Post War Plan No. 1* was actually the fifth detailed postwar plan produced by the Navy since mid-1943.

17. Vincent Davis, *Postwar Defense Policy and the U. S. Navy, 1943–1946* (Chapel Hill: University of North Carolina Press, 1966), 103.

18. Ibid., 5 and 103–5.

19. Ibid., 12–13.

20. Ibid., 21.

21. Adm R. S. Edwards, memorandum for assistant chief of staff, Plans, 22 November 1943, file Demobilization, July 1943–July 1945, series 14, Strategic Plans Division Records, Navy Operational Archives (NOA).

22. Vincent Davis, "Politics and Postwar Defense Policy: The Origins of the Postwar U.S. Navy, 1943–1946" (PhD diss., Princeton University 1961), 243–44; Capt A. D. Douglas, memorandum for Vice Admiral Edwards, 9 October 1944, file Navy Basic Plans June 1943–August 1946 (hereafter Navy Basic Plans), series 14, Strategic Plans Division Records, NOA; for clarification of Moore's role, see Rear Adm Charles J. Moore, USN, retired, interviewed by John T. Mason Jr., 16 July 1966, 1171–84, oral history on file in the NOA.

23. Davis, *Postwar Defense Policy*, 102.

24. Ibid., 98–99.

25. Ibid., 102.

26. Quoted in Arnold Rogow, *James Forrestal: A Study of Personality, Politics, and Policy* (New York: Macmillan Company, 1963), 331; see also Forrestal's letter to Palmer Hoyt, 2 September 1944, in *The Forrestal Diaries*, ed. Walter Millis and E. S. Duffield (New York: Viking Press, 1951), 14.

27. JVF [James V. Forrestal], memorandum for Adm Frederick Horne, 14 May 1944, file Postwar no. 2, box 173, Undersecretary of the Navy Files, 1940–1944, RG 80 (General Records of the Department of the Navy), NA; Davis, *Postwar Defense Policy*, 33–35.

28. Quoted in Davis, *Postwar Defense Policy*, 24.

29. Ibid., 80–88.

30. Robert G. Albion and Robert H. Connery, *Forrestal and the Navy* (New York: Columbia University Press, 1962), 24–25; Paul Y. Hammond, *Organizing for Defense: The American Military Establishment in the Twentieth Century* (Princeton, N.J.: Princeton University Press, 1961), 182.

31. Hammond, chap. 7. The civilian heads of the War and Navy Departments only rarely attended the wartime conferences (Stimson and Forrestal attended the Potsdam Conference, though the latter was not invited), and they were not on the regular distribution list for JCS papers.

32. Henry Stimson Diary (hereafter Stimson Diary), 27 July 1944, 221 (microfilm edition, reel 9), Manuscripts and Archives, Yale University Library, New Haven, Conn.

33. Albion and Connery, 92–93, 124–27; and Ernest J. King and Walter M. Whitehill, *Fleet Admiral King: A Naval Record* (New York: W.W. Norton and Company, Inc., 1952), 629–37.

34. Adm Ernest J. King, memorandum for the Secretary of the Navy, subject: Status of Efforts to Acquire Post War Strategic Bases, 26 September 1944, file 48-1-24, box 90, General Correspondence, 1944–1947, Records of Secretary of the Navy James Forrestal, 1940–1947, RG 80.

35. John Hickerson, memorandum for files, 7 October 1944, file Memoranda, 1944, box 2, Hickerson–Matthews Files, RG 59.

36. King probably saw the *American Magazine* incident as simply "business as usual" for the Office of the Secretary of the Navy. In 1942, Knox had nearly revealed publicly the Navy's ability to read Japanese codes and, on another occasion, had given out classified information about the battleship *Iowa*. See Hammond, 180–82.

37. Capt A. D. Douglas, memorandum for Rear Adm D. B. Duncan, 14 October 1944; and memorandum for F-00 (Edwards) via F-1 (Duncan), subject: Post War Naval Planning, 14 October 1944 (enclosing draft memorandum for the Joint Chiefs of Staff), all in file Navy Basic Plans.

38. Ibid. C. B. Gary, memorandum for Capt A. D. Douglas, 7 April 1945, file National Defense, August 1944–August 1946 (hereafter National Defense file).

39. National Defense file, "Determination," F-14 draft of 26 December 1944, 1–2.

40. Ibid., 5–7.

41. Ibid., 7–10.

42. Ibid., 7–8.

43. Ibid., 8.

44. Ibid. C. B. Gary, one of the F-14 planners, wrote that "the Determination is elastic. It allows for mutation in world naval power that cannot now be foreseen but that will probably occur. The Determination is a long-range one. It is not for V-day or a V-day plus 1-year Navy. It is considered to be as applicable for 1970 as 1950." Gary memorandum, 7 April 1945.

45. Ibid., Determination, 2, 9, and 21–22. For the influence of Mahanian concepts on the Navy's postwar planning, see Davis, *Post War Defense Policy*, 37, 162–65.

46. Determination, 16.

47. Ibid., 14.

48. Ibid., 4–6, 27 and 29.

49. Ibid., 12 and 16–17.

50. Ibid., 9 and 12.

51. Adm A. J. Hepburn, memorandum for Adm R. S. Edwards, 17 January 1945, National Defense file.

52. Adm Ernest J. King to James V. Forrestal, subject: The US Navy (Postwar)—Basis for Preparation of Plans (hereafter US Navy Postwar), 3

March 1945, serial 0604, FF1/A16-3, file A16-3/EN (Jan–May 1945), CNO Records, NOA.

53. Capt A. D. Douglas, memorandum for Admiral Edwards, subject: Basis for Postwar Basic Planning, Condensed Statement, 19 January 1945, US Navy Postwar.

54. Ibid. Capt A. D. Douglas, draft memorandum for deputy COMINCH—deputy CNO, vice chief of naval operations, 19 January 1945, subject: Basis for Post War Naval Planning. The "elements to be studied" were: (1) the probable, absolute, and relative economic and military strength of the larger world powers; (2) the political ideologies of these powers; (3) the probable internal situation of these powers; (4) the probable policies and interests of these powers as a source of solidarity or of conflict; (5) the prospective allies and enemies, and alliances thereof; prospective size, character, and deployment of their forces; probable nature of a war against any enemies; and (6) the probable nature of any postwar international organization and agreements.

55. See ibid., for Moore's and subsequent drafts.

56. Ibid., Captain Douglas, memoranda for Captain Moore, 13–14 February 1945.

57. King to Forrestal, subject: The United States Navy (Postwar)—Basis for Preparation of Plans, US Navy Postwar.

58. See Admiral Willson's draft, n.d., in file Navy Basic Plans.

59. Ibid., Captain Douglas, memorandum for Captain Moore, 13 February 1945.

60. Ibid., Captain Moore, memorandum for Admiral Edwards, 14 February 1945.

61. See chap. 1 this book, 39.

62. The decision on the Philippine bases was not made until August 1945.

63. Minutes of Pacific Conference, San Francisco, Calif., 29 September–1 October 1944, box 182, series 12, Strategic Plans Division Records, NOA.

64. Ibid., minutes of Pacific Conference, San Francisco, 24–26 November 1944.

65. Ibid., Rear Adm D. B. Duncan and Admiral Edwards, memorandum for Adm Ernest J. King, 20 November 1944, attaching study Post War Naval Bases in the Pacific, file Bases General (hereafter Bases General), B-3, box 156. Several of the sites (Espiritu Santo; Manus; Cam Ranh Bay, French Indochina; and Sama Bay, Hainan Island) were in the black-bordered area of JCS 570/2—that part of the Far East where bases might be "required by the U.S. as one of the Great Powers enforcing peace, pending a world wide organization."

66. Admiral King and Admiral Edwards, under pressure from Forrestal to get the Navy's postwar plans completed and facing the prospect of a congressional study of the Navy's postwar base needs in the Pacific, were anxious to get Nimitz's opinion. Admiral King sent Nimitz a message in January 1945 requesting a reply but without any apparent result. Admiral Edwards told Admiral King in February that "with respect to bases outside the U.S., the situation is indefinite. It has been impossible to get CINCPAC to make any definite

recommendations as to his ideas on the matter. Obviously, in view of the magnitude of the operations which he is directing, he has little opportunity to consider postwar problems." See COMINCH-CNO message to CINCPAC 142106, January 1945, file Bases General; and Admiral Edwards's memorandum for Admiral King, 10 February 1945, file Navy Basic Plans.

67. For internal memoranda relating to Forrestal's requests, see Admiral Edwards to F-14, 8 January 1945; Captain Douglas to F-00 (Edwards), 9 January 1945; Captain Douglas to Captain Moore, 9 January 1945; Captain Moore to F-14; and H. Q. I. to Captain Douglas, 18 January 1945; all in file Naval Bases, December 1942–December 1946, series 14, Strategic Plans Division, NOA; and Adm F. J. Horne, memorandum for the Secretary of the Navy, subject: US Post War Military (Naval) Base Requirements, 9 January 1945; Adm F. J. Horne, memorandum for the Secretary of the Navy, subject: US Post War Naval Advance Base Requirements, 26 January 1945; both (quotations from 26 January memorandum) in file CNO, Top Secret (TS), 1945, A4-2/NB, CNO Records, NOA. Documents are now declassified.

68. Edwards pointed out that the planners had already been doing this.

69. Minutes of the 10th meeting, 15 January 1945, box 1, Minutes of the Top Policy Group, Records of Secretary of the Navy James Forrestal, 1940–1947, RG 80.

70. James Forrestal to Admiral King, 8 February 1945, file Navy Basic Plans.

71. Ibid., Admiral Edwards to Admiral King, 8 February 1945.

72. Ibid., Admiral Edwards to Admiral King, 10 February 1945.

73. Admiral Edwards, memorandum for F-1 (Duncan), 10 March 1945, file Bases General; Forrestal Diary, 10 March 1945, vol. 2, Papers of James V. Forrestal (hereafter Forrestal Papers), Seeley G. Mudd Manuscript Library, Princeton University, N.J.

74. Adm E. J. King, Outline of Post War Navy and Overseas Naval Bases, 13 March 1945, file Post War Bases.

75. Forrestal Papers, vol. 1, 27 February 1945; and T. C. Kinkaid to Secretary of the Navy, subject: Proposed Post War Naval Shore Establishments in the Philippine Archipelago, 21 March 1945, file Admiral's Letters, 1945, Papers of Chester W. Nimitz (hereafter Nimitz Papers), NOA.

76. Forrestal Papers, vol. 1, 28 February 1945.

77. JF (James Forrestal): HCO, memorandum, 28 March 1945, file 70-1-1, box 123, General Correspondence, 1944–1947, RG 80.

78. An appendix listing five naval and air bases in the Philippines was added in August.

79. Appendix E, Postwar Overseas Bases in the Pacific, and appendix F, Postwar Overseas Bases in the Atlantic, in *Basic Post War Plan No. 1*, 7 May 1945, serial 00485OD, file A16-3/EN, CNO Records, NOA.

80. Ibid., appendix E.

81. See chap. 3 in this book, 128–29.

82. James MacGregor Burns, *Roosevelt: The Soldier of Freedom* (New York: Harcourt, Brace, Jovanovich, Inc., 1970), 489–90; and William D. Leahy, *I Was There* (New York: Whittlesey House, 1950), 252–53.

83. G. Grant Mason Jr., letter, subject: Letter of Instruction for Special Mission to Capt Oliver J. Lissitzyn, 28 August 1944, in ATC Plans report no. 128 (Mission of Captain Oliver J. Lissitzyn to Alaska), 21 October 1944 (hereafter ATC Plans report no. 128), file 300.123-7, AFHRA.

84. Ibid. Emmons, incidentally, had flown an aerial reconnaissance of the northern Brazilian coast in November 1939, surveying the Natal-Recife area as a site for a major air base. His report affirmed the potential military importance of Pan American Airways facilities in Brazil. See Frank D. McCann Jr., *The Brazilian-American Alliance, 1937–1945* (Princeton: Princeton University Press, 1973), 145–46, 201 and 222.

85. Capt Oliver J. Lissitzyn to Maj Thomas M. Murphy, chief, Policy and Post War Planning, ATC Plans, 21 October 1944, ATC Plans report no. 128.

86. JCS 1295/1, Defense of Alaska, 29 April 1945, sec. 1, file CCS 660.2 Alaska (3-25-45), RG 218 (Records of the United States Joint Chiefs of Staff), NA.

87. Captain Lissitzyn to Major Murphy, ATC Plans report no. 128.

88. See chap. 3 in this book, 106.

89. ATC Plans report no. 128, 16–21.

90. Ibid., 1. Captain Lissitzyn most likely meant China, a resurgent Japan, and Russia (although the latter was the only "Eurasian" nation).

91. Ibid., 17–18.

92. Ibid., 13 and 17.

93. Forrestal to Roosevelt, 19 June 1944, file 8, box 2, series 1, Papers of William D. Leahy (hereafter Leahy Papers), NOA.

94. Copies of Byrd's Report of Special Mission to the Pacific Area are in box 2 of the Papers of Richard E. Byrd (hereafter Byrd Papers), NOA, and in boxes 1836–1837, OPD, Project Decimal File, 1942–1945, RG 165 (Records of the War Department General and Special Staffs), NA.

95. Byrd Papers, book 6, Senior Members' Review of Facts and Findings contained in the preceding five books. Many of Byrd's assumptions in his study of postwar Pacific strategy conform closely to the components of Sherry's "ideology of national preparedness." The polar explorer also saw the preservation of "our way of life (freedom)" as a function of the soundness of the nation's economy. Byrd posited (in section nine) the following connection between the domestic economy and foreign policy:

a. Normal prosperity for all the people is the keystone of freedom.

b. A healthy internal economy (which of course is essential to prosperity) is not enough. There is necessary also a healthy foreign commerce, which in turn must be fostered by our foreign policies: (1) The war has already increased our productive capacity, so we will be dependent on other nations to take care of the surplus.

c. Foreign commerce (both sea and air) and military bases implement each other. For example (1) Worldwide US commercial airlines and a strong merchant marine and national defense are mutually helpful.

d. Thus, in the postwar era political strategy, military strategy, and foreign commerce, being inextricably entwined, will be integrated: (1) But national safety will stand first in importance.

In Byrd's assertion that a nation must have "a healthy foreign commerce" *in addition* to a "healthy internal economy," one is tempted to see an answer to Charles Beard's argument in the *Idea of the National Interest* (1934) and *The Open Door at Home* (1935) that pursuit of overseas markets was a false conception of the "national interest" and that, in fact, "no commerce" meant "no war." Byrd may still have been smarting from Beard's virulent attack in a series of *New Republic* articles and a book (*The Navy Defense or Portent*) in 1932 on the Navy Department and the Navy League. Some scholars see Beard as a precursor of "new Left revisionism." For an insightful article exploring Beard's acquaintance with the ideas of Eckart Kehr, the leading left-wing German historian of German navalism and the Wilhelminian social structure, see Arthur Lloyd Skop, "The Primacy of Domestic Politics: Eckart Kehr and the Intellectual Development of Charles A. Beard," *History and Theory* 12 (1974): 119–31.

96. Maj Gen Thomas T. Handy, assistant chief of staff, memorandum for the chief of staff, subject: Review of Admiral Byrd's Report on Islands in the Southeast Pacific, 30 July 1944, file 580.82TS, sec. 2, box 101, OPD Decimal File, 1942–1944, RG 165. Document is now declassified.

97. General Arnold to Admiral Byrd, 28 July 1944, file Post War Airfields, box 44, Papers of H. H. Arnold, LOC. The PWD prepared the letter for Arnold's signature.

98. Admiral Byrd, memorandum for Admiral Leahy, file 8, box 2, series 1, Leahy Papers.

99. Admiral King, memorandum for Admiral Leahy, subject: British Activities at Clipperton Island, 23 October 1944, serial 003090, file Bases 1945 and 1946, box 12, Leahy Files, RG 218; and Admiral Leahy (for JCS) to Secretary of State Hull, 4 November 1944, file 580.82TS, sec. 2, box 101, OPD Decimal File, 1942–1944, RG 165. Documents are now declassified.

100. Admiral Leahy, memorandum for the secretary of war, 27 November 1944, enclosing Roosevelt's message to Churchill of the same date, file OPD 336TS, sec 8, box 40, OPD Decimal File, 1942–1944, RG 165. Document is now declassified.

101. SWNCC l06 (hereafter SWNCC 106), 13 April 1945, file CCS 093, Clipperton Island (4-13-45), RG 218.

102. President Roosevelt, memorandum to secretary of state, 1 January 1945, *Foreign Relations of the United States, 1945*, vol. 4, *Europe* (hereafter *Foreign Relations of US, 1945*, vol. 4, *Europe*) (Washington, D.C.: Government Printing Office, 1968), 184–85.

103. Ibid., 783–84. Memorandum of conversation by the ambassador to Mexico, temporarily in the United States, 19 December 1944.

104. Ibid., 788–89. Ambassador to France (Caffrey), memorandum to secretary of state, 22 January 1945.

105. Ibid., 792–93. Secretary of State, memorandum to President Roosevelt, 15 March 1945; Diary of Edward R. Stettinius Jr., sec. 6 (7–23 January 1945) and sec. 7 (week of 11–17 March 1945), box 29, Records of Harley A. Notter, 1939–1945, RG 59.

106. SWNCC 106, assistant secretary of the Navy for air, memorandum, subject: Exchange of Ownership of Clipperton Island in Part Settlement of French Lend-Lease Obligations to the United States, 13 April 1945; and SWNCC 106/1 (memorandum from the State Department), same title, 19 April 1945, file CCS 093 Clipperton Island (4-13-45), RG 218.

107. Acting secretary of state (Dean G. Acheson) to the secretary of the Navy (Forrestal), 19 September 1945, *Foreign Relations of US, 1945*, vol. 4, *Europe*, 793–94.

108. William Roger Louis, *Imperialism at Bay: The United States and the Decolonization of the British Empire, 1941–1945* (New York: Oxford University Press, 1978), 373.

109. Quoted in SWNCC 106/1.

110. P. L. Carroll, memorandum for Mr. Hickerson, 24 February 1944, sec. 3, file CCS 360 (12-9-42), RG 218.

111. Diary entry for 22 February 1944, Beatrice B. Berle and Travis B. Jacobs, *Navigating the Rapids, 1918–1971: From the Papers of Adolf A. Berle* (New York: Harcourt, Brace, Jovanovich, Inc., 1973), 485.

112. D. S., memorandum for Mr. Lovett, 15 April 1945, box 199, file Plans, Policies and Agreements; Records, Office of Assistant Secretary of War for Air, RG 107 (Records of the Secretary of War).

113. See McCann for an outstanding analysis of US relations with Brazil during and before World War II. See especially the chapter titled "Airlines and Bases," 213–39, for US government and Pan American Airways efforts (under the latter's secret Airfield Development Program Contract with the War Department) in 1939–1941 to arrange for the use of strategically located northeastern Brazilian airfields. McCann discusses the June 1944 postwar agreement only briefly (pages 330–31), but thinks that the Brazilians acquiesced to the continued presence of US forces in their country after the war because they thought that strong postwar ties with the United States would help to assure security against Argentina or even "preeminence" in South America.

114. G. A. B. (George A. Brownell), memorandum for Mr. Lovett, 29 March 1945, file Plans, Policies and Agreements, box 199, RG 107.

115. JCS 1015, United States Post War Military Base Requirements in Iceland, 23 August 1944, sec. 2, file CCS 660.2 Iceland (8-20-43), RG 218; and JCS 994, United States Postwar Military Requirements in Areas Under the Control of New Zealand, 12 August 1944, sec. 4, file CCS 360 (12-9-42), RG 218.

116. For a copy of the JPWC study The Post War Strategic Posture of the U.S. Armed Forces, dated 5 October 1944, see file Navy Basic Plans, June 1943–August 1946, series 14, Strategic Plans Division Records, NOA. The paper was forwarded to the JCS through the JSSC on 17 October 1944 but not acted upon. See secretary JPWC memorandum for secretary, JCS, sub-

ject: Summary of the Work of the Joint Post War Committee, 30 December 1944, file CCS 334, Joint Post War Committee (3-16-44), RG 218.

117. Quoted in Burns, 287. For Roosevelt's inclination to put off decisions on postwar issues, see Burns, 358–59.

118. Berle and Jacobs, 484. Diary entry for 22 February 1944.

119. Stimson Diary, 4 March 1943, 12–13, reel 8.

120. For documentation on Stimson's irritation at being bypassed in this manner, see Stimson diary entries 21 and 22 August, 11 and 26 October, and 30 November 1944. Quotations are from, respectively, 21 August 1944 diary entry and Stimson's letter to Hull, 22 August 1944. Both are in the Stimson Diary, reel 9, 11–14.

121. Stettinius to secretaries of war and Navy, 29 November 1944, copy enclosed in JCS 1224, Procedure—Joint Chiefs of Staff and State-War-Navy Coordinating Committee, 7 January 1945, sec. 1, file CCS 334, SANACC (12-19-44), RG 218.

122. Stimson Diary, 26 October 1944, 186, reel 9.

123. According to one scholar, the "significance of Stettinius' effort was that it brought diplomatic military decision making into a closer relationship at the very time when many men in the State, War and Navy Departments as well as in the Joint Chiefs were seeking ways to focus their rising doubts about communism." See Thomas M. Campbell, *Masquerade Peace: America's UN Policies, 1944–1945* (Tallahassee: Florida State University Press, 1973), 72.

124. G. A. B. (George A. Brownell), memorandum for Mr. Lovett, 27 July 1944, file Plans, Policies and Agreements, box 199, RG 107.

125. George A. Brownell, memorandum for the assistant secretary of war for air, subject: "Airfields in Foreign Countries," 13 February 1945, and George A. Brownell, memorandum for Mr. McCloy, 16 February 1945, both in file Plans, Policies and Agreements, box 199, RG 107.

126. Quotations from Brownell, memorandum for assistant secretary of war for air, 13 February 1945.

127. Robert A. Lovett, memorandum for the deputy commander, AAF, and chief of Air Staff, 27 February 1945, file Plans, Policies and Agreements, box 199, RG 107.

128. Minutes of the 13th Meeting of SWNCC, 9 March 1945, sec. 1, file CCS 334, SANACC (12-19-44), RG 218.

129. Ibid., corrigendum to minutes of 13th Meeting of SWNCC, 19 March 1945.

130. Interdepartmental memorandum regarding organization of ACC, 27 March 1945 (signed by Acting Secretary of State Joseph C. Grew, Stimson, Forrestal, and Secretary of Commerce Henry A. Wallace), file SWNCC 334, Air Coordinating Committee, box 83, SWNCC/SANACC Records, RG 353 (Records of Interdepartmental and Intradepartmental Committees–State Department), NA. The ACC was the nominal successor to the Interdepartmental Committee on International Aviation, which had lapsed into inactivity before the Chicago Conference on International Aviation in the fall of 1944. The designated members of the ACC were William L. Clayton, assistant secretary of state; Lovett, Gates,

and William A. B. Burden, assistant secretary of commerce. T. P. Wright, administrator of civil aeronautics, was the ACC's executive secretary.

131. George A. Brownell, "The Air Coordinating Committee: A Problem in Federal Staff Work," *Journal of Air Law and Commerce* 14 (autumn 1947): 405–35.

132. Acting Secretary of State Grew to the president, 26 June 1945, file Matthews Papers Miscellaneous, box 6, Hickerson-Matthews Files, RG 59; minutes of the 19th Meeting of the SWNCC, 18 June 1945, file CCS 334 SANACC (12-9-42), RG 218; Acting Secretary of State Dean G. Acheson, memorandum for the president, subject: Continuation of Construction of Airfield at Dhahran, 21 September 1945; and H. S. T., memorandum for the acting secretary of state, 28 September 1945; both in file State Department Correspondence, 1945–1946, box 33, Confidential File, Papers of Harry S. Truman, Truman Library, Independence, Mo. Documents are now declassified.

133. Acting Secretary of State Grew to the president, 26 June 1945, file Matthews Papers Miscellaneous, box 6, Hickerson-Matthews Files, RG 59.

Chapter 3

Base Planning Takes Shape, 1945

In the fall of 1945, the JCS, under constant pressure from civilian government officials since the spring, replaced JCS 570/2 with a new overall base plan. The plan required months to complete, with interservice rivalry accounting for much of the delay. Other factors affecting the planning were the uncertain implications of awesome new weapons; the deterioration of the Grand Alliance (the view of Russia as the next enemy emerged slowly); and the planners' expectation that postwar defense funding would be severely limited. The belief that military budgets would be tight caused the planners to speak mostly in terms of acquiring base "rights" instead of specifying bases to be developed. They hoped that the US civil airlines would come to their aid by maintaining some overseas locations. Planning by both for routes and facilities often coincided, but with increasing frequency their requirements diverged. Finished in October 1945, the new base plan—designated JCS 570/40— reflected a definite shift in the geographic orientation of American strategy. The regional concept of American security was gone, probably forever. But what took its place could not properly be called globalism.

* * *

The dissatisfaction over the condition of the US postwar overseas base program, first voiced by Colonel Brownell in February 1945, spread rapidly throughout the executive branch during the spring of 1945. Some expressed concern at the lack of tangible results produced by the JCS and State Department groups working on postwar bases, while others zeroed in on the need to revise JCS 570/2.

The status report on base negotiations, furnished by the State Department to the State-War-Navy Coordinating Committee (SWNCC) in March, was the first official word civilians in the war and Navy Departments received of progress on the yearlong base acquisition effort.[1] The nearly empty slate, after a year of waiting, aroused considerable displeasure among members of the SWNCC. Brownell, as we have seen, faulted the State Department (the report, he told Assistant Secretary of War for Air Lovett, "shows on its face that the State Department has not sufficiently pressed the necessary work on this entire subject").[2] R. Keith Kane, Forrestal's assistant, reached the same conclusion. In a memorandum for Forrestal and Assistant Secretary of the Navy for Air Gates, summarizing the State Department's report, Kane said, "In effect nothing is being done on one of the most important specific security questions for this country. . . and this at a time when our bargaining power has probably passed its peak and is really due to become weaker." The State Department, he thought, was preoccupied with preparations for the upcoming United Nations Conference at San Francisco, California, and needed to be "jacked up."[3]

Due no doubt to the increased interest shown by the SWNCC, the Joint Post War Committee (JPWC) stepped up its activity. Between early March and mid-April 1945, the JCS submitted additional statements of maximum and minimum requirements to the State Department via the SWNCC, including bases on Canton, Christmas, and Penrhyn Islands in the South Pacific, in Peru, and in the Azores.[4]

The pace was not fast enough for the Air Coordinating Committee. The intragovernmental committee suggested that the JCS should be "requested to press their studies on the JCS 570 series to a conclusion at the earliest possible date, including needs for facilities necessary for the operation of proposed bases and needs for military air routes."[5] If the ACC hoped to integrate the nation's overseas civil and military aviation structure, obtaining the military's requirements was the necessary first step. The ACC was forced to wait for the military to specify what it wanted because President Roosevelt had stated that military requirements for bases, facilities, and transit rights must take precedence over civil aviation needs. Nor were negotiations for military rights to be "postponed or retarded" in deference to those needs.[6] The JCS, however, was not about to be rushed, responding to the ACC's request for more action on bases by simply forwarding copies of the completed statements of maximum and minimum requirements, saying the situation was under control, and stating that the ACC would be informed of further developments.[7]

Calls to reexamine JCS 570/2 paralleled the campaign to speed up base acquisition. The Office of the Assistant Secretary of War for Air was the first to raise the issue, but the Navy also wanted to revise the base bible, seeking to realign the blue-, green-, and black-bordered areas of JCS 570/2 more closely to its *Basic Postwar Plan No. 1*.[8] In April, Admiral King recommended to the JCS that Manus in the Admiralty Islands and the Ryukyu Islands (both within the black-bordered area of JCS 570/2 and planned to be among the Navy's postwar operating bases in the Pacific) be incorporated in the blue-bordered area.[9]

Officers in the Operations Division of the War Department General Staff also believed JCS 570/2 required updating. When the Joint Strategic Survey Committee originally drew up JCS 570/2, noted Col Max Johnson of OPD, the plan had "expressed uncertainty as to the position and attitude of Russia" and had held out the possibility of difficulties with other former Allies following the defeat of Germany and Japan. "In the light of present events," he said, "it is considered that some of these uncertainties currently exist."[10] Johnson did not specify what "present events" he had in mind; although, in the case of the Soviet Union, he probably meant Russia's increasingly arbitrary and exclusionary actions in Eastern Europe (particularly Poland), the tensions produced by unilateral Anglo-American actions relative to the surrender of the German army in northern Italy, and roadblocks thrown up by the Russians as the United States attempted to assist US prisoners of war liberated by Soviet forces.[11] There was yet no consensus within the American military as to the meaning of Soviet behavior (nor would there be even by war's end).[12] Nonetheless, these and other developments during the winter and spring of 1944–45 were like a stone cast into a pond, creating ever widening circles of suspicion regarding Soviet postwar intentions.

Johnson offered other reasons for recommending revision of JCS 570/2, noting, for example, that Assistant Secretary of War John McCloy felt the United States should think about acquiring outright some of Great Britain's and France's strategically located Western Hemisphere possessions, such as Ascension Island in the South Atlantic and Clipperton Island in the Pacific.[13] If the United States were to assume sovereignty over these islands, it would have to reexamine JCS 570/2 because the 1943 plan had indicated American base rights were to be only on a "participating" or "reciprocal" basis in those two locations. General Marshall, evidently convinced by these arguments, proposed and the JCS approved a new overall examination of postwar base requirements. The Joint Staff Planners (JPS) and their subsidiary, the Joint War Plans Committee (JWPC), in collaboration with the JPWC, would conduct the study. The study was to consider: (1) bases required by conditions under which the United States would find itself at war with a major power or powers, and (2) bases required by the United States as a participant in a peace enforced by the major powers, possibly through participation in a world security organization. Unlike JCS 570/2, the new plan would indicate the priority to be attached to individual bases.[14] Marshall omitted naming the "major power or powers" with whom the United States might find itself at war. But in light of Colonel Johnson's comments, there seems little doubt that War Department planners, as had the Navy's F-14 planners months earlier, were beginning to focus on the Soviet Union as the next enemy.

Bob Lovett, who was quite unhappy with the JCS's initial response to the ACC's request for greater speed by the military in determining overseas base requirements, found one flaw in Marshall's proposal.[15] The Army chief of staff's memorandum, he wrote General Arnold, "does not call for a statement (which was asked for by the ACC) of our requirements for *military air routes* and for *bases and facilities* [emphasis in original]."[16] Information about routes and facilities along them, such as radar, communications, and weather stations was essential because US aircraft would have to transit through and use aids to navigation located in foreign countries that did not host an American base.[17] This made negotiations for transit rights and rights to install supporting facilities just as important as negotiations for the overseas base itself. One may infer that route and supporting facilities data would have some bearing on negotiations for commercial rights since civil aircraft would naturally use military support facilities and vice versa. To correct the omission in Marshall's proposal, Arnold, acting on Lovett's cue, recommended that the JCS consider providing for supporting air routes and facilities, and put the report "in such form that. . . it can be submitted to the Air Coordinating Committee. . . so that civilian air requirements can be incorporated; and then a single comprehensive document can be forwarded to the State Department."[18]

Despite the apparent need to hurry, six months would pass before the JCS completed work on the revision of its master base plan. Moreover, although the military recognized that JCS 570/2 needed updating, Lovett's office had initiated the process. The uniformed military rarely took the lead in postwar base matters. In 1943 President Roosevelt prompted the investigations by the Joint Strategic Survey Committee and the Navy's General Board that had produced JCS 570/2. In 1944 the JPWC had coasted until the State Department asked for statements of maximum and minimum base requirements for particular countries. Now, as the war drew to a close, war and Navy Department civilian officials (or civilians in uniform like Colonel Brownell) and such interdepartmental bodies as the SWNCC and the ACC pushed the professional military hard on the subject of postwar bases.

* * *

With Lovett and Brownell leading the charge for a coordinated civil and military air-rights program, it is not surprising to find the AAF under considerable pressure to do its part to promote early determination of military base needs. They hoped to speed up the JCS by having Air Staff planners rapidly complete an assessment of postwar air bases and routes. When completed the results would be forwarded to the JCS committees working on the revision of JCS 570/2. This was the same suggestion Lovett made the preceding February, which the Air Staff did not act on.[19] Now in May 1945, Lovett and Brownell were not about to allow any foot-dragging by the Air Staff.

Following General Marshall's recommendation that the JCS reexamine JCS 570/2, the Air Staff planners had, in fact, begun to restudy the postwar base question on their own.[20] Nevertheless, Lovett and Brownell wanted to make sure the Air Staff effort would have the highest priority. After a visit from Brownell, Brig Gen Lauris Norstad, General Kuter's successor as assistant chief of the Air Staff Plans, told Colonel Moffat, chief of the AAF's Postwar Division, "The current rate of progress under normal procedure indicates that a comprehensive and effective report may not be completed soon enough to assure the protection and furtherance of our military interests in the field of international aviation." Norstad directed Moffat to set up "special procedures" for producing a study within 30 days.[21]

Moffat responded by organizing an ad hoc study group drawn largely from personnel of the Air Staff's Postwar Division and from Air Transport Command's planning unit.[22] One exception was Capt Oliver J. Lissitzyn (then attached to the Office of Strategic Services) who Moffat requested for special duty on the project.[23] In alerting the rest of the Air Staff to the importance of the ad hoc study group's work, Moffat wrote that the United States "needs an integrated pattern of bases, strategically and politically sound, into which piecemeal gains may properly be fitted. Military and naval bases other than air, as well as civil aviation requirements will affect this pattern."[24]

Completed on 11 July 1945 (about three weeks past the deadline initially imposed by Norstad), the ad hoc study group's plan, "U.S. Requirements for Post War Military Air Bases and Rights in Foreign Territory," was a revealing document.[25] Clearly showing what the AAF thought should constitute the American defense frontier, it indicated the relative importance of specific overseas bases within that frontier, and illustrated the principal military air routes connecting one base with another.

The proposed base-rights network, when tied together with the supporting system of military air routes, formed a giant web (in appearance similar to one that might be woven by a deranged spider) stretching over northwest Canada and Alaska; the West, Central, and South Pacific; Central and South America; and the Atlantic from Ascension Island in the south, to the west African bulge, and north to Iceland and Greenland.[26] The plan was similar to previous postwar overseas base blueprints in two major ways—namely, the largest concentrations of bases were in the Western Hemisphere and the Pacific area, and there was no mention of rights to bases on the European continent. On the other hand, the AAF planners broke away from the strictly regional orientation of the earlier plans by recommending that the United States negotiate for transit rights at airfields along two routes zigzagging from bases in the Eastern Atlantic across Africa, the Middle East, and South Asia to the western fringes of the American defense perimeter in the Far East.[27] Such rights would enable US aircraft to traverse the globe, but the AAF planners assigned them to the third and lowest priority of military importance.[28]

Bases along several key routes across the Pacific and on three major transatlantic routes were included in the category of first priority rights. In the Pacific, the United States already controlled the Great Circle route through Alaska and the Aleutians, and a Central Pacific route via Hawaii and other US possessions to the Philippines. The AAF also wanted to obtain rights to bases along an alternate southern route from Vera Cruz, Mexico, or the Panama Canal to Clipperton Island, Nuku Hiva in the Marquesas Islands, and points west. Additionally, the AAF sought base rights on Formosa and Okinawa at the extreme western edge of the nation's defense perimeter. Top priority in the Atlantic went to base rights in Greenland and Iceland on the northern route, the Azores in the mid–Atlantic, and rights to airfields on Ascension Island and the West African coast along the southern route. In short, although the AAF stuck pretty much to the Western Hemisphere–Pacific–Far East concept of America's defense zone, it also emphasized base rights at the outer edges of the perimeter.[29]

If the AAF were to obtain all of the first-priority rights, significant changes would have to be made to JCS 570/2. The 1943 JCS base plan provided simply for "participating" rights on Okinawa, Clipperton Island, and the Azores, but the July 1945 AAF plan called for "exclusive" US rights at these locations.[30] The airmen did not address the obviously touchy question of how US military aircraft would be able to have "exclusive" access to a French possession (Clipperton), nor did they suggest how the Americans might exclude the British from an airfield in the Azores in the face of long-standing Anglo-Portuguese diplomatic ties. These types of problems, presumably, would be resolved by the diplomats. In all, the AAF planners identified more than 125 sites (excluding those in US territories or possessions and those for which postwar arrangements had already been made) where the United States would require postwar air rights, ranging from exclusive use to the simple right of transit and technical stop. But the total number, especially when depicted on a map, is quite misleading. Some have even suggested the AAF used recommendations for a large number of overseas bases as a way to justify a huge independent postwar air force.[31] While there is no doubt that a parochialism sometimes bordering on paranoia existed in the AAF, so facile an interpretation hardly approaches the complexity of historical reality.[32]

Actually, the AAF did not intend to maintain air forces at 125 overseas locations (more than 150 if one counts those overseas areas under American control); its concern was to obtain the *right* to establish a base or use an airfield as a transit point. "At the present time," declared the AAF planners, "it is the acquisition of rights that is of importance. With these rights once secured, the garrisoning or development of individual bases can be left for future determination."[33]

The AAF emphasized base rights for two major, intertwined reasons. First, Lovett and Brownell were anxious to have a consolidated listing of military and civil requirements so American negotiators could get the maximum possible advantage from the presence of American forces and US-financed air facilities on foreign soil. Once the war ended, most US military personnel would return home, and many installations would be dismantled; consequently, the United States would lose its diplomatic leverage. Secondly, if the AAF became too specific about its postwar base plans, the government's entire military and civil air rights acquisition program might become entangled in postwar roles and missions squabbles between the services. Focusing on base rights might prevent this kind of delay. The concentration on base rights also reflected the widely shared beliefs in the military establishment that the

American people would be reluctant to sanction a high rate of defense expenditures after victory and about the nature of the next war. The likelihood of sharp budget cutbacks heavily influenced AAF calculations. "It is not to be assumed," the ad hoc study group pointed out, "that the will of the people will support a United States military establishment adequate to construct, maintain, and garrison complete military bases at every point from which we should be prepared to strike down any threat to our security."[34] Just as their Navy counterparts, the AAF planners saw overseas base rights as a solution to the dilemma posed on the one hand by the promise of fiscal penury, and on the other by the need to be able to apply force quickly and with maximum flexibility in an uncertain postwar international environment.[35] Extensive base rights thus served the demands both of the preparedness ideology and of the American tradition of sparse peacetime military appropriations.

In 1943 one of the principal themes in the ATC's study of air bases was that a postwar economy drive would require the civil airlines to maintain overseas air facilities for the military.[36] Captain Lissitzyn was one of the authors of ATC's report and currently a member of the ad hoc study group. His involvement in both groups raises the question to what extent did commercial aviation interests intrude on the AAF's base planning during the summer of 1945.

There was considerable pressure within the AAF to boost postwar civil aviation. Most came from a belief that the military would need to depend on the airlines to operate many overseas routes and facilities, but some was unvarnished economic opportunism. For example, Maj Gen C. R. Smith, deputy commander of ATC (but within months to resume leadership of American Airlines), told the Air Staff in March 1945 that Abadan (an Iranian island at the head of the Persian Gulf) promised to be a key "crossroads" for postwar commercial air traffic. For this reason, he thought the United States should do everything possible to obtain postwar operating rights there, even to the point of constructing an additional airfield.[37] This was, in effect, a rather transparent bid for a kind of "GI Bill of Rights" for the airlines. Although General Kuter forwarded Smith's proposal to Lovett, it was not acted on, probably because the airfield planned for Dhahran, Saudi Arabia, would satisfy the same need.

The ad hoc study group's July 1945 plan is an excellent yardstick for measuring the degree to which commercial aviation concerns impacted military planning. The AAF planners claimed to have excluded from their deliberations "all matters pertaining to present or future civil or commercial aviation except to the extent that the military may utilize facilities maintained by civil agencies or airlines."[38] But, in view of the ad hoc study group's contention that funds for the military would be very tight after the war, was the recommendation for rights at more than 125 locations made with the conviction that most facilities would be operated by the airlines and, therefore, would be a blueprint for the expansion of postwar American commercial aviation?

Clearly, both military and civil aviation would benefit from well-developed, Great Circle air routes from the Pacific Northwest to the Far East and from the northeastern United States to Europe. The AAF planners stated, for example, that a North Pacific route to the Far East via the Aleutians and the Kurile Islands would save 2,000 or more miles over any other transpacific route to Japan or the Philippines.[39] A route across the Middle East and South Asia to the Far East would also be mutually attractive. On the other hand, the ad hoc study group listed many bases and routes of doubtful commercial value. These included a host of West, Central, and South Pacific sites making up at least seven transpacific routes; alternate northeastern and northwestern Great Circle routes through the Canadian interior; and a route linking the eastern and western edges of the American defense perimeter across Central Africa and the mid-Indian Ocean.[40]

The Central African route was an alternate to the primary route the AAF planners wanted across North Africa (Casablanca, Algiers, Tunis, Tripoli, Benghazi, Cairo), the Middle East, and the Indian subcontinent.[41] No airline was eager to fly the North African portion, let alone the Central African segment, of an east-west route. The airlines preferred instead a route through the Azores to Lisbon, Portugal and the other capitals of southern Europe, connecting eventually with Cairo, Egypt. Indeed, just prior to awarding the right to operate the North African route (the least desirable of the three Atlantic routes awarded) to Trans World Airlines (TWA) in June 1945, the Civil Aeronautics Board pointed out that "the economic justification for a route along the North African coast to Cairo appears very doubtful and is being established primarily because of the national defense considerations."[42] Most significant, the ad hoc group named no requirements for military-air rights on the European continent—the plum commercial market the civilian airlines wanted most to penetrate.

The ad hoc study group's plan demonstrates: (1) how military preparedness and private profit sometimes went hand in hand in military planning but also (2) how military requirements differed from commercial needs. Those who thought the prewar pattern of smooth cooperation between the civil airlines and the military regarding routes and facility maintenance would continue were wrong. Pan American would no longer be the only American airline operating overseas; 11 companies had bid to operate the North Atlantic routes.[43] For the United States to ask an airline to maintain an unprofitable route, was to ask too much in so competitive an environment—patriotism, after all, had its limits.

National security, not economic expansion, was the driving force motivating the AAF's planners in the summer of 1945. If the United States obtained all the postwar air rights identified in the ad hoc study group's document, then it could "move a striking force . . . to outposts from which we can effectively smash any threat."[44] Curiously, the ad hoc study group failed to name any future enemy—Russia was not mentioned in the report. The planners' position seemed to be that the United States must be ready to oppose threats coming from any direction: a "wagons-in-a-circle" posture. Why they were so vague about potential threats is not clear; others within the military establishment were considering the USSR as the next enemy. This apparent strategic ineptitude on the part of the ad hoc study group, however, would be remedied during the coming month. Before Japan's surrender, the Air Staff's Intelligence Division produced a document indicating without a doubt that AAF planners were considering how to apply strategic airpower against the Soviet Union if needed. The paper was an analysis of the size, composition, and deployment of US air units that would be included in an international police force. Its author, in an unmistakable reference to the Soviet Union, said the American contingent of this force ought to be able to protect the United States "from the only power which is conceivably capable of threatening our security." But how would the United States do this while part of a world security force? The AAF analyst's answer was for the United States to secure base rights through the world organization on the west, east, and to the south of the "threatening power" (a term Major General Fairchild, AAF member of the JSSC, had used in referring to the USSR) ostensibly for the postwar policing of Germany and Japan. The difficulty, as the document's author recognized, would be to justify bases south of the USSR (he specifically mentioned Cairo, Egypt; Dhahran, Saudi Arabia; Karachi and Calcutta, India; and Rangoon, Burma). The United States might argue, he suggested, that as the main contributor to an international police force, it would require access to a worldwide chain of bases.[45]

The AAF intelligence document was important for several reasons. It revealed the contempt and suspicion with which some military men viewed internationalism; it showed that AAF thinking about the next war was turning the corner from an amorphous preparation to take on all comers to the concentration on a specific enemy; and it demonstrated that a military planner always operates in more than one temporal dimension. While the paper's author conceded that within a few years "the development of aircraft ranges, and even of nonpiloted air weapons may render the possession of air bases outside the United States unnecessary for defense," the nation should not anchor current policy "on an as yet unrealized dream of the future."[46] For the immediate future, he pointed out, even base rights in Greenland, Iceland, the Azores, or on the West African coast "are considered useful primarily for defensive and ferrying, rather than for offensive purposes."[47] In 1945 the B-29, with a "combat" or "effective" radius of between 1,500 and 2,000 nautical miles, was the AAF's most advanced bomber.[48] Based on this radius of action, a B-29 flying from

Iceland (the closest location to Europe at which the United States planned in 1945 to acquire postwar base rights) could not reach much beyond Moscow and, therefore, could not attack Soviet industrial targets beyond the Ural Mountains. Assuming, then, that bases in Europe would not be available to "strike effectively" at many targets in the Soviet Union, the B-29 had to attack from bases in North Africa, the Middle East, South Asia, or the far western Pacific (at targets in the Soviet Far East).[49] Thus Cairo, Karachi, and other bases on the southern rim of Asia—not Iceland, Greenland, or Alaska—would be the main bases from which the United States should plan to launch offensive operations against the Soviet Union.[50] In the first few years after World War II, the JCS war plans, as we shall see, were geared to use Middle Eastern and South Asian bases in the event of war with the USSR.

The AAF Intelligence Division's analysis (dated 11 August 1945) came too late to have any effect on the ad hoc study group's base rights planning completed on 11 July 1945. The completion date may have been influenced by a letter from Assistant Secretary of War for Air Lovett to Maj Gen Ira C. Eaker, deputy commander of the AAF. Lovett reemphasized the urgent need for the military, particularly the AAF, to pin down postwar base requirements. He called Eaker's attention to a report by the Mead Committee (the Senate Special Committee to Investigate the National Defense Program) in which the senators strongly affirmed their belief that the United States should derive every possible advantage in postwar military and civil air rights from the facilities constructed overseas by the United States during the war.[51] Fortunately, the ad hoc study group's work was complete, or nearly so, when Eaker received Lovett's letter, and the plan was submitted to the JCS.[52] In addition to communicating its desires to the JCS, the AAF would soon have the opportunity to present its views on postwar overseas bases directly to the secretary of state.

* * *

In the critical summer of 1945, overseas bases were very much on the minds of President Truman and James F. Byrnes (who would become secretary of state early in July) much more so than historians have previously recognized. Both were convinced the United States must have the rights to bases their military advisers believed essential for US security. Like FDR, Truman also appreciated the great potential of postwar international air transport, referring to it as: "together with reparations, the most important postwar international problem."[53] Yet the president, once the head of the Special Committee to Investigate the National Defense Program, was apt to interpret international civil aviation more in terms of American national advantage than in the context of the global community occasionally envisioned by Roosevelt.

The Navy, as noted previously, briefed both Truman and Byrnes on postwar base requirements early in June. Shortly after the Navy's presentation to the president, Truman's naval aide asked Admiral Edwards, supervising the Navy's postwar planning for Admiral King, for some ideas on Pacific bases other than in the Japanese Mandates (Marina, Caroline, and Marshall Islands).[54] He replied in a memorandum that the United States should have exclusive military rights in the Ryukyu Islands, Bonin-Volcano Islands, and Manus in the Admiralty Islands. Edwards claimed the Yellow Sea would be the most critical of the approaches to the Pacific because of "the involved and possibly conflicting political interests in the land areas adjacent thereto." With a strong line of Pacific bases, argued Edwards, the United States would be "in position either to take a hand in Asiatic affairs or, alternatively, if so desired, to stand between the Japan-Asia trouble zone and the Pacific." Edwards's memorandum reflected the consistent thrust of all naval postwar planning up to that point—an active role for the Navy on behalf of US interests in the Pacific.[55]

After receiving the Navy's views, Truman told Harry Vaughan, his military aide and poker-playing confidant, to obtain the Army's opinion.[56] In a response edited personally by General Marshall, the Army seconded much of what the Navy had said (including the estimate of the strategic importance of the Yellow Sea), but stressed that "primary reliance" should be on "air power complemented by naval surface power." (Like young siblings who constantly poke and push at each other, the services rarely ignored an opportunity for intramural scratching and clawing, but there was no discord between them over the firmness of the US postwar grip on the Pacific.) The Army also told the president that a system of bases would secure the American position in the Pacific and make it possible for the United States "to project its military power into any troubled area" in the Far East. Other powers were to be discouraged from setting up bases "anywhere within the periphery of our Pacific frontier."[57]

Through mid-1945 civilian and military leaders devoted most of their attention to the question of Pacific versus Atlantic military bases. The concentration on the Pacific can be accounted for by the memory of Pearl Harbor, a tradition of expansion into the Pacific, FDR's aversion to postwar involvement in Europe, and such pressing issues in the first half of 1945 as the controversial question of an international trusteeship for the Japanese Mandates, and the need to provide for postwar bases in the Philippines. However, during the Potsdam Conference near Berlin, Germany, in July, American leaders were to become quite concerned about the eastern portion of the base network.

Throughout the voyage to Europe on the cruiser USS *Augusta,* American leaders prepared thoroughly for the Big Three (England, Russia, United States) meeting at Potsdam. Truman, Byrnes, and Admiral Leahy studied massive briefing books prepared by the State Department, conferring at least once and sometimes twice a day.[58] The president also received advice from his close political advisers and speechwriters (John Snyder, George Allen, and Samuel I. Rosenman). In a memorandum they listed key issues, in order of importance, likely to come up at the conference: Russian entry into the war against Japan, the economic stabilization of Europe, full participation by the British in the Pacific, policy toward Germany, holding the peace conference in the United States, and, finally, "some military and naval bases if possible." They also reminded the president that "as a well-known Missouri horse trader, the American people expect you to bring something home to them."[59] The very day Truman's advisers wrote their memorandum, the Mead Committee published its report on the disposition of US installations abroad. It was, moreover, known within the White House that public-opinion polls showed 53 percent of the American people now favored the acquisition of new military bases, whereas in 1942 only 34 percent had been so inclined.[60]

Neither the State Department nor the military was eager to raise the subject of postwar bases at Potsdam. In June, Secretary of State Stettinius had written that the American delegation to the Potsdam Conference should be ready if the issue came up, but "it would be preferable for the United States not to take the initiative in proposing the discussion of any questions relating to international bases at *this* time"(emphasis in original).[61]

One reason the diplomats and soldiers were reluctant to discuss bases is obvious: the military had not yet decided what it wanted.[62] Additionally, little enthusiasm remained for the idea of international military bases.[63] This noble vision had foundered (as far as the United States was concerned) on the rock of American military insistence on exclusive control of the Japanese Mandates.

In line with the preconference plan, the United States did not raise the base issue at any of the formal sessions at Potsdam. Truman, however, confronted British Prime Minister Winston Churchill with the subject at a private luncheon on 18 July. Unfortunately, we have only Churchill's account of this meeting, but it shows how civil and military matters could become entangled in a discussion of postwar aviation. Truman, recalled the prime minister, brought up "air and communication," explaining that as president he has "great difficulties to face about airfields in British territory, especially in Africa, which the Americans had built at enormous cost." The president thought, wrote Churchill, that the two countries should develop "a firm plan for common use." Churchill responded that if he continued in office, he was certainly willing to discuss this but believed "it would be a great pity if the Americans got worked up about bases and air traffic and set themselves to make a win of it at all costs." To this point, Truman had been referring, not primarily to common military bases, but to access for American airlines to British-controlled civil airports. The prime minister, by speculating next about the benefits that would come from the common use of naval facilities, skillfully shifted the conversation to the ground of military bases alone. Truman, who wanted to avoid the appearance of a postwar Anglo-American military alliance, now began to retreat, saying, as Churchill remembered it, that although he (Truman) favored a continuation of the reciprocal use of facilities established during the war, any arrangement would have to be consistent with UN organization policy.[64] The Truman-Churchill "military bases" colloquy demonstrates the very real rivalry between Great Britain and the United States for postwar economic advantage.[65] It also reveals a Harry Truman still much influenced by the "they hired the money, didn't they" mentality of the Mead (formerly Truman) Committee. Finally, their conversation shows how a civil airfield could be easily perceived as a military base and vice versa. If friends were able to recognize this fact, then how about enemies?

Potsdam offered the "Missouri horse trader" an opportunity to pressure the British on postwar civil aviation, but it also provided the occasion for a noticeable turning of American attention to Atlantic military bases. Byrnes, Averell Harriman (American ambassador to the Soviet Union), and Generals Marshall and Arnold apparently discussed the problem of postwar bases at a dinner on the evening of 22 July.[66] Byrnes, who already knew what bases the Navy wanted, evidently asked for the other services' requirements. The next day, Marshall gave Byrnes a copy of JCS 570/2 and the memorandum on Pacific bases that the Army had prepared for the president.[67] Similarly, Arnold (also perhaps the next day) sent the secretary of state a "hurriedly prepared map indicating air base requirements."[68] After his return to the United States, Arnold had a better map prepared for Byrnes (one based on the ad hoc study group's report) and provided him with data on "certain military air bases which we discussed." Arnold listed the bases in the following order: Iceland, the Azores, Dakar, Ascension Island, the Cape Verde Islands, and Nuku Hiva in the French Marquesas group.[69] Only the last was a Pacific base—the rest were all in the Atlantic.

The priority Arnold attached to long-term base rights in Iceland received reinforcement from an unlikely source. On 28

July, James Forrestal flew into Potsdam, sans invitation from President Truman.[70] The Navy secretary had not yet wormed his way into the highest American political-military decision-making circle; he had, however, gotten along well with Byrnes, and the latter evidently thought Forrestal, as the head of the Navy Department, deserved a larger role in the defense policy-making arena. Forrestal told Byrnes that retention of the American bases in Iceland was of great importance.[71] Byrnes agreed and authorized Forrestal to discuss the question with the British.[72] On his way home, the Navy secretary stopped in London and stressed to Clement Atlee, Churchill's successor as prime minister, and Sir Alexander Cadogan, a permanent undersecretary in the British Foreign Office, the significance of Icelandic bases both to England and the United States in any future war.[73]

The flurry of behind-the-scenes activity at Potsdam regarding base rights in Iceland could be attributed to the increasing American concern for the postwar European balance of power. But the immediate catalyst probably was arrival of word from Washington that the Soviets had plans for their own outposts on the roof of the world.

In the first week of July, the American ambassador in Oslo, Norway, reported to the State Department that the Norwegian foreign minister had told him of Soviet demands made in November 1944 for Norway to cede Bear Island to the USSR, for joint rule by the two countries over Spitsbergen, and for Norway to renounce the 1920 multilateral treaty recognizing Norwegian sovereignty over the Spitsbergen Archipelago.[74] The State Department, anticipating that the Soviets might raise these demands at Potsdam, wanted to get the military's evaluation of the strategic implications of Soviet bases at these locations and the bearing such a Soviet move might have on US efforts to obtain base rights in Iceland and Greenland.[75]

JCS committees in both Washington and Potsdam considered the State Department query. The military pointed out that Bear Island's strategic importance was its control of the route through the Barents Sea; and the Spitsbergen Archipelago might have significance as a stepping-stone along postwar arctic commercial and military aviation routes.[76] Most of the JCS officers believed that Soviet bases on Bear Island or Spitsbergen would have little strategic impact *if* the United States could secure bases in Iceland and Greenland. The military preferred not to discuss Spitsbergen at Potsdam but to postpone postwar bases and other territorial questions to a later meeting of the Council of Foreign Ministers (by then the United States would know what it wanted).[77]

If, however, the Soviets should bring the matter up at Potsdam, Admiral Willson, one of the three "elder statesmen" on the JSSC, was disposed to take a strong stand:

> We should oppose the Russian proposals not only as untimely, but as unnecessary for Soviet security and contrary to long-range and over-all security considerations from our point of view. This war has been fought to prevent an aggressive nation from dominating Europe, and ultimately threatening the Western Hemisphere. From the long-range security point of view, and until the postwar situation and Soviet policy can be seen more clearly, we should, insofar as practicable, resist demands and policies which tend to improve the Soviet position in Western Europe.[78]

Willson obviously rejected any notion that Russian bases along the Soviet Union's northern frontier may have been as justifiable as American bases on the arctic fringes of the North American continent. Furthermore, he clearly believed the United States should take an active role in postwar Europe.[79] This view was endorsed by the JCS.[80]

Not all top-level American military leaders agreed that national security either demanded strong bases in the North Atlantic or continued US involvement in European affairs. In June, Lieutenant General Embick (Willson's Army colleague on the JSSC) wrote to the State Department's John Hickerson that, in light of American-Russian relations and the many difficulties ahead for the United States in occupying Germany, "it would be unwise for us to press at this time for base facilities in Iceland." Embick argued that if the United States acquired base rights in Iceland unilaterally, it "will project the United States into the European Theater, cannot be defended as essential to our own national security, and may be expected to arouse Russian suspicion as to Anglo-American intentions."[81]

Throughout a career that had begun in 1895, Embick had frequently found himself at odds with his military and civilian superiors. But Embick's dissents were more than just the outbursts of a contentious crank. In the 1920s and 1930s, Embick consistently supported a limited boundary for the US Pacific defense perimeter: a line drawn from Alaska through Hawaii to Panama. In Embick's opinion, US interests in the Far East were not worth the high cost it would take to defend them. In short, he was an arch regionalist, even a continentalist, when it came to the application of American military power.[82] By the end of World War II, Embick's idea of the proper extent of America's defense frontier had enlarged appreciably. Yet, unlike many military planners and civilian policy makers, he did not agree that an American military presence close to a troubled area would necessarily be a force for peace and stability. His objection to an American base in Iceland is consistent with this view. While undoubtedly in the minority in maintaining that the United States should not assume a belligerent posture toward the USSR, Embick's was by no means, as we shall see, a lone voice in this respect within military planning circles.

Still, the balance was tilting away from the kind of regionalism that saw no long-term role for the United States in Europe and the Middle East toward a more active and aggressive policy in a sphere traditionally subject to relatively brief American incursions. John McCloy, assistant secretary of war, reacted negatively to Embick's views. The former's aide reported that McCloy felt Embick's ideas represented "a rather restricted concept of what is necessary for national defense."[83] At Potsdam, General Marshall told the other joint chiefs that Byrnes, in a discussion of the Spitsbergen development (probably on the evening of 22 July), had said rather than reacting to Soviet demands with counter claims, the United States should initiate its own proposals for base requirements.[84] Another remark Byrnes made at the dinner sums up this attitude: "what we must do now is not make the world safe for democracy, but make the world safe for the USA. Russia is like a greedy kid—never satisfied. When it gets one concession, it always has a couple more to request."[85]

That President Truman proposed to heed the secretary of state's recommendation and develop a strong overseas military base system became clear as he addressed the American people by radio following his return from Potsdam. After describing the devastation he had seen in Germany and announcing his determination to prevent such a fate from befalling the United States, the president (even before mentioning the atomic bomb) declared "Though the United States wants no territory or profit or selfish advantage out of this war, we are going to maintain the military bases necessary for the complete protection of our interests and of world peace. Bases which our military experts deem to be essential for our protection, we will acquire. We will acquire them by arrangements consistent with the United Nations Charter."[86] But at the time of Truman's speech, the "military experts" in the JCS organization had not yet determined what the US postwar base structure should be. The revision of JCS 570/2 was barely under way.

* * *

During the late summer and early fall of 1945, an atmosphere of uncertainty and intense pressure enveloped the American military, especially the JCS staff officers striving to come up with a base plan. The horrifying destructive force revealed by the dropping of the atomic bombs on Hiroshima and Nagasaki, Japan, filled the military with apprehension for future American security.[87] In other quarters, possession of the bomb encouraged smug complacency. With the war's end, there was no resisting the popular clamor to "bring the boys home," even though some protested that rapid demobilization might adversely affect the nation's ability to fulfill its postwar military commitments.[88] For what purposes, to what extent, and for what duration the United States would have to maintain military forces abroad became problematical as the Grand Alliance broke apart, torn by a snarl of competing interests and ambitions. On 20 August, the president (inspired by his zealously cost-conscious budget director, Harold D. Smith) asked the services to submit an integrated proposal for their postwar needs. This was a moment of truth for the military. On the one hand, the president's request forced more coordination of postwar planning, most notably in the development of a long-range strategy and plans for an overseas base network. On the other hand, the president's order also exacerbated interservice rivalries because joint plans would mean the concrete definition of each service's postwar roles, missions, and force levels.[89] The AAF, driving hard for an autonomous and coequal status in the postwar military structure, was determined to have a healthy slice of defense expenditures. The Navy, fearing submersion by the Army and AAF in a unified military establishment and put on the defensive by charges that the atomic bomb made it (and the Army) obsolete, prepared to fight for its life. Inevitably, overseas base planning was caught up in the turmoil of change affecting the American military as the war ended.

To some observers, the effort to replace JCS 570/2 with a new overall plan for postwar bases seemed to be in disarray. "It is quite apparent to me after my conversations with the Secretary of State and the conferences with the Joint Chiefs of Staff," wrote General Arnold, "that the ideas of everyone in any way connected with the subject are very hazy when it comes to bases required by the future security of the United States."[90] The Navy, of course, had a completed base plan, and the AAF had submitted its recommendations for air base rights to the JCS, but the War Department had not merged Army and AAF requirements. As for the study initiated in the JCS by General Marshall in May, at least three sets of base papers were circulating by August. "They are not tied together," Arnold said, "and not being submitted by these committees when they should be. We must have a policy. Certainly if the Joint Chiefs of Staff haven't a clear-cut conception of what our postwar requirements are we can't expect any higher echelons to have one."[91] Bob Lovett seconded the AAF commander's irritation at the lack of progress, pointing out once again that military lethargy was holding up negotiations for both postwar military and commercial rights.[92]

Agreement on a basic postwar military policy and overall strategic concept logically had to precede completion of a joint base plan. A JCS committee had begun to work on these guiding principles in May, and by the end of August had made enough progress to give the base planners a foundation on which to build a base structure.[93] JCS 1496/3, "Basis for the Formulation of a Military Policy," and JCS 1518/3, "Strategic Concept and Plan for the Employment of United States Armed

Forces," are filled with the tenets of the "ideology of national preparedness." New and powerful long-range weapons had shrunk the ocean barriers that had previously protected the United States. The war had also seriously weakened traditional European allies who had formerly stood between aggressors and America. Senior military officers believed the United States was now highly vulnerable to surprise attack and probable devastation in any future war. To avoid this fate, the United States must have sufficient armed strength to deter aggressors who might ultimately threaten national security. So great was the potential danger that if deterrence was not successful, then the United States must be ready to start "preventive" (first strike) war against any hostile opponent.[94]

The two JCS documents unquestionably envisioned an enormously expanded role for American military power as compared to the prewar period. According to the JCS, the aggregate of US national policy, from which military policy was derived, was "directed toward the maintenance of world peace, under conditions which insure the security, well-being, and advancement of our country."[95] This was an ambitious goal. The deterrence and "preventive" war strategy, outlined in JCS 1496/3 and JCS 1518/3 and designed to fulfill the ends of national policy, amounted to what historian Sherry describes as "a brief for the United States to become the world's policeman and peacemaker."[96] Yet, there is a fine line of interpretation regarding the purposes for which the military believed armed force would be employed outside the United States after the war.

To argue that the American military saw itself as the "world's policeman and peacemaker" in 1945 is to overstate the case. The JCS recognized that keeping the peace of the world was not up to the United States alone, or even to all nations acting through the UN. "In the last analysis," JCS 1496/3 states, "the maintenance of . . . world peace will depend upon mutual cooperation among Britain, Russia, and the United States."[97] If relations between the major powers, particularly between Russia and America should break down, the United States would have to be prepared to confront an aggressor threatening American security without help from allies or the UN. In 1945, Russia posed the only foreseeable danger to US safety—the

American military's overwhelming concern was to be able to handle this threat. "If equipped to deal with any problem presented by the eventuality of a conflict with Russia," said the JCS, "the United States would also be equipped to deal with any other power due to the comparatively weaker position of all other powers."[98] Providing a force to accomplish this objective fell well short of planning a postwar military establishment "for unilateral enforcement of world peace."[99] The evidence shows the military to have been willing, even eager, to police the Far East, insofar as events there affected US security and interests in the Pacific. Many military leaders, largely in the context of perceived Russian capabilities, were also ready to become permanently entangled in postwar Europe. But the globalism of later decades was the consequence of blending both apprehension about American physical safety *and* the fear of a worldwide communist conspiracy directed from the Kremlin. In 1945 the latter dread festered only in the minds of a few.

What the JCS primarily wanted was military power adequate to forestall an attack on the United States—a posture for which overseas bases were critical. The JCS knew the American people would not support armed forces anywhere near the size the military believed desirable.[100] For this reason the limited military forces available must be highly trained, well equipped, and "so disposed strategically that they can be brought to bear at the source of enemy military power, or in other critical areas in time to thwart attack by a potential aggressor."[101]

New weapons also influenced the JCS's attitude toward bases abroad. JCS planners considered the implications the atomic bomb and other technological developments might have on an overseas base system at a special meeting attended by Vannevar Bush, civilian director of the wartime Office of Scientific Research and Development, and other members of the JCS's Joint New Weapons Committee. Bush told the military that whatever the potential of new weapons, a need for advance bases would still exist. The maximum range of the German V-2 rocket was only 400 miles; and even if a guided missile with a 2,000-mile range were developed, the United States would still require an overseas base from which to launch it.

In Bush's opinion, "the closer we get to a potential enemy the better." Maj Gen Leslie Groves, head of the Manhattan Project and a man almost obsessed with the idea of security, added, "We should get our bases now and plan not for 10 years but for 50–100 years ahead."[102] The atomic bomb, then, made possession of far-flung bases even more urgent.

In formulating a long-range military strategy, the JCS planners saw a postwar American base network as having two general characteristics. First, it must contain an outer perimeter of bases "from which to reconnoiter and survey possible enemy actions, to intercept his attacking forces and missiles, to deny him use of such bases, and to launch counteractions which alone can reach a decision satisfactory to us." Second, outer perimeter bases suitable for both defensive and offensive purposes were to be part of an integrated system made-up of "well-developed primary bases" supported by "connecting secondary bases" serving as "stepping stones" between the primary and perimeter bases. The whole arrangement would provide "security in depth, protection to lines of communication and logistic support of operations."[103] Its practical effect would be to extend the US strategic frontier outward to the fringes of Europe, Africa, and Asia.

Once the guiding strategic concept and rationale for an extensive system of overseas bases had been determined, the JCS then debated the number of bases required, whether civil aviation needs should be included, the priority to attach to particular overseas bases, and the best way to maintain the base system in the face of scarce resources. These discussions, lasting throughout September and October, reveal both the acrimony of interservice rivalry and the sensitivity some high-level military leaders had regarding the impact of an expanding American defense frontier on other nations.

The initial draft of the JCS base plan was ready by the end of August.[104] The immediate reaction by senior JCS staff officers was that the JWPC team preparing the study had proposed acquiring rights to too many bases. Lt Gen J. E. Hull, Army assistant chief of staff for operations, reviewed the paper and commented that "we should start by cutting requirements in half and then start cutting."[105] Brig Gen George A. Lincoln, the

Army's representative on the JPS, thereupon directed his subordinates to reduce requirements to a level acceptable to the president and Congress.[106] The Navy's top planner, Rear Adm M. B. Gardner, was also taken aback by the large number of bases, wryly suggesting the use of a gazetteer showing exceptions rather than a lengthy base list.[107] The JWPC's overenthusiasm probably stemmed from an attempt to combine the bases contained in all previous JCS studies, the Navy's *Basic Postwar Plan No. 1*, and the AAF's ad hoc study group document. Later drafts of the JCS base plan would show significant reductions in the number of bases, though not enough to satisfy civilian superiors in the War and Navy Departments.[108]

General Hull also detected the ambition of civil aviation expansionists in the first draft of the JCS study. "How much of this is national security and how much is commercial aviation?" he asked. [109] Hull's question underlines the close relationship the military believed it and American air carriers would have after the war. But his suspicion that the interests of civil aviation were being put forth under the "national security" umbrella seems unfounded. Both the military and commercial air carriers, of course, stood to profit from reliable North Atlantic and North Pacific air routes. Hull, however, was challenging the need for rights to routes across Africa and the Indian subcontinent.[110] But "national defense" and not economic consideration was the primary reason the CAB awarded the North African route to TWA. A report prepared by the CAB's Air Transport Information Division and submitted to the JCS by the ACC in August 1945 pointed to Africa's comparative insignificance in the world economy, remarking that for the "immediate future" the "volume of air traffic touching that continent would be relatively small."[111] The CAB report found it "conceivable" that a route across Mediterranean Africa might have some importance since it would act as "a bridge to Europe, the Near East, and the Far East."[112] But as far as the CAB's analysts were concerned, the African route of most economic interest was north-south along the west coast of Africa—not east-west.[113] Moreover, the ACC showed no desire for a route across Central Africa (one the military wanted) and, in fact, recommended no commercial rights be sought there.[114]

The consensus among the JCS staff officers was that however useful the civil airlines might be in the postwar period, a distinct line should be drawn between military and civil requirements. Admiral Gardner and his AAF counterpart on the JPS, Brig Gen Charles P. Cabell, agreed civil needs could not be easily included in the JCS study. Furthermore, military base rights, declared Gardner, were "vital to the defense of the United States and should be kept separate and clear."[115] The vision held by some officials early in the war of an integrated system of civil and military overseas air facilities was beginning to fade as the military more vigorously asserted the priority of "national security" while the commercial air carriers pursued the goal of economic advantage.

If the JCS planners could agree on some issues, they were sharply at odds on others. Differences surfaced, for example, in a debate over the designation of "primary" bases. Interservice rivalry and divergent attitudes regarding the effect US outposts would have on other nations were at the heart of these conflicting views. According to the JCS's strategic concept, the "danger areas" for the United States included (1) the Arctic air approaches to North America, (2) the Atlantic and Pacific approaches to North America, and (3) Latin American and Atlantic and Pacific approaches to the Panama Canal.[116] General Lincoln pinpointed the meaning of the overall strategic guidance when he told the other JPS planners, "We should give the weight of our attention to the north as any future threat would be most likely to come from the northeast or the northwest and not from the south."[117] Assertion of this general principle, however, sparked a controversy that eventually involved Generals Marshall and Arnold and Admiral King.

The battle lines were not always clearly defined, but generally the AAF pushed to have the Azores, Iceland, and Greenland named as primary bases and Dakar upgraded to a secondary base. The Navy adamantly opposed attaching so much importance to these areas. The Army usually sought to mediate between the other two services, though its Operations Division did not at first concur with putting the Ryukyu Islands into the primary category—a step the Navy and the AAF were eager to take. The Navy fought hard to deflect the AAF's effort to boost the status of the North Atlantic bases. It argued that the Azores should not be a primary base because the islands lacked adequate harbor facilities and construction during peacetime would entail enormous cost. Moreover, the United States was also likely to encounter the same difficulties in negotiation for rights in the Azores that had been experienced during the war.[118] To Admiral King's proposal to list the Azores as a secondary base, General Arnold countered, "I consider that we should keep the strategic concept clearly before us. . . . We must be in a position to deliver damaging counter blows possibly within a matter of 24 hours to any source of influence controlling aggression against us and at the same time we must have adequate forward bases for warning and interception of enemy assaults."[119] As for Greenland, King maintained adverse terrain and unfavorable weather eliminated the Danish possession from consideration as a primary base.[120] The AAF's rebuttal was that the island already had bases capable of expansion and that recent War Department, Headquarters AAF, and ATC surveys indicated previously unrecognized base possibilities there. Additionally, the development of new weapons with longer ranges and more destructive power substantially increased the island's strategic significance.[121]

In resisting primary base status for Iceland and the upgrading of Dakar, Admiral King advanced a startling argument. In a base system to defend the United States and the Western Hemisphere, he felt "a balance must be struck between the security afforded thereby and the aggressive threat to other powers implicit in the degree of activation and use of certain forward base areas in time of peace." Though he admitted Iceland's and Dakar's strategic significance "from the viewpoint of possible offensive air operations," King believed it "politically" unwise to upgrade their status: "I feel that as a practical matter, the inclusion of these locations in a higher category would not serve to increase either the development or the utility of these bases for their intended purpose while their designation in the higher categories might well have, when known, undesirable implications abroad. The same considerations apply to the Azores."[122] Obviously, King did not confine himself to strictly military assessments. Such willingness to take "political" factors into account was not uncommon for the military in this period.[123] What is so striking about the admiral's stance is its divergence from the position of his civilian superior, Forrestal, who in July had been in England lobbying for an Anglo-American agreement on the postwar use of bases in Iceland.

Was Admiral King sincerely concerned that far-flung American bases might appear to threaten other powers or was there some other explanation for his attitude? Some US military leaders were quite reluctant to have American military power poised on their neighbors' doorsteps. General Embick had doubts about Iceland. General Lincoln, in contrast, was all for bases in the North Atlantic but had reservations about the Far East. He advised against the AAF and Navy proposition that Okinawa become a primary base. "It places too much stress on a base area," he told General Hull, "which in the coming years may be considered, with some justification, by Russia and China, as a threat to them rather than as a reasonable element in the US security system."[124]

Adm Raymond A. Spruance, a leading combat commander in the Pacific during the war, also thought the Ryukyu Islands should not be fortified. At a press conference in Manila, Philippines, in late August, Spruance had called for a sharp reduction in the size of the postwar Navy and had declared that the United States should refrain from building up bases near Asia, such as Formosa and Okinawa, so as not to alarm the Russians and the Chinese. "It would be a sore point with us if a foreign power held a string of islands blockading our coasts," according to Spruance. For expressing views so apparently contrary to Navy policy, Spruance, according to his biographer, Thomas Buell, had his knuckles "vigorously rapped by his superiors in Washington."[125] Spruance was out of step with the Navy's position regarding Okinawa and the size of the postwar fleet, but not with the general idea that forward bases might produce adverse reactions abroad. Admiral King would soon join him in raising this last point, but King's sensitivity to the potentially negative political consequences of overseas bases was quite selective. The Navy's military chief, for example, was not at all bothered by Russian reaction to a strong US base on Okinawa, and in 1943 had recommended that the United States maintain postwar bases in Iceland.[126] Thus, something other than empathy for Russian or other foreign powers' feelings must explain his hostility to North Atlantic bases. What seems to have disturbed King most was the likelihood that emphasis on bases in Greenland, Iceland, the Azores, and Dakar would increase the AAF's claim on the postwar defense budget and give it a preeminent place in the American military structure.

The purpose of the JCS base plan was to provide military advice to the State Department in negotiations to obtain postwar base rights. But any enumeration of priorities for obtaining rights or designation of certain locations as primary base areas might be interpreted by some as implying that those bases having top priority would also be developed more fully. In other words, they would receive more funds and larger contingents of US forces than bases in a lesser status. No such determination could be made, however, until the peacetime size, composition, and deployment of US military forces had been decided. The JCS planners recognized this difficulty.[127] To make this clear and probably to dampen the fires of interservice rivalry, Marshall told the other joint chiefs "the strategic importance of some of the sites is not a direct guide to the expenditures which are desirable or the active use to which the site is put in peace or war." In Marshall's view, simply denying an area to a foreign power might well satisfy US strategic requirements.[128]

Marshall's calm voice did not reassure the Navy because, unlike the Army and the AAF, it had already submitted a proposal for a postwar force level to the president and Congress. Additionally, on 5 September 1945, the Navy had publicly announced the bases in the Pacific and Atlantic that it intended to develop as major overseas installations. The Atlantic bases were Argentia; Newfoundland; Bermuda; Roosevelt Roads and San Juan, Puerto Rico; Guantanamo Bay, Cuba; and Coco Solo, Canal Zone.[129] Navy Secretary Forrestal, reported the *Washington Post*, was "not prepared to discuss the possibilities of Iceland or Greenland, but he implied that it [the Navy] was interested in additional Atlantic bases."[130] In the fall of 1945, the Navy was indeed preparing to maintain other Atlantic facilities in Greenland, Iceland, the Azores, and Port Lyautey on French Morocco's Atlantic coast. These were to be largely naval air or auxiliary air stations in reduced operational or caretaker status.[131] When ordered by Admiral Edwards to cut the number of personnel assigned to Atlantic bases, Captain Douglas pointed out that the 10,000 Navy personnel planned for the Atlantic facilities represented less than 2 percent of the Navy's projected postwar strength of 558,000. "I feel that our position in the Atlantic should be strengthened rather than weakened," Douglas protested.[132]

In contrast to the Navy, the AAF and the Army had big plans for North Atlantic bases. When the War Department finally produced a coordinated Army and AAF plan for the deployment of overseas forces in February 1946, it planned for Iceland, Greenland, and the Azores each to have one very heavy bomber (VHB) group and approximately 15,000 personnel.[133] Given so great a disparity between Navy and War Department plans for North Atlantic bases and Admiral King's inconsistency regarding the effect American bases might have on other nations, it is reasonable to conclude his resistance to placing Iceland, Greenland, and the Azores in the primary base category stemmed mostly from institutional motives.

In addition to considering base priorities, whether to include civil needs, and the number of bases for which postwar rights were to be requested, the JCS also discussed how a large base network might be maintained under a tight defense budget. Marshall had warned all along that money would be scarce and the Army and AAF would have to take this into account as they drew up their postwar plans. In November 1944, he had brusquely rejected the War Department Special Planning Division's proposal for an Army and AAF numbering a combined total of 1.1 million as too expensive and therefore politically unrealistic.[134] General Lincoln reported in June 1945 Marshall's desire for the number of bases to be held down and for rights, rather than bases, to be sought where possible.[135] The AAF's July 1945 plan, emphasizing acquisition of base rights was squarely in-line with this guidance. Marshall, according to Lincoln, believed "we might be able to get what we want cheaper by letting someone else [i.e., another country]. . . hold the bases and arrange to have landing and similar rights for which we will pay them."[136]

Brig General Cabell, the AAF member of the JPS, elaborated at length on the Army chief of staff's idea as the JCS officers struggled to come up with a revised base plan during the summer of 1945. Citing the litany of arguments constituting the preparedness ideology, Cabell affirmed that the United States must have ready access to "bases from which the sources of power on the major land masses of the world may be reached." To do this, Cabell said, the United States might have to operate from bases in the United Kingdom, France, Italy, West Africa, and China. But he also admitted it to be "incompatible both with US policy and with the requirements of national security . . . to maintain US military forces on the continents of Europe and Asia after the occupation needs have ceased." Cabell's solution to this dilemma paralleled Marshall's proposal and could have been inspired by the Army chief of staff's view. Under a concept known as a "Maintenance Covenant," Cabell said another nation would maintain bases on its territory meeting American requirements. In return, the caretaker nation might receive forgiveness of lend-lease debts, abrogation of payment for surplus equipment, or a US agreement to train members of its armed forces. Cabell conceded that numerous obstacles stood in the way of arranging maintenance covenants, with adverse Soviet reaction foremost among them. Giving the "appearance of 'ringing' a certain power by a series of these bases, or a leak to her of negotiations concerning the establishment of such," he wrote, "might precipitate the very action which this was designed to prevent." For this and other reasons, Cabell thought rights would have to be acquired under the cover of civil air transport needs.[137]

The JCS did not specifically endorse the commercial aviation subterfuge, but Marshall suggested the following recommendation be included in the JCS paper: "In view of the political complications and difficulties involved in maintaining US personnel and installations in foreign territory in peacetime and because of the elements of cost and manpower, it is believed that the State Department should give serious consideration to arrangements by which other nations undertake the load of maintaining required installations in certain areas in return for payment in one form or another by the United States."[138] Use of American money to attain military objectives abroad would become an important feature of US postwar foreign policy. George Marshall, first as Army chief of staff and later as secretary of state, was one who consistently advocated this approach.

Under pressure from the Mead Committee, the State Department, and the Office of the Assistant Secretary of War for Air, the JCS resolved the issues preventing completion of the base paper at a meeting on 23 October 1945. An account of what was said by Leahy, Marshall, King, and Arnold apparently does not exist, but the nation's four leading military figures evidently were able to agree since they approved the base plan, designated JCS 570/40.

The JCS had resolved the controversy over primary base areas by compromising. All agreed the Ryukyu Islands should be a primary base, and Admiral King gave way before Army and AAF insistence on placing the Azores in the same category. The Army's Operations Division had advised Marshall to side with King in classifying both Iceland and Greenland as secondary bases, but Marshall seems to have rejected some of the advice because the JCS elevated Iceland to primary base status.[139] The AAF did not get all it wanted because Greenland remained a secondary base and Dakar was not upgraded. In addition to the Ryukyus, Azores, and Iceland, the JCS identified several other primary base areas: the Panama Canal Zone, Hawaiian Islands, Mariana Islands, Philippine Islands, Southwestern Alaska-Aleutian area, Newfoundland, and Puerto Rico-Virgin Islands.[140] The choice of primary base areas demonstrates the swing of the strategic pendulum from the Pacific orientation of earlier plans to a greater concentration on the Atlantic. But the strategic shift went beyond equal division between east and west; fully half of the primary bases focused American power astride the northern approaches to the United States and its possessions.[141] Moreover, more than half of the primary bases were at the outer edge of the American defense perimeter— unmistakable evidence of the preparedness ideology's hold on strategy.

To support the primary base areas, the JCS recommended 60 additional secondary, subsidiary, and minor bases and base areas about equally divided between the Pacific and the Atlantic.[142] Almost one-third blanketed the Caribbean and Pacific approaches to the Panama Canal, though none of the Central and South American locations extended south of an east-west line drawn from the Natal-Recife area of Brazil to Talara, Peru. Several of the 60 support bases, particularly those in the Pacific south of the equator (e.g., Manus in the Admiralty Islands, Guadacanal and Tulagi in the Solomon Islands, Espiritu Santo in the New Hebrides, Noumea in New Caledonia, and Bora Bora in the Tuamotu Archipelago) were of dubious value from a strategic standpoint. This was a fact already discerned by some JCS staff officers.[143] Within months the military would find rights to these bases expendable.

Of the 70 bases or base areas listed in all categories, the United States possessed sovereignty or enjoyed right of use by conquest or previous agreement in half. The State Department would need to negotiate for US rights in the 35 remaining areas. The JCS indicated the priority for obtaining rights in these areas by distinguishing, somewhat esoterically, between bases that were "essential" and those that were merely "required."[144] (Greenland, even though a secondary base, fit into the essential category.) Additionally, as with all previous base papers, the JCS identified whether US rights were to be exclusive, joint, or participating.[145]

The JCS argued that bases enumerated in JCS 570/40 were not sufficient to assure American security without other conditions being met. First, the United States must have "exclusive strategic control" of the Japanese Mandates and other islands captured from Japan. Second, there must be a provision for additional base rights in Latin America through the inter-American defense pact contemplated under the Act of Chapultepec. Third, current US-Canadian defense agreements must be extended. Fourth, the United States must arrange for base rights to fulfill military commitments incurred through participation in the UN organization.[146] Beyond these stipulations, the JCS also explained that the military would require as yet unspecified rights to operate navigation, communication, weather, and warning facilities.[147] The base system detailed in JCS 570/40, concluded the JCS, was not only necessary for American security if the UN should fail to keep the peace, but would also "contribute materially to the effectiveness of that organization in maintaining peace throughout the world."[148]

The long-awaited military base plan met little resistance from civilian officials. The SWNCC approved the study on 25 October and forwarded it to the secretary of state (a copy also went to the ACC).[149] With the statement of military base requirements, the government presumably had all the information needed to provide for American physical security. Now, presumably, the government could begin to seek advantages for the US postwar international commercial air system.

As extensive, even grandiose, as JCS 570/40 was, the plan had two significant omissions: (1) rights to bases along a route across North Africa, the Middle East, and South Asia, and (2) rights to bases in Europe. The SWNCC on the advice of Gates, assistant secretary of the Navy for air, informed the State Department that "in order to operate the U.S. system of bases and to provide alternate routes for movement of U.S. aircraft, the United States should have rights for air transit and technical stop at certain non-United States air bases and air base sites."[150] These were to be in addition to the base rights listed in JCS 570/40.

In January 1946, the JCS provided the State Department with a list of supplemental air transit rights. Most were for bases along the North Africa–India route: Algiers; Tripoli; Cairo, Egypt; Dhahran, Saudi Arabia; Karachi, Agra, and Kharagpur, India; Bangkok, Thailand; and Saigon, Indochina. Successful negotiations for transit rights at these locations would give the United States a route (described as "highly desirable because of strategic considerations" by the JCS) linking the eastern and western edges of the American base network. The JCS expected all of the transit airfields to be "operated by commercial or foreign military interests."[151] None of the supplemental rights, however, were for bases on the European continent.

In late 1945 the long history of American aversion to permanent involvement in Europe still enveloped military planners. In the fall of 1944 officers assigned to the United States Strategic Air Forces in Europe, commanded by Lt Gen Carl Spaatz, had drawn up plans for permanent postwar European air bases. But more than distance separated the planners in the field from those in Washington. When General Arnold received word of this proposal, he told Spaatz the subject was "filled with dynamite." Reminding Spaatz of the US commitment to support an international peacekeeping organization and to withdraw from Europe as soon as possible after the war, Arnold called planning for permanent postwar European air bases "inadvisable."[152] From then on, Spaatz's staff officers confined their work to recommendations for air bases to support the occupation of Germany. General Cabell's comments to the JPS in September 1945 suggest that the military believed the stricture against permanent air bases in Europe was still in effect.

Although a long-term European presence appeared out of the question, a requirement for temporary occupation air bases remained. In April 1945 Spaatz forwarded to AAF Headquarters a "Periphery Base Plan" to meet occupation needs. It called for US air forces to be stationed at airfields in Germany and Austria and in a ring surrounding the defeated enemy at bases in Italy, France, Denmark, and Norway (US policy was to close down bases in Great Britain immediately after the war).[153] By June the JCS and the SWNCC had endorsed the AAF plan.

Over the summer, however, the Periphery Base Plan ran into difficulties. Acting Secretary of State Grew felt bases in Norway and Denmark "would open the door to Russia" and, from a political point of view, he was "much opposed to obtaining bases in Scandinavia even though only for the period of the occupation."[154] Grew asked Stimson and Forrestal to have the military reconsider its plans, but, amazingly, the program was not suspended. When the American ambassador to Norway cabled the State Department in August 1945 that the plan for air bases in that country was still alive, and, if carried through, might subject the Norwegians to unwanted Soviet demands, State again requested the military to reexamine its requirement.[155] Only then did the military drop plans for bases in Norway and Denmark.[156] Negotiations for rights to two air bases in France also did not go smoothly.[157] By June 1946 the military, which had in the meantime secured use of two Italian air bases and was planning to deploy two VHB groups to bases in Germany, concluded that the State Department could discontinue negotiations for the French air bases. The peripheral base concept had been abandoned.[158]

Given the persistence of the US policy of no long-term European involvement and the international political obstacles created by the plan for occupation bases, it is no wonder that JCS 570/40 failed to mention postwar base rights in Europe. Although military planners saw the advantages of European bases, they also knew obtaining them was not possible for political reasons in 1945.

* * *

JCS 570/40, the JCS's 1945 base plan, represented the military's conviction that to guarantee national safety and to be prepared for the next war, the United States had to extend its strategic frontier significantly. In contrast to previous studies, JCS 570/40 focused more on bases in the Atlantic, the northern approaches to the Western Hemisphere, and on acquiring strong points near the edges of the defensive perimeter. Military strategy, however, was not the sole basis for the JCS's recommendations—bureaucratic, domestic, and international political factors were also important influences. Admiral King doggedly resisted assigning high priority to North Atlantic bases apparently because doing so would result in advantage for a rival service, the AAF. The possibility of interservice bickering and expected tight postwar budgets were the reasons all the services put their requirements in terms of obtaining base "rights." Even though European bases were closest to the probable future enemy, the JCS refrained from asking for rights on the Continent so as not to contravene what seemed to be national policy.

Sometimes the military was as politically diffident as it was astute. Although government leaders almost unanimously supported the idea of a far-flung postwar base system, the military was slow in naming its requirements. Civilians had to push and prod constantly, and occasionally the military even ignored civilian requests for action. Resentment over an inability to completely control the military, particularly the JCS, when it came to matters having "political" content increasingly infuriated high officials in the War and Navy Departments.

By failing to respond rapidly to the ACC's request for detailed information on bases, the military appeared indifferent to the economic dimension of American security. An overriding concern for physical security, however, and not indifference to economic security largely explains the military's slow response. Top policy makers shared the same apprehensions but also had to devote part of their attention to assuring postwar economic prosperity. Overseas air bases, routes, and other facilities played an important part in postwar American foreign policy, precisely because policy makers sought to combine physical and economic security requirements (even though the former always enjoyed top priority).

The drives for overseas military bases and commercial air facilities reinforced each other, contributing to America's outward surge after World War II. Open-door economic expansion, which had always had a global reach, was now joined by a search for physical security not bound by geographical limits. Yet, this is not to say the military contemplated policing the globe; the frantic pace of demobilization could foster no such illusion. Transit rights in North Africa, the Middle East, and South Asia would connect the eastern and western borders of the defense system. These same transit rights would also promote maintenance of airfields that someday might be used to carry out air attacks against the Soviet Union. The air facilities might also contribute to achieving economic goals; for example, the airfield at Dhahran promised access to Middle Eastern oil, and commercial air rights at Cairo, Karachi, Rangoon, and Bangkok would be important links in an air transport route between Europe and the Far East. Similarly, northern Great Circle routes from the United States to Europe and the Orient could serve both military and civil purposes.

Notes

1. State-War-Navy Coordinating Committee (SWNCC) 38/3, 27 March 1945, sec. 5, file CCS 360 (12-9-42), Record Group (RG) 218 (Records of the United States Joint Chiefs of Staff), National Archives (NA).

2. G. A. B. [George A. Brownell], memorandum for Mr. Lovett, 29 March 1945, file item 4, sec. l, box 199, Plans, Policies and Agreements File; Records, Office, Assistant Secretary of War for Air, RG 107 (Records of the Secretary of War), NA.

3. R. Keith Kane, memorandum for the secretary and Mr. Gates, 11 April 1945, file CNO Top Secret (TS) 1945, NB/EF, CNO Records, Navy Operational Archives (NOA), Washington, D.C. Document is now declassified.

4. D. S., memorandum for Assistant Secretary of War for Air Lovett, 15 April 1945, file item 4, sec. 1, box 199, Plans, Policies and Agreements File, RG 107.

5. T. P. Wright, executive secretary, ACC, memorandum to Secretary, Joint Chiefs of Staff (JCS), 27 April 1945, in enclosure to JCS 570/16, 12 May 1945, sec. 5, file CCS 360 (12-9-42), RG 218.

6. See chap. 1, in this book, 36.

7. JCS 570/16, 12 May 1945, sec. 5, file CCS 360 (12-9-42), RG 218.

8. Capt A. D. Douglas, memorandum for Admiral Edwards via Admiral Duncan, subject: Post War Fleet Base at Manus, 13 March 1945, series 14, Strategic Plans Division Records, NOA. Bases in the blue area of JCS 570/2 were required for defense of the United States and its leased areas and possessions. The green area contained bases vital for Western Hemisphere defense, while the black area covered those military facilities to be used by the United States as "one of the Great Powers enforcing Peace."

9. Adm Ernest J. King, memorandum for the JCS, 1 April 1945, FF1/A14, serial 00804, sec. 5, file CCS 360 (12-9-42), RG 218.

10. Col Max S. Johnson, memorandum for the chief, Strategy and Policy Group, Operations Division (OPD) (hereafter Colonel Johnson, memorandum, OPD), 7 May 1945, sec. 1A, box 611TS, file ABC 686 (6 November 1943), ABC Decimal File, 1942–1948, OPD, RG 319 (Records of the Army Staff), NA. Document is now declassified.

11. Michael S. Sherry, *Preparing for the Next War: American Plans for Postwar Defense, 1941–1945* (New Haven, Conn.: Yale University Press, 1977), 169–78.

12. Ibid.

13. Colonel Johnson, memorandum, OPD.

14. JCS 570/17, 14 May 1945, sec. 5, file CCS 360 (12-9-42), RG 218. The reentry of the Joint Staff Planners (JPS) and the Joint War Plans Committee (JWPC) into postwar base planning is significant because it shows a general upgrading of postwar matters in the JCS organization. The JPS and the JWPC were the key JCS wartime planning groups.

15. Robert A. Lovett, memorandum for General Arnold, 17 May 1945, file item 4, sec. 1, box 199, Plans, Policies and Agreements File, RG107. The JPWC's answer to the ACC, said Lovett, "is quite inadequate and misses the point entirely."

16. Ibid.

17. Lt Col George A. Brownell, memorandum for the assistant secretary of war for air, subject: Airfields in Foreign Countries, 13 February 1945, file item 4, sec. 1, box 199, Plans, Policies and Agreements File, RG107.

18. Gen Henry H. Arnold, memorandum for secretary JCS, 23 May 1945, sec. 5, file CCS 360 (12-9-42), RG 218.

19. Robert A. Lovett, memorandum for deputy commander, AAF, and chief of Air Staff, 27 February 1945, file item 4, sec. 1, box 199, Plans, Policies and Agreements File, RG 107.

20. R. C. Moffat, memorandum for Colonel Cork, subject: Re-evaluation of Recommendations in JCS 570 Series, 17 May 1945, file 145.86-33B, vol. 2, 1943–1946, USAF Historical Research Agency (AFHRA), Maxwell AFB, Ala.

21. Lt Col George A. Brownell, note to Robert A. Lovett, 21 May 1945, file item 4, sec. 1, box 199, Plans, Policies and Agreements File, RG 107; and Brig Gen Lauris Norstad, memorandum for chief, Post War Division, 21 May 1945, file 145.86-29, Directives, 1943–1946, AFHRA.

22. R. C. Moffat, memorandum for assistant chief of Air Staff, Plans, 21 May 1945; and R. C. Moffat, memorandum for Gutru, Shepley, Snyder, and Lissitzyn, 22 May 1945 (hereafter Moffat memorandum Gutru, Shepley, Snyder, and Lissitzyn), both in file 145.86-33B, vol. 2, 1943–1946, AFHRA.

23. Reference found in 21 May 1945, Moffat memorandum. After participating in the preparation of General Emmons's Alaskan report, Capt Oliver J. Lissitzyn had been assigned to the OSS. R. C. Moffat described him to General Norstad as "for many years an authority on international air routes . . . a specialist in this type of work." His presence on the ad hoc study group testified both to the need to fulfill Lovett's requirement that military air routes as well as bases be designated, and to the firm conviction in the AAF, born of the pre–World War II experience in the South Pacific and Latin America, that military aviation would once again have to rely on routes and facilities maintained by the commercial lines.

24. R. C. Moffat to AC/AS, M & S; AC/AS, CC & R; AC/AS Intelligence; Air Communications Officer, 29 May 1945, file 686.9, Foreign Aviation Fields, box 293, Army Air Forces (AAF) Air Adjutant General, Classified Decimal File, RG 18 (Records of the AAF), NA. Document is now declassified.

25. Assistant Chief of Air Staff Plans, Post War Division, U. S. Requirements for Post War Military Air Bases and Rights in Foreign Territory, 11 July 1945, (hereafter U. S. Requirements for Post War Military Air Bases and Rights in Foreign Territory, RG 107), file item 4, sec. 2, box 199, Plans, Policies and Agreements File, RG107.

26. Ibid., see appendix E, Map of Total Requirements (Mercator Projection), and annex D to appendix E, Map Indicating Space Relationships (Polar Projection), dated 20 June 1945.

27. Ibid., 8.

28. Ibid., see appendix D, Map of Third Priority Requirements.

29. Ibid., see appendix B, Map of First Priority Requirements.

30. Ibid.

31. Perry McCoy Smith, *The Air Force Plans for Peace, 1943–1945* (Baltimore: Johns Hopkins University Press, 1970), 75.

32. Ibid., passim.

33. U. S. Requirements for Post War Military Air Bases and Rights in Foreign Territory, RG107, 4–5.

34. Ibid.

35. See chap. 2, in this book, 69–70.

36. Ibid., chap. 1, 27.

37. Maj Gen C. R. Smith, memorandum for Maj Gen L. S. Kuter, 21 March 1945; and Maj Gen L. S. Kuter, memorandum to Maj Gen C. R. Smith, 27 March 1945, both in file 21-162-5, Air Transport Military Civil Operations (ATC), box 10, Records of the Air Coordinating Committee, RG 340 (Records of the Office of the Secretary of the Air Force, 1942–1956), NA. The author's government security clearance permitted access to the records of the ACC that had not yet been reviewed for declassification. At the author's request, the above documents were declassified. Abadan already had an airfield, but it was controlled by the British. For background on the Abadan airfield, see T. H. Vail Motter, *The Persian Corridor and Aid to Russia* (Washington, D.C.: Office of the Chief of Military History, Department of the Army, 1952), 54–55, 128–29, 256–57, and 270–73.

38. U. S. Requirements for Post War Military Air Bases and Rights in Foreign Territory, RG107, 1.

39. Ibid., 8.

40. Ibid., appendix E, Map of Total Requirements.

41. Ibid.

42. L. Welch Pogue to secretary of the Navy, 9 May 1945, sec. 5, file CCS 360 (12-9-42), RG 218, NA.

43. Henry Ladd Smith, *Airways Abroad: The Story of American World Air Routes* (Madison: University of Wisconsin Press, 1950), 227.

44. U. S. Requirements for Post War Military Air Bases and Rights in Foreign Territory, RG107, 4.

45. Unsigned memorandum for the deputy chief of the Air Staff, subject: U.S. Air Force Contingent for Combined International Enforcement Action of the United Nations, 11 August 1945, file 142.0302-13, Assistant Chief of Air Staff, Intelligence, Intelligence Memoranda, AFHRA. Although the memorandum is not signed, the initials *g m* appear in the authenticating block. Maj Gen George MacDonald was then the assistant chief of the Air Staff, Intelligence.

46. Ibid.

47. Ibid.

48. First flown in August 1946, the B-36, with a "combat" or "effective" radius of 3,700 nautical miles (NM), did not come into regular service until 1948. See Marcelle Size Knaack, *Encyclopedia of U. S. Air Force Aircraft and Missile Systems*, vol. 2, *Post-World War II Bombers, 1945–1973* (Washington, D.C.: USAF, Office of Air Force History, 1988), 25. Combat or effective radius refers to the maximum distance an aircraft carrying bombs can fly to a target and still have enough fuel to return to its base. Because an aircraft's combat or effec-

tive radius is a function of several factors (e.g., fuel capacity, weight of bomb load, winds, flight altitude), one can find different combat or effective radius figures for the same aircraft. For the B-29, the AAF used 2,000 NM. See the Spaatz Board Report, 23 October 1945, file October 1945, Personal, box 22, Diaries, Papers of Carl Spaatz (hereafter Spaatz Papers), LOC. The JCS also used 2,000 NM (see JWPC 416/1, Revised, Military Position of the United States in the Light of Russian Policy, 8 January 1946, sec. 3, file CCS 092 USSR, 3-27-45, RG 218), and sometimes 1,700 NM (see JCS 1518, 19 September 1945, sec. 2, file CCS 381, 5-13-45, RG 218). Admittedly, the AAF flew some spectacular long-range missions in the fall of 1945. In late September, three B-29s flew nonstop from Japan to Chicago, Illinois. Lt Gen Curtis E. LeMay, pilot of one of the aircraft, was quoted as saying: "I believe we could fly from the United States to Europe in a B-29 right now, drop an atomic bomb and return safely." Even so, Russia was well beyond Europe. In November, another B-29 flew nonstop from Guam to Washington, D.C.—a distance of nearly 8,200 miles (see *New York Times*, 2 October 1945, 1, and 20 November 1945, 1). However, these were one-way missions with no bombs aboard and little related to the realities of military planning.

49. Unsigned memorandum for the deputy chief of the Air Staff, subject, U.S. Air Force Contingent for Combined International Enforcement Action of the United Nations, 11 August 1945, file 142.0302-13, Assistant Chief of Air Staff, Intelligence, Intelligence Memoranda, AFHRA.

50. Ibid.

51. Robert A. Lovett, memorandum for Lt Gen Ira Eaker, 9 July 1945, file SAS 686, Case 521, box 150, Papers of Henry Harley Arnold (hereafter Arnold Papers), LOC. The following is that part of the Mead Committee report quoted to Eaker by Arnold:

> Studies should have been in process months ago surveying our future requirements, both from a military and a commercial point of view. For the military, it may be desirable for the Army or the Navy to maintain bases at some points in the European theater, and now, while we are still in a good bargaining position, negotiations could be engaged in with the countries involved for rights, to maintain them. Our international air commerce will find many of the airfields built for war air transport indispensable to any network of international air routes . . . time is of the essence. As our forces withdraw and are redeployed, one installation after another will be abandoned, unless positive action is taken in advance to insure its proper disposition.

For the complete text of the Mead Committee report, see Senate, *Special Committee to Investigate the National Defense Program: Investigation of the National Defense Program*, 79th Cong., 1st sess., Senate Report No. 110, part 2, Investigations Overseas, 6 July 1945.

52. Lt Gen Ira C. Eaker, memorandum for the assistant secretary of war for air, 24 July 1945, file item 4, sec. 1, box 199, Plans, Policies and Agreements File, RG107.

53. Diary entry, 27 April 1945, in Henry A. Wallace, *The Price of Vision: The Diary of Henry A. Wallace, 1942–1946* (Boston: Houghton Mifflin, 1973), 437.

54. Extracts of a conversation between Admiral Duncan and General Lincoln, 18 June 1945, file OPD 336TS, case 126, box 143, OPD Decimal File, 1945, RG 165 (Records of the War Department General and Special Staffs), NA. Document is now declassified.

55. R. S. Edwards, memorandum for the naval aide to the president, FF1/A14-7, serial 00512, 12 June 1945, file COMINCH TS 1945, AF-2, COMINCH Records, NOA. Document is now declassified.

56. Col Harry Vaughan, memorandum for the chief of staff, 16 June 1945, file OPD 336TS, case 126, box 143, OPD Decimal File, 1945, RG 165. Document is now declassified.

57. Ibid., memorandum for the military aide to the president, subject: Pacific Bases, 3 July 1945. See also R. W. P., memorandum for the record, 30 June 1945, same file; and Col R. J. Wood, memorandum for Colonel Johnson, subject: Pacific Bases, 18 June 1945, sec. 3B, file ABC 686 Philippines (8 November 1943), ABC Decimal File, 1942–1948, OPD, RG 319.

58. Charles L. Mee Jr., *Meeting at Potsdam* (New York: Dell Publishing Co., Inc., 1975), 23–25.

59. Memorandum for the president (J. S., G. A., S. I. R.), 6 July 1945, file Report to the Nation on the Potsdam Conference, 9 August 1945, box 4, Subject File 1945, Papers of Samuel I. Rosenman, Harry S. Truman Library, Independence, Mo.

60. Edward R. Stettinius, secretary of state, memorandum for the president, subject: Latest Opinion Trends in the U.S.A., 23 April 1945, file Trends (Public Opinion), box 138, President's Secretary's File, Papers of Harry S. Truman (hereafter Truman Papers), Truman Library, Independence, Mo.

61. Edward R. Stettinius, letter to Joseph C. Grew, acting secretary of state, 22 June 1945, in *Foreign Relations of the United States, Conference of Berlin (Potsdam), 1945*, vol. 1 (Washington, D.C.: Government Printing Office [GPO], 1960), 185. Byrnes did not officially become secretary of state until 3 July 1945.

62. Compilation of Subjects for Possible Discussion at Terminal, tab 85, Post War Base Requirements, July 1945, file 143-502-3A, AFHRA.

63. The State Department, in the proposed conference agenda prepared for the president, had declared:

Before the Conference at Dumbarton Oaks, it was generally believed in Government circles in the United States that after the war, in the territories taken from Japan, there would be two classes of bases: (1) U.S. bases under the exclusive control of the U.S., and (2) international bases, under the joint administration of two or more of the United Nations.

At present, however, the idea of international bases has been abandoned. It is envisaged that all bases will be held by some one of the United Nations and that certain of these bases will be open to the use of other United Nations.

"Background Information, The Far East: Postwar International Bases in Territories Taken from Japan," in "The Berlin Conference Agenda Proposed by the Department of State," vol. 2, box 1, President's Naval Aide: Office Files (Security File), Truman Papers.

64. Winston S. Churchill, *The Second World War: Triumph and Tragedy* (Boston: Houghton Mifflin Company, 1953), 631–34; see also Lord Moran, *Churchill: Taken from the Diaries of Lord Moran: The Struggle for Survival, 1940–1945* (Boston: Houghton Mifflin Company, 1966), 293–94; and Mee, 103–4. That same afternoon, General Arnold recalls he "had a long talk with Air Chief Marshal Sir Charles Portal, Britain's top air commander, about how to reconcile the operations of our Air Force as well as our commercial airlines in time of peace. It was not a simple problem, for we had conflicting ideas. We agreed we should both have bases throughout the world the R. A. F. and the U. S. A. F. could use, but the ways and means of securing these bases when operating under peacetime conditions stymied us, because our State Department and the Foreign Office in Great Britain had methods of doing things which were not conducive to helping the military in advance of a war." Gen H. H. Arnold, *Global Mission* (New York: Signet, New American Library, 586). Whether the Arnold-Portal conversation was directly related to the Truman-Churchill exchange is not certain.

65. For discussions of Anglo-American economic rivalry, see Gabriel Kolko, *The Politics of War: The World and United States Foreign Policy, 1943–1975* (New York: Random House, Vintage Books, 1968); and William Roger Louis, *Imperialism at Bay: The United States and the Decolonization of the British Empire, 1941–1945* (New York: Oxford University Press, 1978). For the specific issue of postwar international air competition, see John Andrew Miller, "Air Diplomacy: The Chicago Civil Aviation Conference of 1944 in Anglo-American Relations and Postwar Planning" (PhD diss., Yale University, 1971), and Smith, *Airways Abroad*, for the period from 1945.

66. Chief of Staff, memorandum for Mr. James F. Byrnes, 23 July 1945 (hereafter Chief of Staff memorandum for Byrnes), file OPD 336TS, case 126, box 143, OPD Decimal File, 1945, RG 165; H. H. Arnold Diary of the Terminal Conference, box 249, Report File, 1943–1945, Arnold Papers; Arnold, *Global Mission*, 589; and H. H. Arnold to James F. Byrnes, 20 August 1945, file Post War Airfields, box 44, Official File, 1932–1946, Arnold Papers. Document is now declassified.

67. See Chief of Staff memorandum for Byrnes. Document is now declassified.

68. H. H. Arnold to James F. Byrnes, 20 August 1945, Arnold Papers.

69. Ibid.

70. Walter Millis and E. S. Duffield, *The Forrestal Diaries* (New York: Viking Press, 1951), 76–77.

71. Forrestal Diary, entry for 30 July 1945, vol. 2, Papers of James V. Forrestal (hereafter Forrestal Papers), Seeley G. Mudd Library, Princeton University, Princeton, N.J.

72. Ibid.

73. Ibid. During the Potsdam Conference, Churchill and his Conservative Party were defeated in a general election by the Labor Party. Clement Attlee became the new British Prime Minister and immediately joined Truman and Stalin at Potsdam. Ernest Bevin became the new foreign secretary.

74. Appendix A, Paraphrase of Top Secret Telegram no. 204, 5 July 1945, from the American Ambassador Oslo to the secretary of state, enclosure to SWNCC 159, 13 July 1945, sec. 1, file CCS 092, Spitsbergen (7-13-45), RG 218. The ambassador also reported Soviet foreign minister V. M. Molotov had told the Norwegian foreign minister that the USSR wanted to protect its lines of communication and that the United States and Great Britain were taking similar measures in the Pacific and Mediterranean. Document is now declassified.

75. Ibid., SWNCC 159, 13 July 1945.

76. During World War II, Bear Island was used as a fueling and turn-around point for destroyers on convoy duty on the northern run to Murmansk and Archangel.

77. JWPC 389/l/M, 16 July 1945; JCS 1443/1, 17 July 1945; JCS 1443/2 (Terminal), 22 July 1945; and minutes of JCS 201st meeting, 23 July 1945, all found in sec. 1, file CCS 092 Spitsbergen (7-13-45), RG 218.

78. Ibid., enclosure B to JCS 1443/1, 17 July 1945.

79. Ibid.

80. Memorandum by the JCS to the SWNCC, 23 July 1945, in file *Foreign Relations of the United States, 1945*, vol. 5, *Europe* (Washington, D.C.: GPO, 1967), 96–97.

81. Lt Gen Stanley D. Embick, memorandum for Mr. J. D. Hickerson, subject: U.S. Base Facilities in Iceland, 30 June 1945, sec. 1B, box 623TS, file ABC 686 (6 November 1943), ABC Decimal File, 1942–1948, OPD, RG 319. Document is now declassified.

82. Ronald Schaffer, "General Stanley D. Embick: Military Dissenter," *Military Affairs* 37 (October 1973): 89–95.

83. Col Harrison Gerhardt, executive to the assistant secretary of war, memorandum for General Hull, 16 June 1945, section 1B, box 623TS, file ABC 686 (6 November 1943), ABC Decimal File, 1942–1948, OPD, RG 319. Document is now classified.

84. Minutes of JCS 201st meeting, 23 July 1945, sec. 1, file CCS 092, Spitsbergen (7-13-45), RG 218.

85. H. H. Arnold Diary of the Terminal Conference, 22 July 1945, box 249, Report File, 1943–1945, Arnold Papers.

86. *Public Papers of the Presidents of the United States, Harry S. Truman, 1945* (Washington, D.C.: GPO, 1961), 203. Examination of successive drafts of the president's Potsdam address shows, in microcosm, the evolution of the American attitude not only toward overseas bases but also the shift from an almost exclusive concern with the Pacific and Far East to at least an equal concern for the Atlantic then under way throughout the military establishment. Rosenman probably wrote the first draft of the speech, but Leahy and Byrnes also worked on it, though at what point is not clear. (See

the diary of William D. Leahy, 7 August 1945, The Papers of William D. Leahy, LOC.) In the first draft, the paragraph on bases was buried in the middle of the text and referred only to Pacific bases:

> And incidentally let no one worry about whether the United States is going to get all the bases it needs in the Pacific for our complete future protection. I can assure you that whatever our experts tell us is reasonably necessary will be ours. We do not propose to give up what we have gained at such cost—so long as we need it for our own safety.

Significantly, in the third draft, the paragraph on bases had been moved to the prominent position we have seen that it occupied in the final version; the restrictive reference to the Pacific was also deleted. See the file Presidential Speeches: Drafts, box 32, Speech File, President's Secretary's File, Truman Papers.

87. Sherry, 191.

88. Ibid., 191–95.

89. Ibid., 196–98.

90. General Arnold to General Norstad, subject: Post War Bases, 22 August 1945, file Post War Airfields, box 44, Official File, 1932–1946, Arnold Papers.

91. Ibid.

92. Lovett, memorandum for the deputy chief of staff, 24 August 1945, enclosure to JCS 570/28, 28 August 1945, sec. 7, file CCS 360 (12-9-42), RG 218.

93. Sherry, 197; JWPC 361/4, Over All Examination of U.S. Requirements for Military Bases, 25 August 1945, sec. 7, file CCS 360 (12-9-42), RG 218.

94. Sherry, 198–202; *Preventive* is Sherry's word, not the JCS's. The JCS said, "When it becomes evident that forces of aggression are being arrayed against us by a potential enemy, we cannot afford through any misguided and perilous idea of avoiding an aggressive attitude to permit the first blow to be struck against us. Our government, under such conditions, should press the issue to a prompt political decision, while making all preparations to strike the first blow if necessary." See JCS 1496/3, Basis for the Formulation of a Military Policy, 20 September 1945, 27, sec. 2, file CCS 381 (5-13-45), RG 218.

95. JCS 1496/3, 24. "We are now concerned," said General Marshall in his final report on the war, "with the peace of the entire world." Quoted in Sherry, 202.

96. Ibid.

97. JCS 1496/3, 24 and JCS 1518/3, Strategic Concept and Plan for the Employment of United States Armed Forces, 9 October 1945, 0113612, both in sec. 2, file CCS 381 (5-1-45), RG 218.

98. Ibid., JCS 1518/3, 0113616.

99. Sherry, 203.

100. JCS 1496/3, 26–27, sec. 2, file CCS 381 (5-13-45), RG 218.

101. Ibid.

102. Minutes of JPS 215th meeting, 22 August 1945, sec. 1, file CCS 334 Joint Staff Planners (8-2-45), RG 218.

103. JCS 1518/3, 0113615, sec. 2, file CCS 381 (5-13-45), RG 218.

104. JWPC 361/4, Over All Examination of U.S. Requirements for Military Bases, 25 August 1945, sec. 7, file CCS 360 (12-9-42), RG 218.

105. G. A. L. [George A. Lincoln], memorandum for chief, Strategy Section, 26 August 1945, box 611TS, file ABC 686 (6 November 1943), ABC Decimal File, 1942–1948, OPD, RG 319. Document is now declassified.

106. Ibid.

107. Minutes of JPS 217th meeting, 1 September 1945, sec. 1, file CCS 334 Joint Staff Planners (8-2-45), RG 218.

108. G. A. L. [George A. Lincoln], memorandum for General Hull, subject: Military Bases and Rights During the Peacetime Period, 19 September 1945, sec. 1B, box 612TS, file ABC 686 (6 November 1943), ABC Decimal File, 1942–1948, OPD, RG 319. Late in 1947 General Lincoln conceded that the bases were planned "on such a grandiose scale that a world map showing what we wanted looked like a smallpox victim." Brig Gen George A. Lincoln, "Postwar Planning" lecture, Air War College, Maxwell AFB, Ala., 3 November 1947, file K239-716247-49, AFHRA. Document is now declassified.

109. G. A. L. [George A. Lincoln], memorandum for chief, Strategy Section, 26 August 1945, sec. 1A, box 611TS, file ABC 686 (6 November 1943), ABC Decimal File, 1942–1948, OPD, RG 319. Document is now declassified.

110. Ibid.

111. Report of the Air Transport Division, Economic Bureau, Civil Aeronautics Board, Dealing with the United States Military Air Bases on the Continent of Africa, enclosure to JCS 570/31, 1 September 1945, 0101967, sec. 7, file CCS 360 (12-9-42), RG 218.

112. Ibid., 0101971.

113. Ibid., 0101968.

114. ACC no. 9/9, Postwar Civil and Military Air Rights Abroad Other Than at Destroyer Bases—African Air Bases on which U.S. Funds Expended Where Commercial Rights are Desired, 14 August 1945 enclosure to JCS 570/31, 1 September 1945, sec. 7, file CCS 360 (12-9-42), RG 218.

115. Minutes of JPS 217th meeting, 1 September 1945, sec. 1, file CCS 334 Joint Staff Planners (8-2-45), RG 218.

116. JCS 1518/3, 0113615, sec. 2, file CCS 381 (5-13-45), RG 218.

117. Minutes of JPS 217th meeting, 1 September 1945, sec. 1, file CCS 334 Joint Staff Planners (8-2-45), RG 218.

118. Ibid. For evolution of the Navy's position on the Azores, see minutes of JPS 218th meeting, 5 September 1945, and 219th meeting, 12 September 1945; memorandum by COMINCH and CNO, enclosure A to JCS 570/36, 8 October 1945; JCS 570/38, memorandum by CNO, 12 October 1945; JCS 570/39, memorandum by the CNO, 19 October 1945, all in sec. 9, file CCS 360 (12-9-42), RG 218; and R. J. W. [Vice Adm Russell Wilson] memorandum for record, 20 October 1945, enclosing extract of Admiral Gardner–General Lincoln telephone conversation, 20 October 1945, sec. 1B, box 623TS, file ABC 686 (6 November 1943), ABC Decimal File, 1942–1948, OPD, RG 319. Document now declassified.

119. JCS 570/37, memorandum by the commanding general, AAF, 10 October 1945, sec. 9, file CCS 360 (12-9-42), RG 218.

120. Ibid., JCS 570/39, memorandum by CNO, 10 October 1945. See also Admiral King memorandum for JCS, FFl/A4-2, serial 002115, 1 September 1945, file COMINCH, TS, 1945, A4-2, COMINCH Records, NOA. Document is now declassified.

121. Briefing paper prepared for General Arnold, subject: Support for Iceland, Greenland, Azores as Primary Bases, n.d., sec. 3, file 686 (10-10-43), Air Force Plans and Operations Division, RG 341 (Records of Headquarters USAF, 1942–1956), NA.

122. JCS 570/39, memorandum by the CNO, 19 October 1945, sec. 9, file CCS 360 (12-9-42), RG 218.

123. In a memorandum concerning an upcoming visit by Australia's minister for external affairs (Dr. Herbert V. Evatt), Col K. W. Treacy, one of General Marshall's staff officers, told his chief, "It is a salient point that international military matters are now practically all very closely tied in with political matters." See K. W. T. (Col K. W. Treacy), memorandum for General Hull for the chief of staff, 30 October 1945, file OPD 336TS, case 207, box 145, OPD Decimal File 1945, RG 165. Document is now declassified.

124. G. A. L. [George A. Lincoln], memorandum for General Hull, 9 October 1945, sec. 1C, box 612TS, file ABC 686 (6 November 1943), ABC Decimal File, 1948, OPD, RG 319. Document is now declassified.

125. Thomas B. Buell, *The Quiet Warrior: A Biography of Admiral Raymond A. Spruance* (Boston: Little, Brown and Company, 1974), 371–72.

126. See chap. 1 in this book, 10.

127. G. A. Lincoln, memorandum for the Joint Staff Planners, 1 September 1945; George A. Lincoln, memorandum for Gardner, Cabell, and Campbell, 10 September 1945; G. A. L. [George A. Lincoln], memorandum for General Hull, 10 September 1945, all in sec. 1B, box 612TS, file ABC 686 (6 November 1943), ABC Decimal File, 1942–1948, OPD, RG 319; minutes of JPS 218th meeting, 5 September 1945, and 219th meeting, 12 September 1949, both in sec. 1, file CCS 334 Joint Staff Planners (6-2-43), RG 218; G. A. L. [George A. Lincoln], memorandum for the assistant secretary, War Department General Staff, 6 October 1945, file item 4, sec. 1, box 199, Plans, Policies and Agreements File, RG 107. Document is now declassified.

128. JCS 570/36, enclosure B, memorandum by the chief of staff, US Army, 8 October 1945, sec. 9, file CCS 360 (12-9-42), RG 218.

129. *Washington Post*, 6 September 1945, 1 and 4.

130. Ibid.

131. CNO to Distribution List, subject: *Basic Post War Plan No. 1*, Development Plan, Atlantic Bases, Op-4OY/elg/gms, (SC) A16-3/EN, serial 091P40, 5 December 1945, file CNO Confidential A16-3/EN, 1945, CNO Records, NOA. Document is now declassified.

132. Ibid., Admiral Edwards, memorandum for Admiral Cooke, 20 November 1945; and Capt A. D. Douglas memorandum for Op-30, subject: Missions for Post War Atlantic Bases, 23 November 1945.

133. AG 322 (4 February 1946) TS, War Department Plan for U.S. Peacetime Overseas Bases, 14 February 1946, box 16, Report/Project File RG 407 (Records of the Adjutant General's Office, 1917–1958), NA. The exact planning figures were: Iceland 15,510; Greenland 13,131; and the Azores 14,516. Document is now declassified.

134. Sherry, 101–8.

135. G. A. L. [George A. Lincoln], memorandum for record, 30 June 1945, sec.1A, box 611TS, file ABC 686 (6 November 1943), ABC Decimal File 1942–1948, OPD, RG 319. Document is now declassified.

136. Ibid.

137. Brig Gen C. P. Cabell, memorandum to JPS, 14 September 1945, file item 4, sec. 1, box 199, Plans, Policies and Agreements File, RG 107.

138. JCS 570/36, enclosure B, memorandum by the chief of staff, US Army, 8 October 1945, sec. 9, file CCS 360 (12-9-42), RG 218.

139. H. A. C. [Howard A. Craig], memorandum for the chief of staff, 23 October 1945, sec. 9, file CCS 360 (12-9-42), RG 218.

140. Ibid., JCS 570/40, Over All Examination of U.S. Requirements for Military Bases and Rights, 25 October 1945 (hereafter JCS 570/40), 204.

141. JCS 570/40 depicts the American base system on both polar and Mercator maps.

142. Ibid., 205–6.

143. G. A. L. [George A. Lincoln], memorandum for Joint Staff Planners, 1 September 1945, sec. 1B, file ABC 686 (6 November 1943), ABC Decimal File, 1942–1948, OPD, RG 319; and minutes JPS 217th meeting, 1 September 1945, sec. 1, file 334 Joint Staff Planners (8-2-45), RG 218.

144. JCS 570/40, 209 and 212–13.

145. Ibid., 212. The difference between "joint" and "participating" was that in the latter case the United States would enjoy rights, along with other nations, on the most-favored-nation principle.

146. Ibid., 206 and 210–11.

147. Ibid., 206 and 211.

148. Ibid., 210.

149. SWNCC 38/22, 25 October 1945, sec. 9, file CCS 360 (12-9-42), RG 218, NA.

150. Ibid., SWNCC 38/25, 8 November 1945, sec. 11.

151. SWNCC 38/30, 11 February 1946, *Foreign Relations of the United States, 1946*, vol. 1, *General: United Nations* (Washington, D.C.: GPO, 1972), 1142–45.

152. General Arnold to General Spaatz, 8 November 1944, file Post War Civil Airlines, box 44, Official File, 1932–1946, Arnold Papers.

153. General Spaatz to commanding general, AAF, subject: Occupation Period Requirements of U.S. Air Forces in Europe, 10 April 1945, enclosure to JCS 1332, 30 April 1945, file SWNCC 134 (hereafter SWNCC 134) Series, 323.3 Air Bases Europe, box 24, SWNCC/SANACC Records, RG 353 (Records of Interdepartmental and Intradepartmental Committees-State Department), NA.

154. Minutes of Meetings of Committee of Three, 1944–1947, 26 June 1945, Diplomatic Branch Reference File, NA.

155. Ambassador Osborne to secretary of state, 30 August 1945, appendix to SWNCC 134/2, 20 September 1945 in SWNCC 134; minutes of SWNCC 23d Meeting, 5 September 1945, sec. 2, file CCS 334 SANACC (formerly SWNCC), RG 218.

156. SWNCC 134/3, 29 October 1945, in SWNCC 134.

157. Ibid., SWNCC 134/4, 30 October 1945; SWNCC 134/8, 26 February 1946. Acting Secretary of State Acheson to Secretary of War Patterson, 29 March 1946; Col J. M. Reynolds, memorandum for record, 1 April 1946, both in file Plans and Operations Division 686, cases 2-11, box 137TS, OPD, 1946–1948, RG 319; Brig Gen Reuben C. Hood, summary sheet for OPD, chief of staff, secretary of war, 8 April 1946; and Patterson to secretary of state, 12 April 1946, both in SWNCC 134.

158. SWNCC 04/9, 17 June 1946, in SWNCC 134.

Chapter 4

Postwar Adjustments, 1946–1948

Although the military completed a postwar base plan by the fall of 1945 (JCS 570/40), it was never to be implemented. As the outline of the postwar world became clear between 1946 and 1948, base planning underwent significant changes. Pressures from civilian defense officials, concerned both about the cost of so extensive a base system and the reaction of foreign countries to American requests for base rights, forced the military to reduce its requirements. The reduction would require a geographic reorientation of American overseas base strategy. Rather than emphasizing far northern bases, military planners shifted their attention to bases along Russia's southern rim. This change was of major importance, allowing base planning to integrate with overall war planning in 1948. Until then, overseas base planning had taken place in relative isolation from other aspects of strategic planning—giving base planning an aura of detached unreality.

* * *

Since JCS 570/40, the JCS's 1945 base plan had been endorsed by the State-War-Navy Coordinating Committee, it ostensibly had the approval of the top civilian officials in the state, war, and Navy Departments. But early in 1946 those officials, prompted by differing motives, challenged the overseas base plan and forced the JCS to reevaluate and reduce requirements.

Secretary of State Byrnes, who at Potsdam had encouraged the military to be more aggressive in naming overseas base requirements, was among the first to have second thoughts. At the end of January, Byrnes, having recently returned from London and the first session of the UN General Assembly, called Robert P. Patterson, Stimson's successor as secretary of war, to ask for military assistance in future talks with Great Britain, Australia, and New Zealand concerning postwar base rights.[1]

During the conversation, Byrnes left Patterson with the impression that he believed the military wanted too much in the way of base rights abroad—a criticism Patterson also initially appeared to adopt. "I believe," Patterson told Gen Dwight D. Eisenhower, the Army's new chief of staff, "that the original [base] list is one prepared by the JCS. It probably is much too long and represents a far more ambitious program than the Army and Navy can support."[2]

Top military planners were angered and frustrated at this evidence of a changed attitude by the civilian secretaries. General Lincoln reported that both he and Admiral Gardner had "noted a somewhat spineless attitude on the part of the State Department and an apparently definite reluctance to put up to the British facts such as our great contributions to them . . . and the stand that we expect their cooperation."[3] What others failed to understand, wrote Lincoln, is that at most locations "we don't want sovereignty or even much say in what goes on . . . what we are looking for is the right to land and get off."[4] Patterson, who had had nothing to do with postwar strategic planning while serving as undersecretary of war, may not have fully understood this point either. OPD staff officers drafted a letter for his signature to the secretary of state explaining the situation. In this letter, Patterson explained to Byrnes that although he recognized "there were difficulties involved in international negotiations of this nature," he did not believe the JCS's requirements to be "excessive" since they "have *not* recommended that you seek sovereignty or exclusive rights to bases in the majority of cases under consideration." The secretary of war urged Byrnes "to press this question of base rights to a successful conclusion."[5] Patterson was aware of the reason for Byrnes's altered outlook: approaches made to other nations on the subject of postwar American base rights were encountering "difficulties." The British, for example, reacted negatively to an American request for help in persuading the Portuguese to grant base privileges in the Azores and Cape Verde Islands. Ernest Bevin, Great Britain's foreign secretary, told Lord Halifax, British ambassador to the United States, that he thought it "bad in the interests of world peace," to set up military bases at those locations. Bevin preferred they be treated as a "great air communications station" or "a free-for-all civil aviation station." This, according to Bevin, was "the rather bigger view."[6] Halifax passed Bevin's views to Byrnes.[7] The American secretary of state was learning that it was not going to be easy to "make the world safe for the U.S.A."

James Forrestal soon joined Byrnes in criticizing the JCS's base plans. The Navy secretary's motives were complex. They originated partly from a wish to protect the Navy's interests but also from his desire to uphold the principle of civilian supremacy over the military, particularly in relations with the JCS. Few men were more committed to the idea that civilians must control the military than Forrestal; his experiences with Admiral King had left a lasting impression. When President Truman asked him to become the first secretary of defense in July 1947, Forrestal recalled querying the president "whether he intended that control of the military establishment should be in civilian hands, because I said that was the way I proposed to exercise the powers in this job."[8] Integral to Forrestal's concept of civil supremacy was a belief in the existence of a "civil" as opposed to a "military" view of policy issues and a conviction that, although military advice should be sought before political decisions were made, civilians ought to make the decisions.

Forrestal had been quite active on the civil-military front throughout the last half of 1945. His most important victory was securing presidential approval for reorganization of the Navy Department. The post of commander in chief of the US fleet with its prerogative of direct access to the president (so jealously guarded by Admiral King) was abolished; an executive order in September provided for a chief of naval operations who was to be "responsible to the President *and to the Secretary of the Navy*" (emphasis added).[9] Forrestal made sure Adm Chester W. Nimitz understood the new ground rules before nominating him to replace King.[10] Beginning in 1946, Nimitz, unlike King, met almost daily with Forrestal and at a regular time.[11] To end the confusion within the Navy Department over responsibility for those matters bearing on the relationship between international politics and armed force, Forrestal sanctioned the creation of an assistant chief of naval operations for political-military affairs who would report not only to the CNO

153

but also directly to Forrestal and under Secretary of the Navy Gates. King had sought to retain control of this function under the CNO, but Forrestal insisted that the secretary's office be the central contact point for liaison with the State Department, the SWNCC, and other government agencies.[12] In this way, Forrestal was able to achieve better coordination within the Navy Department on political-military questions, and thereby to increase his own influence in the making of national policy.

Although Forrestal had become master of the Navy Department, controlling the JCS was a more difficult problem. The reorganization of the Committee of Three and establishment of the SWNCC had resulted from resentment over the JCS's tendency to bypass the civilian secretaries.[13] The SWNCC's authority was further clarified in October 1945 when the three secretaries approved a new charter for the subcabinet body.[14] Yet on the postwar base issue Forrestal moved to check the JCS, not through the SWNCC, but directly at the cabinet level. During a February 1946 meeting of the Committee of Three, the Navy secretary announced the JCS was "all over the map" on base requirements and should be made to "come down to earth." He suggested the three secretaries meet with Eisenhower and Nimitz to cut down the base list. To assure cooperation by the military, Forrestal also thought Byrnes should address a letter to him and Patterson formally requesting a reduction in base requirements to the number considered absolutely necessary. Patterson, with moistened finger in the air, also agreed that the base list needed to be "pruned."[15] At this time, Forrestal knew nothing about the secretary of war's recent strong defense of the JCS's base plans (he found out three days later when one of his aides obtained a copy).[16]

At their next meeting, the three secretaries again discussed postwar bases at great length, with Forrestal and Patterson both reiterating the need to reduce base requirements to realistic cost and manpower dimensions. In something of a surprise move, Forrestal presented a letter to Byrnes separately identifying the Navy's base requirements.[17] His independent action was not, however, primarily a response to Patterson's earlier letter since he had planned to send a list of the Navy's base needs to the secretary of state even before finding out what

Patterson had done.[18] Forrestal's letter to Byrnes was the second occasion in five months that the Navy secretary had short-circuited the JCS on overseas bases. In October 1945, before the JCS had completed its base plan, Forrestal had written Byrnes about the Navy's requirements.[19] The Navy, of course, had long since finished its own base plans and announced them publicly. The October letter probably reflected frustration at the lack of results coming from the JCS and a fear that the slow pace might decrease the Navy's chances of getting the base rights it wanted. Now, in February 1946, Forrestal saw an opportunity to present the Navy in a favorable light and to demonstrate that on so important a political-military question as overseas bases, the secretary of the Navy, not the JCS, would speak for the Navy.

Forrestal's maneuver produced some ill feelings in the War Department. At the three secretaries' meeting, the only response had come from Howard C. Petersen, assistant secretary of war (present with Patterson), who said Army and Navy base requirements should be advanced jointly.[20] Within OPD, the reaction was much stronger. General Lincoln compared Forrestal's letter with JCS 570/40, discovering it to contain, with a few exceptions, the same base requirements identified in the JCS plan. Forrestal had omitted only Yap-Ulithi in the Pacific; Belem, Brazil; the Edmonton-Whitehorse route to Alaska; the Fort Chimo-Frobisher Bay route to Greenland; Batista Field, Cuba; Curaçao; and Surinam. The Navy, observed Lincoln, "did nothing but present the joint requirements of JCS 570/40 as a 100 percent Navy requirements, leaving out a few places that are entirely Army Air."[21] In other words, the Navy list only appeared to be of more modest proportions than that of the JCS. Lincoln next drafted a letter upbraiding Forrestal for this deviation from the established practice of having the JCS present overseas base requirements to the secretary of state via the SWNCC.[22] He then took the draft to Petersen, emphasizing the necessity for handling overseas base matters jointly and for "adopting a policy of coming back at the Navy on every point of aggression."[23] A few days later Lincoln confided to General Hull, the Army's assistant chief of staff for operations, "The Navy action in this case is completely unilateral and also gets the base business out of the hands of the JCS into the hands of the Departments. We do not understand Mr. Forrestal's action." Furthermore, according to Lincoln, Admiral Gardner, assistant chief of naval operations for strategic plans and Navy member of the Joint Staff Planners, also had no idea what Forrestal was up to. Lincoln himself thought the Navy secretary might be "striving to weaken the power of the JCS or by cutting out the air bases he strengthens the stand of the Navy in the current interservice controversy."[24]

Although the situation was potentially explosive, the mixture of interservice bickering and civil-military friction resulting from Forrestal's letter did not develop into a major confrontation. First, the three civilian secretaries agreed that the military must cut back their base plans; Byrnes worried about foreign opposition, Forrestal and Patterson about cost. Second, Forrestal, without sacrificing anything to the principle of civilian control, offered a compromise. He suggested, during the Committee of Three gathering on 28 February, that General Hull and Vice Adm Forrest P. Sherman, deputy CNO for operations, ought to get together with Fred Searles Jr., who was supervising base negotiations in the State Department, to iron out the problem.[25] Finally, the letter drafted by Lincoln for Patterson's signature was apparently never sent, probably because the proposed State Department conference ordered by the three civilian secretaries would include top JCS officers and would meet the War Department's principal demand for joint treatment of base matters.

What to reduce became the next key question. In this case the State Department, not War or Navy, led the charge. Searles had persuaded Byrnes that bases in the Pacific south of the equator were of little strategic importance.[26] Although both Forrestal and Patterson defended the need for rights at other locations, neither objected to the general idea of reductions in the South Pacific.[27] Rights to South Pacific bases, Searles had explained to Byrnes, could only be useful against Japan, whereas the real danger the United States faced was from the Soviet Union. For this reason, Searles urged that the United States seek military rights in India, specifically to airfields at Karachi and Calcutta. Byrnes quoted Searles as saying, "If Stalin knows we have airfields in India that fact will serve as a greater deterrent to him than the United Nations Charter."[28] Whether Searles reached this strategic insight independently or after conferring with some military officers is not clear (Byrnes indicated that the AAF agreed with Searles). So convincing was Searles's argument that Byrnes had asked Bevin in January if the British might persuade India to make airfields available to the Security Council. At that time, Bevin did not think it wise for his government to do this. Byrnes, however, was now no longer inclined to wait on the British and was prepared to approach the Indian government directly. Besides British reluctance, the secretary of state pointed out that another drawback of requesting military rights at Indian airfields might cause the Soviet Union to "assert that we are closing in on her."[29]

Nonetheless, a direct approach to India could be easily justified. Early in February, Soviet premier Joseph Stalin delivered a speech that shocked many. Supreme Court Justice William O. Douglas described it to Forrestal as a "Declaration of World War III."[30] George Kennan's famous Long Telegram, with its gloomy assessment of Soviet intentions, arrived in Washington on 22 February and was read by Byrnes and Forrestal before 28 February.[31] Former prime minister Winston Churchill had been in the United States since late January preparing (with Truman, Byrnes, and Leahy's knowledge) the "Iron Curtain" speech he would deliver at Fulton, Missouri, on 5 March 1946.[32] Thus, the focus on South Asian bases at the Committee of Three meeting reflected clearly the direction American policy was moving in regard to the Soviet Union.

Following the mandate from the civilian secretaries to reduce base requirements and to specify the vital ones quickly, State Department and military representatives met to discuss the problem. Searles contrasted the importance of transit rights across North Africa, the Middle East, and India with the higher category rights the military wanted in the Pacific south of the equator. Admiral Sherman conceded that naval requirements in the South Pacific could be "thinned down considerably," though Hull did not think the rights the War Department sought in that area would be difficult to acquire. Everyone present agreed on the importance of Greenland, Iceland, and the Azores to national security and on the need to oppose British insistence that the United States be content with only commercial air rights in the Portuguese possessions.[33]

JCS staff officers, while aware for some time of State Department dissatisfaction (and surely also that of Forrestal and Patterson) with JCS 570/40, decided not to undertake any revision until directed by the JCS. General Lincoln explained that, after all, the State Department had not submitted any comments on JCS 570/40, nor had it "communicated with the Joint Chiefs of Staff with regard to any of the aspects of the base plan." This, of course, was true in a formal, written sense only. Such considerations were irrelevant to Admiral Gardner, who did not think the JCS needed to "appease the State Department in presenting the plan most acceptable to it, notwithstanding the military implications." In his opinion, the fact that the JCS had identified requirements was sufficient; the State Department's job was to conduct the negotiations and tell the JCS what had been obtained. Nonetheless, Lincoln knew that General Eisenhower disapproved of certain features of the plan, and Gardner admitted some misgivings on the Navy side about South Pacific bases. Lincoln decided to recommend to General Eisenhower that the chief of staff take up the base question with the other joint chiefs.[34] Two days later, the JCS directed the Joint Staff Planners to review JCS 570/40 to reduce requirements for base rights to a minimum.[35]

The JCS did not completely revise JCS 570/40. The objective was to modify the requirements for rights to be negotiated with foreign countries. In other words, the JCS amended the listing of "essential" and "required" rights intended to serve as a guide for the State Department. They did not alter the categories of primary, secondary, subsidiary, or minor bases designed to structure the services' postwar base planning in support of the overall strategic concept. As usual, the JCS planners worked at a glacial pace. The modification went through several drafts and was not approved by the JCS and forwarded to the SWNCC until June 1946.[36]

The JCS modified JCS 570/40 in two principal ways. First, within the categories of essential and required, the JCS reduced the maximum and minimum degree of control sought at particular locations in terms of exclusive, joint, participating, or transit rights. Second, the JCS shifted some sites between the essential and required divisions, entirely eliminating a few places from the latter. The two major modifications reflected military acknowledgment of the adverse reaction likely to result from either the United States requesting to maintain forces on the territory of other nations or asking a nation to restrict use of its territory in favor of the United States. Most of the changes affected rights to bases in the Pacific south of the equator and represented the first stage of the general strategic shift from the south and west to the north and east. The JCS, believing many civilian officials did not understand the difference between "bases" and "rights," felt compelled to explain the distinction at length.

> The utilization of the word base [in JCS 570/40, SWNCC 38/25] in connection with the areas in which military rights are desired was not intended to imply necessarily the permanent garrisoning of troops or stationing of aircraft or naval vessels in foreign territory during peacetime or even wartime. There is a distinction between "rights" desired which can be exercised when necessary, and the actual establishment, garrisoning or maintenance of bases. Whether or not the United States intends to take advantage of rights at any particular site will depend on a number of factors, such as the current strategic concept, the international situation, new weapons of war, and the material and manpower resources available to the armed forces of the United States.[37]

If confusion existed at this point, then some of the fault belonged to the JCS who had not forwarded the complete text of JCS 570/40 to the State Department.[38] On the other hand, there was no avoiding State's objection that the rights the military desired were too much of an infringement on other powers' sovereignty. Capt Robert L. Dennison, the Navy's new assistant chief of naval operations for political-military affairs and actively involved in assisting the State Department in negotiations for base rights, informed the Navy's strategic planners: "I should like to suggest that our desires regarding the 'right of control' in various base areas be re-examined. The minimum acceptable conditions stipulated for various bases require that the 'right of control' be always vested in and exercised at the option of the United States. This is not realistic, and in my opinion will be impossible to negotiate in many instances."[39]

159

By way of example, Dennison pointed out that the British were objecting to US insistence on the right of control in current negotiations.[40]

To answer criticism surrounding the right of control attached to the essential and required bases in JCS 570/40, the JCS now abandoned requests for exclusive rights of any kind—"joint" rights would now constitute the highest degree of desired US control. The JCS, however, expanded the meaning of this term by specifying that all other nations were to be denied use of the base unless mutually agreed to by the United States and the nations exercising jurisdiction. Thus, for Iceland, Greenland, the Azores, airfields in the Republic of Panama, and the Galapagos (all identified as essential), the maximum military requirement was now joint rights. In most of those places deemed required, the JCS stuck to their request for maximum joint rights but dropped the minimum from joint or participating to simple "transit" rights.[41]

The JCS also altered the lineup of essential and required bases by dropping Canton and Manus Islands in the South Pacific and Ascension Island and the Cape Verde Islands in the Atlantic from the essential to the required category. In contrast, Casablanca-Port Lyautey, North Africa moved up to join the five remaining essential locations. Three bases dropped altogether from the new list of military requirements: Clipperton Island, Bora Bora in the French-owned Society Islands, and Formosa.[42] The removal of Clipperton and Bora Bora was further evidence of the military's de-emphasis on the South Pacific. Rights to bases in Formosa, while strategically justifiable and strongly desired by the AAF, were politically unacceptable.[43] In Formosa's case, said General Lincoln, "we must realize that the matter of extraterritoriality is involved; that we have fought for many years to terminate extraterritoriality in China and that we must try to avoid setting a precedent, which may embarrass us politically later." Moreover, he pointed out, no formal agreement could guarantee the United States the right to use Formosa if, in the next war, China was to be allied against the United States.[44] Just as in the summer and fall of 1945 when they drew up JCS 570, military planners again subordinated strategic to political considerations in reaching decisions about bases required for US security.

By mid-1946, the JCS had concluded that little strategic need existed for extensive base rights in the Pacific south of the equator. Yet the JCS had made no move to cut back requirements in this area (despite questioning by some JCS staff officers of the necessity for such base rights as early as September 1945) until pressured to do so by the secretaries of state, war, and Navy. The three civilian department heads each saw the problem from somewhat different perspectives. Byrnes was apprehensive about the negative reaction American requests for postwar base rights were producing overseas. The State Department even suggested that cuts in the South Pacific might be appropriate both politically and strategically. Forrestal and Patterson showed concern for the base network's overall cost, although the former was probably also inspired by the desire to restrict some of the JCS's independence from civilian control. Outside pressure, however, had only limited impact on the JCS who, it was clear, could be pushed—but not too rapidly. The JCS considered the changes made to JCS 570/40 in June 1946 to be amendments only, not a full-scale revision of that document. Pressure for a complete overhaul of JCS 570/40 would come from the AAF. In its view, the 1945 base plan was especially deficient in the number of primary bases programmed for the arctic approaches to the North American continent.[45] In May 1946, Gen Carl Spaatz, the AAF commander, told officers on the Air Staff that the AAF's primary objective for the next three or four years would be to develop defenses on the polar frontier.[46] In fact, he had approved the June 1946 amendments to JCS 570/40 only on the condition that action be taken to designate Greenland and central Alaska as primary base areas.[47] For airmen, the so-called "Polar Concept" had become an article of faith.

* * *

In the first few years following World War II, planning for, acquiring the rights to, and establishing bases across the Western Hemisphere's far northern frontier became high-priority

161

concerns within the American military establishment. The AAF, contending that airpower could best exploit the region's defensive and offensive potential, let few chances slip to educate the other services and the general public on the strategic significance of the far north. AAF claims that the United States was "wide open at the top" surrounded the whole matter with a sense of dramatic urgency.[48] Yet, by the end of 1947, the newly independent Air Force's experience in the Arctic revealed the existence of a huge gap between the recognition of the strategic importance of far north bases and the ability to develop and to operate from these forward outposts.

Soldiers and civilians alike had realized transpolar and other northern air routes were likely to be militarily and economically important once the war with Germany and Japan ended. In addition, as we have seen, the rapid deterioration in relations with the Soviet Union, startling advances in weapons technology, and bitter interservice rivalry heightened interest in the far north bases. The AAF, in a campaign lasting from late 1945 through 1947, sought to make the most of the situation.

In the fall of 1945, air leaders began to speak and write publicly about the danger from the north. They assumed the next war would be much like the last—a total conflict whose aim would be destruction of the opponent's war-making capacity. Using polar projections of the earth's surface, the airmen showed that the world's major industrial and population centers lay north of 30 degrees, with the shortest distance between these centers being by air over the pole. Thus, attack was likely to come from that direction, given the range and speed of modern aircraft (and eventually guided missiles). The onset of war would be swift, with the resulting outcome nearly complete devastation. In a December 1945 magazine article, General Spaatz pointed to the recent flight of four B-29s from Japan to Washington, D.C., as evidence that "a range of only 6,500 miles is sufficient for an aircraft to take off from a base below the Arctic Circle, fly across the Polar regions on a one-way trip, *and reach every great industrial-political-military Center on the other side of the world.*" With near-Arctic bases, said Spaatz, an enemy could bomb key American cities, and "U.S. bombers based near the 65 degree North line could retaliate in kind against the largest cities of any possible adversary." This, noted Spaatz, "might be done today." In the future, advanced aircraft like the B-36 would be able to fly two-way missions from such bases.[49] For these reasons, possession of extreme northern bases had enormous defensive and offensive implications. Spaatz thought air defenses stretching from Alaska, across Canada, to the North Atlantic might be able to intercept some of the enemy's aircraft or missiles, although many would get through.[50] "The only real defense," he maintained, "has become a total offense, one that would be aimed at smashing the enemy's whole organism and would 'counter' his offense incidentally in the process."[51] For the AAF, then, the ultimate importance of far north bases lay in their potential as launching sites for offensive air operations.

Many seemed convinced that the next battleground might well be the skies over the Arctic. John L. Sullivan, assistant secretary of the Navy for air, reported that "a large portion of the American public has come to think that a future threat might come through Canada or Alaska."[52] The AAF pounded the point home with spectacular flights, demonstrating its transpolar capability. In October 1946 a B-29, named *Pacusan Dreamboat,* flew over 9,500 miles nonstop from the Hawaiian Islands over the north polar regions to Cairo, Egypt. Spaatz was gratified that "the nation's press saw the performance as an object lesson in the need for adequate air defense of the Arctic Frontier."[53]

The Navy was much less awed by the prospect of polar warfare. The two naval members of the Joint Staff Planners resisted AAF initiatives to have JCS 570/40 revised for the purpose of adding more primary base areas on the northern frontier.[54] In a speech at the National War College, Washington, D.C., Admiral Spruance played down the polar threat, calling the Arctic regions wastelands and pointing out that the Bering Strait (the part of Eurasia closest to the United States) was still some 2,000 miles from any continental American city.[55] Nonetheless, top naval officers conceded that, "with the passage of time and the expected development of aircraft and airborne missiles, the importance of the northern approaches to the U.S. will increase." For this reason, said Admiral Sherman, "the Navy was making every effort to improve its capability to operate in the arctic environment."[56]

In contrast to the Navy, the War Department had few doubts about the wisdom of rapidly implementing the Polar Concept. Comparison of deployment figures in the War Department's February 1946 and May 1947 plans for US peacetime overseas bases illustrates the emphasis being placed on the far north. While in February 1946 the War Department planned to deploy a total of 299,000 Army and AAF personnel to all overseas military bases, the pressure of budget cutbacks reduced this figure to 198,000 by May 1947.[57] Even so, the number of personnel destined for duty in Alaska increased from 23,000 to 39,000.[58] Additionally, in 1946 the War Department planned to deploy less than one full very heavy bomb (VHB) group and less than two complete fighter groups to Alaska out of a total of 13 VHB groups and 16 fighter groups identified for overseas duty. In May 1947, the planned overseas deployment had dropped to five VHB and nine fighter groups, but two of the VHB groups and two of the fighter groups were scheduled for Alaskan duty.[59]

In 1946–47 the AAF sought to develop Arctic bases. The Air Transport Command received permission to establish an alternate air route between Iceland and Alaska. Additionally, the Air Proving Ground Command built a climatic hangar in Florida to simulate the Arctic environment and to run preliminary tests.[60] In the summer of 1946, Strategic Air Command (SAC) units, including the 28th Bombardment Wing, a VHB unit, deployed to Ladd Field, Alaska.[61] The Polar Concept was about to be tested—and was found wanting. During the winter of 1946–47, as historian Harry Borowski has so well described, the AAF discovered it could not operate effectively in the Arctic. The airmen and machines suffered great stress, because they were inadequately prepared for the harsh climate. Prior to departure for Alaska, instructions given to aircrews regarding cold-weather effects on the body and equipment had been skimpy. The men did not sufficiently realize the importance of wearing proper clothing or handling equipment carefully. Rubber oxygen masks, for example, distintegrated when treated roughly in minus zero temperatures. The Alaskan Air Command, whose mission was to support the SAC deployment, lacked proper equipment. Hangar space was limited, and aircraft exposed to frigid temperatures and high winds for extended periods often broke down. Engines took hours to warm up, tires froze to runway surfaces, and flight controls stuck constantly. The resulting halts in flying operations caused by harsh conditions caused morale to plummet.[62]

When crews were able to fly, the unfamiliar and forbidding aerial enviroment presented obstacles the fliers were slow to overcome. In late 1945 Spaatz had optimistically declared, "Arctic flying itself would present no major problems. Our new electronic navigation instruments, better antiweather controls both in engines and aircraft, and a high level of flying skill would combine to make polar runs generally uneventful."[63] The practical experience gained in 1946–47 painted a much different picture. For one thing, airmen on Arctic missions experienced unusual flying hazards. Extremely cold temperatures caused in-flight equipment malfunctions, and rapid weather changes produced disorientation, making landings risky. With little faith in either their survival equipment or search and rescue units, airmen feared being lost in the vast, thinly-populated, and hostile polar regions. The difficulties of navigating in the Arctic added considerably to this mental stress. There were few ground aids to navigation, and charts and instruments were unreliable near the North Pole. Although new navigation techniques and equipment had been developed, the inexperienced aircrews were reluctant to rely on them. Weather and the fliers' unfamiliarity with polar navigation forced several aircraft to go down. One B-29, returning from a mission to the North Pole and in radio contact with Ladd Field, lost its bearings, eventually crashing in Greenland.[64] Clearly, the problems faced by SAC units in Alaska during the winter of 1946–47 showed the Polar Concept to have a major flaw—the AAF could not yet operate in any meaningful way in the Arctic.

The Alaskan failures did not cause the AAF to abandon its Polar Concept, but they were probably responsible for its de-emphasis in 1947. That summer, Maj Gen Clements McMullen, deputy SAC commander, surveyed islands in the northern Canadian Archipelago suitable for a bomber base. The search for a site was long and frustrating—at one point McMullen admitted nearly having "shed my polar concept."[65] Eventually, he located a site on Cornwallis Island, Canada, and recommended its development: "The international situation is such that all European and Icelandic bases and construction of bases in Greenland are likely to be denied to us. Existing bases within the United States, Canada, Newfoundland, and Alaska are so situated as to preclude access to most priority targets of Europe and Asia even on one-way raids."[66] Spaatz, however, disapproved the project, largely because the money and personnel required to construct and to support the base "would detract from USAF capabilities to accomplish work which may be required in other strategic areas of greater importance."[67]

While Spaatz and other Air Force leaders continued to talk about the polar frontier, they now emphasized its defensive rather than offensive potential.[68] Early in 1948, Forrestal frankly told President Truman that "decisive action over the polar ice cap is not within the limits of practicability for the next several years."[69] In truth, the Polar Concept had been a mixture of reality and fantasy from the very beginning. In December 1945 General Spaatz quite likely had been aware of Soviet designs on Spitsbergen and Bear Island. This prospect provided some basis for his apprehension and desire to establish Arctic bases. He may also be forgiven his glowing assessment of the ease with which air operations could be conducted in the Arctic, for he certainly had no knowledge of how troublesome they would prove. On the other hand, he too easily mixed present with future capability. Conceding his description of transpolar warfare was "hypothetical and oversimplified," he nonetheless claimed it to be based on the "known performance of today's aircraft."[70] The stress on what might take place *today* was less than candid. He failed to point out that the range of a B-29, carrying a bombload of any consequence, would be considerably less than 6,500 miles even on a one-way mission. Furthermore, JCS studies were then showing that the Soviets lacked a strategic air force. Their best bomber could reach targets only 2,000 miles distant—far short of the continental United States.[71]

While Spaatz portrayed the future quite well (in five years long-range aircraft, and in 15 years the ballistic missile could traverse the pole), he exaggerated the immediate danger; undoubtedly, interservice rivalry was partly responsible for the hyperbole. For example, in testimony before the Senate Appropriations Committee in April 1946 Spaatz claimed the polar regions to be an "air frontier" where nature barred "effective operations by surface forces."[72] Overstating the near-term possibility of transpolar air warfare also probably was rooted in a genuine fear that the postwar rush to slash military expenditures and the blistering pace of technological advance would leave the United States without enough time to make up lost ground if a hostile power should become entrenched in polar outposts of its own. For this reason, concern for developing, but especially for acquiring rights to bases along the northern frontier was not misplaced in 1945–47. Yet, the Air Force's over-concentration on a region whose military potential seemed so well-suited to the interests of one service contributed, as we shall see, to delays by the military in stressing bases "in other strategic areas of greater importance."

* * *

While the AAF campaigned for Arctic frontier bases from late 1945 through 1947, the United States and the Soviet Union, already at odds over the future of Central and Eastern Europe, began to confront each other in the Near East and in Southeastern Europe. Historically, this region had been the scene of Anglo-Russian rivalry, but after World War II, Great Britain had lost much of its imperial muscle and was unable to fill its traditional role as the opponent of Russian expansion into the Mediterranean. American policy makers, inspired by a growing conviction that Stalin's Russia was a twin to Adolf Hitler's Germany, by the lure of Middle Eastern petroleum, and by commercial aviation's promise, moved to halt Soviet penetration of the area.

Crisis followed crisis in quick succession in the two years following the war. Strong US opposition to the continued presence of Soviet troops in northern Iran darkened the winter of 1945–46. Then in August, the Soviet Union demanded that Turkey's control of the strategic Dardanelles Strait, guaranteed by the Montreux Convention in 1936, be modified in Russia's

167

favor. Among other things, the Soviets wanted joint rights with Turkey to use bases in the straits. The United States formally objected, and President Truman approved plans to send a naval task force into the eastern Mediterranean. When the Yugoslavs shot down two US aircraft over their territory within days of the US response to Soviet pressure on Turkey, war seemed likely to some high-level American officials.[73] Although the tension produced by the Turkish crisis subsided, alarm bells rang again in Washington in early 1947 at reports the Soviets were behind the collapse of order in Greece.[74] This news, combined with the announcement of Great Britain's decision to end its aid program to the Greek government resulted in swift American action.[75] On 12 March 1947, Truman asked Congress to approve $400 million in aid for Greece and Turkey, and declared that "it must be the policy of the United States to support free peoples who are resisting attempted subjugation by armed minorities or by outside pressure."[76] In proclaiming what came to be known as the Truman Doctrine, writes historian Daniel Yergin, the president "committed the United States to a global struggle with the Soviets."[77] Eastern Europe—solidly within the Soviet sphere—was hardly a favorable arena in which to wage the battle. There were, said Dean Acheson, undersecretary of state, "other places where we can be effective."[78] Some of these lay along Russia's southern rim.

As the focus of the developing Cold War shifted from Eastern Europe to the Near East and eastern Mediterranean in 1946–47, bases and base rights in the area assumed increasing importance. Without bases military force could not be applied to support national policy nor would even the threat of military sanctions have much meaning. Thus, the power with access to bases was (at least in theory) in a better position to achieve its national objectives. The Soviet Union and the United States played this geopolitical game.

Scholars writing about Soviet postwar security objectives have usually concentrated on the Soviet Union's desire to create a buffer between Germany and Russia in Eastern Europe. Yet, the Soviet Union's concept of its own security needs appears to have included more than a protective belt of client states in Eastern Europe (even if one ignores the controversial issue of

Soviet aims in Western Europe). The Soviets, as we have seen, recognized the significance of outposts on the northern frontier; Spitsbergen and Bear Island were the Soviets' Greenland and Iceland. For a time in 1945 and early 1946, Soviet troops occupied northern Norway and the Danish island of Bornholm, strategically situated at the entrance to the Baltic. The Americans viewed these forces as intended primarily to establish a Soviet claim for base rights.[79] Within a year, Soviet troops had departed both places. Russian intentions are not known; perhaps disarming the German garrisons was their only objective. On the other hand, the Soviets may have desired base rights, but like the United States, ultimately found national resistance to the presence of foreign troops too strong.

The major effort by the Soviets in acquiring postwar bases was directed toward the eastern Mediterranean and North Africa. At Potsdam and at the Council of Foreign Ministers meeting in London, in September 1945, the Soviets called for joint control with Turkey of the Dardanelles and for a sole Russian trusteeship over Tripolitania (part of Italy's former colonial holdings in North Africa).[80] The Russian demand for bases in the straits, as we have seen, would precipitate a Soviet-American crisis in the summer of 1946. Great Britain and the United States were united in resisting Soviet advances in North Africa, with Byrnes thinking the Soviets were after access to uranium deposits in the Belgian Congo.[81] British foreign secretary Bevin, bluntly told Soviet foreign minister V. M. Molotov that he knew the Soviets wanted Tripolitania to use as "a base for military purposes." Molotov did not deny the accusation.[82] The Western powers also suspected the Soviets had an interest in the Greek Dodecanese Islands. The Soviets had opposed their demilitarization (because, according to Byrnes, such a step would tie Russian hands if Greece were to go communist).[83] Such evidence suggests the Soviet Union probably had a preparedness ideology of its own that contemplated extension of Russia's strategic frontier not only in Eastern Europe, but also the Arctic region and the Mediterranean. Still, on balance, the Russians did not try to reach out as far as the Americans in their search for security.

Unlike the Russians, the American military initially showed relatively little enthusiasm for bases in North Africa (east of the

169

Atlantic side of Gibraltar), in the eastern Mediterranean or Middle East, or in South Asia. The AAF had consistently argued for transit rights across these areas, but the JCS did not request them in JCS 570/40. Not until early 1946 did the JCS ask the State Department to negotiate for these rights. The United States had secured military rights at Dhahran in 1945, but the airfield had been constructed primarily for economic and not military reasons.[84] With the general rise in tension between the United States and the USSR from late 1945 onward, particularly with the series of crises in the Near East and Eastern Mediterranean in 1946–47, military and civilian leaders paid increasing attention to providing for American bases on the southern periphery of Europe and Asia. Contingency war plans drawn up by the JCS from 1946 to 1948 reflected the growing importance of southern rim bases in postwar US military strategy.

Despite the initiation of efforts within the JCS in late December 1945 to determine what the US military would do in the event of war with the USSR and signs of mounting friction with the Soviet Union in 1946–47, the United States did not have an approved war plan until spring 1948. The preparation of the war plan, begun in the summer of 1947, was preceded by a series of JCS studies designed to provide an analytical framework on which the final plan could be built. The studies, code-named *Pincher*, identified probable Soviet military courses of action in specific geographic areas and the options for counteraction available to US military forces.[85]

The Pincher studies make several common points. The Soviet Union's ultimate objective was world domination, its intermediate aim was to dominate the Eurasian continent, and its short-term objective was to assure security along its borders.[86] The Soviets would not resort to war in the foreseeable future (in this case, the next three years), although war might erupt through miscalculation.[87] If war should occur, then Russian forces, deficient in naval power and lacking a strategic air force, would conduct concurrent overland offensives in Europe and the Middle East.[88] In all probability, Soviet armies would quickly overrun most of Europe (excluding the British Isles), although Western forces would be able to slow down a Russian advance toward the Suez Canal.[89]

For the United States, Soviet aggression would mean total war.[90] But given the generally weakened state of the postwar American military, the United States would initially have to go on the strategic defensive in the Pacific and Far East, while undertaking a counteroffensive against Russia in Europe and the Middle East. The United States would rely on its strength—long-range aircraft carrying atomic and conventional bombs against Soviet urban and industrial targets to destroy Russia's war-making capacity and will to fight. The formal strategic concept, as it evolved throughout 1946–47, was

> to destroy the capacity of the U.S.S.R. and her satellites to continue hostilities by a main offensive effort in Western Eurasia and an active defense in Eastern Asia. Initially to secure Britain, the Cairo-Suez area and the Atlantic Islands; to conduct operations to secure adequate air and naval bases, and provide essential aid to our Allies; undertake a maximum strategic air bombardment effort against vital elements of Soviet military and industrial power; to secure essential sea and air lines of communication; to secure the Bering Sea, Japan–Yellow Sea line; and to conduct political, psychological, and underground operations in the U.S.S.R. and in Russian occupied territories to waste Russian resources.[91]

Since the heart of the US response was to be a strategic air offensive from Western Eurasia, the selection of air bases was a critical element in JCS contingency planning. Admiral Sherman testified in closed session before the Senate Armed Services Committee that "our joint concepts envisage that the principal initial counteroffensive efforts against Russia itself would consist of a strategic air offensive from bases in the British Isles and in the vicinity of Suez, and perhaps from India."[92] In late 1945 and early 1946, bases located in western China and Italy were part of the planning for a strategic air offensive.[93] But the advance of Chinese communist forces evidently ended consideration of China, while Italy's vulnerability to Soviet attack probably forced its elimination from JCS plans. Toward the end of 1947, JCS staff officers included bases in Japan and the Ryukyus in their planning, but bases in the United Kingdom, the Middle East, and India were the most important.[94]

British airfields were attractive for several reasons. Although American forces rapidly departed the United Kingdom after World War II, of all the nations in Western Europe,

Britain would be the most receptive to an American return. The JCS described the United Kingdom as the "keystone" of the initial air offensive against the USSR because of its logistic support capacity and its strategic location.[95] From bases in Great Britain B-29s could reach any overrun area in Western Europe and such key targets as the Ploesti oil fields in Rumania, Moscow, and the Donbass industrial region in the Soviet Union.[96] None of the 140 airfields built in England during World War II were equipped to sustain VHB operations, but many could be easily converted. General Spaatz and Air Marshal Sir Arthur Tedder informally agreed early in 1946 that the Royal Air Force (RAF) would prepare four or five RAF bases in East Anglia to receive B-29s, and Spaatz may have discussed the subject again with the British in June 1946.[97] As a result of these discussions, five British airfields were suitable for VHBs and four others readily adaptable by mid-1947.[98]

Despite distinct advantages, the use of British bases had some drawbacks. Poor weather often hampered flying operations for days and in some cases weeks.[99] Moreover, since the Soviets were expected to overrun most of the continent, missions flown from England would proceed entirely over enemy-occupied territory.[100] Finally, B-29s carrying either 10,000- or 15,000-pound bombloads were limited to a "combat" or "effective" operating radius of between 1,500 and 2,000 NM. This limited range put the Baku oil fields and industries east of the Ural Mountains beyond the range of United Kingdom-based long-range aircraft.[101] "The U.S., Atlantic Islands and other base areas," stated the JCS, "do not provide adequate bases, or coverage of target systems in the U.S.S.R., for a sustained strategic air campaign against vital elements of Soviet military power, of the magnitude estimated to be required, within an acceptable time period."[102]

Possession of bases close to the Soviet Union's southern border could remedy the major disadvantage of using British bases. With the exception of Leningrad and the rest of northwestern Russia, every significant Soviet target was accessible from airfields in Egypt and India.[103] For this reason, southern bases were of equal importance to British airfields in JCS contingency planning from late 1945 through 1947.[104] A crucial

172

point, in fact, is that they would have enjoyed this status even if the postwar Soviet-American confrontation had been confined to Central and Eastern Europe or if no pools of oil had lain underneath Middle Eastern sands. The August 1945 AAF intelligence memorandum, discussed in the previous chapter, that connected proposals for postwar base rights to the B-29's effective combat radius, had foretold as much.

Although highly desirable, use of bases in Egypt and northwest India presented some difficulties of its own; simply acquiring rights, as Byrnes discovered in India's case was likely to be a serious obstacle. Furthermore, while both Egyptian and Indian airfields could accommodate B-29s, the former would require further development "before strategic air operations in strength could be initiated."[105] Finally, war planning was always subject to sudden shifts in national policy. US recognition of Israel in 1948, for example, would imperil the military's plans for relying on bases in the Cairo-Suez area. Nevertheless, these were relatively minor drawbacks compared to the region's overall strategic significance.

The Soviet advance south of the Black Sea was so alarming because it seemed aimed, in part, at denying to the United States advance bases that were critical to the strategic air offensive (perceived then as the only viable US military option).[106] The JCS planners projected their own preparedness ideology onto the Soviets:

> Due to the constantly increasing ranges of aircraft capable of performing strategic bombing missions, the U.S.S.R. feels that the perimeter of Soviet dominated territory must be constantly expanded. In order for the Soviets to accomplish their immediate objective of security, they must attempt to gain control of areas from which the Allies might launch major military operations against Soviet vital areas.[107]

If war should occur, then an early Soviet aim would be "seizure or neutralization of those areas from which the Western powers might swiftly and effectively strike at the U.S.S.R., particularly the Cairo-Suez area."[108] Holding on to the Middle East, consequently, would be a major objective of US and allied forces if, as Forrestal told President Truman, "anything should develop to the north and east." Since the United States had no transpolar offensive capability, the secretary of defense continued,

173

"Any sustained and therefore decisive action against nation 'X' would have to take place largely from the Mediterranean and its environs."[109]

The requirement to acquire bases within striking distance of Soviet targets was not the only stimulus for America's entry into the eastern Mediterranean and Middle East after World War II. The need for oil alone, would have generated pressure for some kind of American military presence in the area. The expansion of US commercial air transport was another powerful lure. All of these factors combined with an overarching fear that events in Iran, Turkey, and Greece were among the first stages of a long-range Soviet master plan for world domination initiated an unmistakable shift in the geographic orientation of American strategy. Between 1945 and the end of 1947, the strategic spotlight passed from the Pacific, to the Arctic and the North Atlantic, and then to British, Middle Eastern, and South Asian bases.[110]

* * *

By 1947 JCS 570/40, the base plan prepared by the JCS in late 1945 (even as modified in mid-1946), was badly in need of major overhaul. The AAF, pressing its Polar Concept, felt much more emphasis should be given to far north bases. At the same time, JCS contingency war planning reflected a requirement for air bases in the United Kingdom, Egypt, and India, that would enable the United States to respond to a Soviet attack with a counteroffensive of its own. Although the JCS revised the overall base plan during the year, the changes only partly addressed these strategic deficiencies. Rather than current military strategy, budget cutbacks, difficulties encountered by the State Department in negotiating for base rights, and interservice rivalry determined the new plan's makeup. By the end of 1947, the odd result was a base plan one step out of phase with the realities of war planning. Not until 1948, when civilian defense leaders pushed the services to agree on a joint war plan, would there be a marriage between base planning and war planning.

Formal work on a revision of the 1945 base plan began in February 1947.[111] The officers assigned to the task received

174

instructions from the JCS Joint Staff Planners to consider "size of forces, availability of funds, the international political situation, new definitions of categories of bases, and the current status of base negotiations."[112] Later, they were also told to come up with a paper that "sets forth the military worth of geographical areas in conformance with the overall strategic concept and with the base requirements which are envisioned in the successful prosecution of a major war."[113] The staff officers labored for more than six months; finally, in September 1947, the JCS approved the fourth draft of the new base plan, JCS 570/83, and submitted it to the State Department through the SWNCC.[114]

JCS 570/83 provided for a system of 53 primary, subsidiary, and transit bases or base areas. This was a considerable reduction (even when several bases were combined into one base area) from the 90 sites identified in JCS 570/40.[115] The nine primary base areas included the Hawaiian Islands; the Mariana-Bonin Islands; the Ryukyu Islands; Alaska and the Aleutians; Canada; Newfoundland and Labrador; Greenland and Iceland; the Azores; and the Caribbean and Panama. The 15 subsidiary bases consisted generally of locations in the South Atlantic, the western Atlantic, and the Pacific; while the 29 transit air bases were largely situated along the North African, Middle Eastern, and South Asian route and in central and northern South America. Forces were to be deployed in peacetime only at primary and subsidiary bases or base areas.[116] In addition to the primary, subsidiary, and transit categories, JCS 570/83 also designated many other locations as strategic base areas to "be kept under surveillance with a view to denying or restricting military development by other powers." These included northwestern Europe; Great Britain; South America; Japan; a belt encompassing all of North Africa and the Middle East; and another belt stretching from the south central Pacific, through the East Indies, to the Malay Peninsula.[117] Finally, the JCS divided those bases requiring State Department negotiation to obtain rights into two categories, required and desired. [118]

According to the joint chiefs, JCS 570/83 constituted a reevaluation of military base planning in the face of cost and manpower limitations, as well as the problems encountered by the State Department in its efforts to acquire base rights on foreign territory.[119] Moreover, a new base plan was needed "so that properly coordinated base development may proceed in conjunction with, and in support of, war planning."[120] Although not a system capable of waging a major war, the JCS claimed JCS 570/83 would provide for a "reasonable defense" of the United States and a means to project "offensive operations within our capabilities" once war broke out.[121] In some ways the JCS's description of the basis on which the plan was prepared was accurate; in other ways quite misleading.

Anticipated reduction in military appropriations was a key element in the design of JCS 570/83.[122] The JCS base planners attempted to predict the probable size of the postwar federal budget and the portion likely to be allocated to national defense.[123] They projected future government exenditures to amount to $18 billion annually and military appropriations to range between $2.1 and $4 billion per year.[124] Yet, the amount required to develop the base system envisioned by JCS 570/40 totaled over $5 billion. Even if as much as $200 million were allocated each year for overseas base construction (the average of the actual appropriations for fiscal years 1946 and 1947), the network would take over 25 years to complete.[125] The conclusion was inescapable: "The capabilities of the armed forces to develop bases are definitely limited as to manpower and money. . . . High priority therefore should be given to the construction of those bases which are vital to the defense of the U.S. *and essential to an early offensive* [emphasis added]."[126] By reducing requirements from the 90 bases or base areas in JCS 570/40 to the 53 in JCS 570/83, the JCS was responding, in part, to the reality of declining defense appropriations. The reduction also showed the military's awareness of the problem the State Department was having in securing base rights in foreign countries. By 1947 the State Department's lack of success greatly concerned the military, particularly the AAF. Air Staff officers felt that General Marshall, who had recently succeeded Byrnes as secretary of state, should be informed of the situation's seriousness before the JCS undertook its review of the base plan.[127]

How to approach Marshall presented a sensitive problem in civil-military relations to the planners. One suggestion was to prepare a letter from Stuart Symington, assistant secretary of war for air to Patterson, secretary of war, asking the latter to forward a summary of the status of base negotiations to Marshall. A second recommendation was to have Generals Eisenhower and Spaatz discuss the matter with the secretary of state. Military planners rejected both of these procedures "on the thesis that they involved initiation of action by the military to the State [Department] and that such action might be untimely."[128] Another method considered and rejected on the grounds that it would probably take too long was to submit a letter to Marshall from the JCS through the SWNCC. Finally, staff officers agreed to informally approach John D. Hickerson, director of the State Department's Office of European Affairs, and ask him to brief Marshall. "By this means" the officers believed, "a purely State Department approach might be presented, as service representation would probably be unwise unless expressly requested."[129] Sensitivity to resentment by War and Navy Department civilian leaders over any effort by the professional military to short-circuit them and to Marshall's status as a career officer, probably explains all of the elaborate maneuvering.

The plan worked! Hickerson told Marshall of the "great difficulties" encountered in attempts to secure long-term base rights. For one thing, reported Hickerson, British foreign secretary Bevin had advised Byrnes that the United States should not seek long-term base rights because to do so might show a lack of confidence in the UN and might encourage the Soviet Union to seek base rights in the Dardanelles, Eastern Europe, and Scandinavia. Moreover, Communist parties around the world had been "bitterly critical" of US efforts to obtain base rights, notably in Iceland. For these reasons, said Hickerson, "we have had to postpone our attempts to obtain long-range base rights in a number of places. . . ." One temporary solution, he noted, was to negotiate for air transit rights in connection with support of US overseas occupation forces.[130]

Seeing that the whole issue reached Marshall's attention was about the best the military could hope for. When the revision of JCS 570/40 got under way in February 1947, JCS planners still recognized that the decreasing likelihood of acquiring long-term rights had to be taken into account in drawing up a new plan.[131] Staff officers directly involved in base planning formally requested detailed State Department advice. In March, Admiral Sherman and General Norstad, representing the JCS, conferred with Hickerson and Paul Culbertson at State to come up with some general guidelines for the revision. Those attending the conference agreed that the only Atlantic locations at which the United States would seek long-term rights would be Greenland, Iceland, and the Azores. Small Pacific bases south of the equator would, as a rule, be deleted. Significantly, the military conferees held transit rights across North Africa, the Middle East, and South Asia to be desirable "if reasonably attainable by negotiations" but did not recommend any "sizable amount of quid pro quo to be offered for these rights."[132]

Not until late June did Hickerson formally reply to the base planners' request for guidance. It was filled with pessimism about the prospects for long-term rights: "I feel that we are now in a situation where the Soviet propaganda machine will chalk up a black mark against us every place where we try to get post war military base rights. In these circumstances I feel that we should severely pare down our requirements to things that are really important to our security." In the Pacific, Hickerson felt that US security requirements had "practically been met" with UN approval of a US strategic trusteeship over the former Japanese Mandate Islands and with the recently signed United States Philippine postwar base agreement. As for the Atlantic, Hickerson conceded that the United States must continue to press for long-term rights in Greenland, Iceland, and the Azores. He was much less enthusiastic about the military's desire for bases on the Atlantic coast of Africa (i.e., Casablanca, Port Lyautey, and Dakar). "I personally never felt," wrote Hickerson, "that it was essential to our defense to obtain these rights and I have been fearful that our trying to get them might be grist for the communist mill, but I acquiesced in our discussing these rights informally with the French." Requests for rights elsewhere in the Atlantic, he concluded, "should be dropped."[133]

So negative an assessment by the State Department clearly influenced the military's new base plan. In transmitting JCS 570/83 to the SWNCC the JCS said they recognized "the difficulties attendant upon negotiations and the reluctance of foreign nations to grant 'rights' to any outside power, and accordingly have established the requirements for a minimum of such rights."[134] In JCS 570/83, the JCS asked the State Department to negotiate for rights in 14 fewer countries than in JCS 570/40 and its mid-1946 modification. Most of the deletions were to sites in the Pacific south of the equator, the Dutch East Indies, Mexico, and Central America. All of these changes conformed to the overall strategic shift from the south and west to the north and east that had been under way since the end of the war.

The strategic orientation of JCS 570/83 focused overwhelmingly on defense of the Western Hemisphere's northern approaches. The four primary base areas blanketing the northern access routes to the United States were (1) Alaska and the Aleutians, (2) Canada, (3) Greenland/Iceland, and (4) Newfoundland/Labrador. During the preparation of the base plan, there was little debate (as there had been in 1945) over the strategic significance of these areas. AAF arguments had won the day. This time interservice conflict revolved around the priority to be attached to areas further to the south. The AAF believed the Ryukyu Islands, Mariana-Bonin Islands, and the Azores should all be classed as primary bases, while the Hawaiian Islands, Caribbean, and Panama were of secondary importance.[135] The Navy and Army, in contrast, did not think the Ryukyus and the Azores merited primary status, but were convinced the Hawaiian Islands, Panama, and the Caribbean belonged in that category.[136] Only the Army opposed classifying the Mariana-Bonin Islands as a primary base area.[137] General Lincoln, in a letter to his JPS counterparts, candidly explained the real issue in the debate over the more southerly base areas:

> The practical result of our attempts to date [to develop a sytem of base categories and assign particular bases to them] has been to establish a system of priorities which every agency connected with the problem has tried to use in connection with its own particular interest. Logically, confusion arises when the same system of priorities is applied to diplomatic negotiations to deployment of forces to the expenditure of

funds. This is particularly true when, in the matter of funds (or construction) we are dealing in shortages and on a year-to-year basis.[138]

In other words, not only was JCS 570/83 to indicate to the State Department what priorities in overseas base rights the military wanted, but it was also to be an overall plan for the development of the US overseas base system. Since the latter involved money, disputes flared up over the less strategically important areas.

The basis for compromise in the debate over priorities to be attached to the base areas not in the far north was obvious—Navy support for classifying the Ryukyus and the Azores as primary bases in exchange for the AAF withdrawing its opposition to designating the Hawaiian Islands, Panama, and the Caribbean as primary. By late May 1947, such a compromise had taken place (the Army apparently being outvoted on the question of the appropriate status for the Mariana-Bonin Islands).[139] This solution was, of course, simply a way of avoiding the problem of allocation of funds, which could be fought out later.

Neither the unity of opinion regarding far northern bases nor the interservice disagreement over the proper status for base areas farther to the south were the most noticeable features of JCS 570/83's strategic dimension.[140] What confounds the historian is the nearly total absence (as the plan was being prepared) of any discussion about bases along Russia's southern rim and the military's failure to express any special urgency to the State Department about acquiring rights to them. Admittedly, the JCS labeled transit rights to bases in North Africa, the Middle East, and South Asia as "desired" but did not intend to deploy forces at these locations in peacetime. Yet, contingency war plans then being drawn-up named bases in the United Kingdom, Egypt, and India as crucial to the success of a strategic air offensive. Furthermore, the JCS themselves proclaimed JCS 570/83 to be a plan providing for base development to "proceed in conjunction with and in support of war planning."

Conceivably, the strategic deficiencies in JCS 570/83 may simply have been an example of the right hand not knowing what the left hand was doing. The JCS base planners were not directly involved in designing war plans. But isolation of the base planners is not a satisfactory explanation since the four members of the JPS reviewed both base plans and war plans before submitting them to the JCS.[141]

More complex factors explain the absence of emphasis on southern rim bases in JCS 570/83. First, the State Department in mid-1947 clearly opposed expansion of overseas military base rights. Military planners, long sensitized to the highly political nature of US bases on foreign territory refrained from pressing the issue except in the case of such northern and mid-Atlantic bases as Iceland, Greenland, and the Azores. Second, if the mid-March conference between high-level military and State Department officials was any indication, the military itself was not convinced that much should be given up to acquire transit rights across North Africa, the Middle East, and South Asia. At this point, the military had higher priorities, particularly the far northern bases. These bases were vital for defense of the United States and the Western Hemisphere. Since JCS 570/83 was to establish priorities both for rights acquisition and base development against a background of international political complications and stringent funds for military spending, priority had to go to bases closer to home—primarily defensive rather than offensive bases. Lastly, interservice rivalry, which came to the fore in war planning, was also partly responsible for JCS 570/83's strategic inconsistencies.

Without a definite war plan, base planning would lack a sharp focus. While studies intended to lay the basis for a war plan had been under way since late 1945, the JCS's Joint War Plans Committee did not begin to draw up the war plan itself until the end of August 1947. The plan was finally presented to the JCS in March 1948, seven months later.[142] Adm C. D. Glover explained the reason for the delay to Maj Gen A. M. Gruenther, director of the Joint Staff:

> I know that it will be a great relief to you, the Joint Chiefs of Staff, and Mr. Forrestal to have the final draft of the Emergency Plan (Brief). . . . I believe it is important for the Joint Chiefs and Mr. Forrestal to know that we still have great difficulty putting out plans involving requirements for forces in the future which may establish the size and composition of the respective services. We [the Planners] therefore hope that the basic questions which involve us in many controversies can be solved in Key West.[143]

The meeting of the JCS and the secretary of defense that same month in Key West, Florida, did not resolve the bitter controversy over the postwar roles and missions of the services—"who will do what with what," as Forrestal put it.[144] It did, according to Paul Hammond, "emphasize the duty of the Joint Chiefs to provide the Defense Department integrated, or unified, military staff plans, rather than compilations of service-oriented plans.[145] The JCS did their duty, approving a short-range emergency war plan for planning purposes on 19 May 1948.[146] The heart of the plan's strategic concept was "initially, to launch a powerful air offensive designed to exploit the destructive and psychological power of atomic weapons against the vital elements of the Soviet war-making capacity."[147] The air offensive would be launched from bases in England and in the Khartoum-Cairo-Suez area.[148]

Even before agreement on a war plan, however, the Air Force had taken some steps to assure access to southern rim bases. At the end of October 1947, Symington told Gen Hoyt S. Vandenberg, Air Force vice chief of staff, that work should begin immediately on establishing a base in North Africa.[149] In early December, after James M. Landis, chairman of the Civil Aeronautics Board, wrote Forrestal asking whether the civil airlines needed to continue to operate the North African coastal route, Symington replied on behalf of the secretary of defense that the Air Force believed operation of this route by an American air carrier to be in the interests of national security and that the Air Force was taking action to reopen Wheelus Field, Tripoli.[150] A few days later, the State Department agreed to instruct the US Embassy in London to finalize negotiations with the British for the continued use by the USAF of Wheelus Field and Mingaladon Field, Burma.[151] At the crucial meeting in January 1948 between Forrestal, Symington, Spaatz, and Vandenberg, when all conceded the importance of the Mediterranean since "decisive action over the polar ice cap" was not then practical, the Air Force objective was identified as getting "a footing in North Africa and then look[ing] for bases closer to the enemy from which the war could be brought home to him."[152] The next day, however, Major General Gruenther, Joint Staff director, told Forrestal he thought "the question of air bases in North

Africa implies a narrow limitation on our needs in the event of war. He said what we were really talking about was bases in the Eastern Mediterranean and in the Middle East."[153]

Once the JCS had decided on a war plan, base planning became less diffuse, more realistic, and more closely tied to war planning. In August 1948, when the JCS again submitted requirements for overseas base rights to the State Department, the military asked for joint or participating rights at 19 locations—all but one along Russia's southern rim.[154] In the spring of 1949 the JCS completed another overall review of overseas base requirements. The spotlight was clearly on bases in the United Kingdom, along the North African, Middle Eastern, South Asian routes, and in the far north. Among the rights the JCS declared to be "a matter of urgency" was:

> the right to supplement the British effort to improve the medium bomber bases of Abu Sueir, Suez Canal Zone; Khomaksar, Aden; and such other air bases in this area as may be necessary to implement current emergency war plans; and the following bases in the U.K.: Brize Norton, Upper Heyford, Fairford, and one additional base [not specified].[155]

In April, the National Security Council reinforced the military's desire for the development of British and Egyptian airfields, necessary for emergency war plans, recommending that "the President direct the Secretary of State to undertake negotiations with the British Government regarding the provision of funds required for the construction of the airfields envisaged."[156] Base planning seemed, finally, to be heading in a clear and purposeful direction.

* * *

Between 1946 and 1948 military base planning adjusted (often slowly) to postwar realities. The JCS accommodated sharply lower postwar defense expenditures and hostile foreign reactions to American requests for base rights by reducing base requirements. The lack of funding and difficulties in securing base rights contributed to a shift in strategic emphasis from far northern bases to bases along Russia's southern rim. The low defense budget, for example, forced reliance on a strategic air offensive which, in turn, called for bases in the United Kingdom,

North Africa, the Middle East, and South Asia. Resistance to an American military presence in such strategic locations as Iceland also prompted strategists to look elsewhere for base rights. So too did the harsh reality of the Arctic environment and perceived Soviet aggression in Iran, Greece, and Turkey.

Yet, the geographic reorientation of American strategy had little impact on base planning until its marriage to war planning in 1948. The road to a symbiotic relationship between base planning and war planning had been a long one. In 1947, the lack of a war plan was probably the most important reason for JCS 570/83's strategic unreality (although the critical shortage of funds required to develop a base system and the State Department's aversion to negotiating for an expanded program of base rights were also significant influences). Throughout this long process, military staff officers drew up their plans in an environment interlaced with international, domestic, and bureaucratic politics. But unlike their predecessors in 1943–45, the postwar architects of plans such as JCS 570/83 openly acknowledged the result of their work to have been shaped by influences other than a purist's conception of the requirements of military strategy.

Notes

1. Secretary of War Robert P. Patterson, memorandum for the chief of staff, 30 January 1946, file 686, box 326, Army Chief of Staff Decimal File, 1946, Record Group (RG) 165 (Records of the War Department General and Special Staffs), National Archives (NA).

2. Ibid.

3. G. A. L. [George A. Lincoln], memorandum for General Hull, 31 January 1946, sec. 1E, box 613 Top Secret (TS), file ABC 686 (6 November 1943), ABC Decimal File, 1942–1948, Operations Division (OPD), RG 319 (Records of the Army Staff), NA. Document is now declassified.

4. Ibid., General Hull, memorandum for Colonel Tate, n.d., sec. 9, box 622TS. Document is now declassified.

5. Robert P. Patterson, to secretary of state, letter, 11 February 1946, file SWNCC 38 Series, Navy Operational Archives (NOA), Washington D.C.

6. Message from Ernest Bevin, British foreign secretary to Lord Halifax, British ambassador to the United States, 27 November 1945, in annex to memorandum of conversation, by the secretary of state, 29 November 1945, *Foreign Relations of the United States 1945*, vol. 6, *The British Common-*

wealth; The Far East (hereafter *Foreign Relations, 1945,* vol. 6), (Washington, D.C.: Government Printing Office (GPO), 1964), 216–17.

7. Ibid.

8. Walter Millis and E. S. Duffield, eds., *The Forrestal Diaries* (New York: Viking Press, 1951), 295. Forrestal once referred to President Truman as "the most rocklike example of civilian control the world has ever witnessed." Quoted by John Lewis Gaddis, "Harry S. Truman and the Origins of Containment," in Frank J. Merli and Theodore A. Wilson, eds., *Makers of American Diplomacy from Theodore Roosevelt to Henry Kissinger* (New York: Charles Scribner's Sons, 1974), 207.

9. Quoted in Robert G. Albion and Robert H. Connery, *Forrestal and the Navy* (New York: Columbia University Press, 1962), 240.

10. Ibid.

11. Forrestal Diary, September 1946–1947, passim, Papers of James V. Forrestal (hereafter Forrestal Papers), Seeley G. Mudd Library, Princeton University.

12. Albion and Connery, 158, 190–93; and minutes of the 33d Meeting of the Top Policy Group, 24 September 1945, box 2, Records of Secretary of the Navy James Forrestal, 1940–1947, RG 80 (General Records of the Department of the Navy), NA.

13. See chapter 2, 84–85.

14. Minutes of the 25th Meeting of the SWNCC (State-War-Navy Coordinating Committee), 21 September 1945, sec. 2, file CCS 334 SANACC (12-19-44), RG 218 (Records of the United States Joint Chiefs of Staff [JCS]), NA; The Operation of the SANACC, 17 February 1948, box 5, SWNCC-SANACC, RG 353 (Records of Interdepartmental and Intradepartmental Committees-State Department), NA. Leo Pasvolsky, special assistant to the secretary of state for international organization and security affairs, suggested in November 1945, that perhaps the time had come for the JCS to be represented on the SWNCC. But James C. Dunn, the State Department member of the SWNCC, said the secretaries of war and Navy would not agree. The two service secretaries, said Dunn, thought the JCS should be consulted but "wished to keep political decisions in their own departments and had set up SWNCC for the purpose of excluding the Joint Chiefs of Staff from actual formulation of such decisions." Minutes of the 167th Meeting of the Secretary of State's Staff Committee, 13 November 1945, *Foreign Relations of the United States, 1946,* vol. 1, *General, The United Nations* (hereafter *Foreign Relations, 1946,* vol. 1) (Washington D.C.: GPO, 1972), 1122.

15. Minutes of the Meetings of the Committee of Three, 1944–1947 (hereafter, Minutes, Committee of Three), 20 February 1946, Diplomatic Branch Reference File, NA.

16. "It [Patterson's letter] would certainly have been pertinent to the last Top Three meeting of February when it was decided that every effort would be made to prune down our requirements to a minimum," the aide noted. Memorandum to the secretary, from Edward Hidalgo, 23 February 1946, file CNO TS 1946, A4-2/NB, CNO Records, NOA. Document is now declassified.

17. Minutes, Committee of Three, 28 February 1946; Forrestal Diary, vol. 4, 28 February 1946, Forrestal Papers; James Forrestal, secretary of the Navy, letter to the secretary of state, 28 February 1946, file ABC 686 (6 November 1943), sec. 1G, box 614TS, ABC Decimal File, 1942–1948, OPD, RG 319. Document is now declassified.

18. Adm D. C. Ramsey, memorandum for the secretary of the Navy, 20 February 1946, folder Postwar Bases, file CNO TS 1946, A4-2/NB, CNO Records, NOA; JF [James Forrestal] to Admiral Ramsey, 21 Feburary 1946, file 48-1-24, box 90, Records of Secretary of the Navy James Forrestal, 1940–1947, RG 80; unsigned memorandum for the secretary of the Navy, 22 February 1946, folder U.S. Post-war Base Requirements, file CNO TS 1946, A16-3/EN, CNO Records, NOA. Documents are now declassified.

19. The JCS received a copy of this letter, but from the State Department through the SWNCC. SWNCC 38/20, 9 October 1945, sec. 9, file CCS 360 (12-9-42), RG 218.

20. Minutes, Committee of Three, 28 February 1946.

21. G. A. L. [George A. Lincoln], memorandum for record, 2 March 1946, file ABC 686 (6 November 1943), sec. 1G, box 614TS, ABC Decimal File 1942–1948, OPD, RG 319. Document is now declassified.

22. Ibid., proposed memorandum for the secretary of the Navy from the secretary of war, 2 March 1946. The draft for Patterson's signature stated in part:

> In accordance with the directive of the President, dated 1 February 1944, that, subject to the approval of the Secretaries of War and the Navy on matters involving departmental policy, the Joint Chiefs of Staff will be the coordinating agency in regard to military guidance to be furnished to the State Department. On the matter of military bases, the Joint Chiefs of Staff studies on these matters presenting a joint integration of requirements, have been prepared and forwarded to the Secretary of State after approval of the War and Navy Department's members of the State-War-Navy Coordinating Committee. . . . It appears there should be a clear meeting of minds as to whether it is proposed to continue along the lines of the President's directive . . .; or, alternately, whether the War Department should now parallel the separate action initiated by the Navy Department, leaving to the State Department and other governmental agencies the problem of assuring adequate coordination. I question the soundness of the latter procedure. [Document is now declassified].

23. Ibid., G. A. L. [George A. Lincoln], memorandum for General Craig, 2 March 1946.

24. Ibid., G. A. L. [George A. Lincoln], memorandum for General Hull, 9 March 1946.

25. Minutes, Committee of Three, 28 February 1946; Forrestal Diary, vol. 4, 28 February 1946, Forrestal Papers.

26. Minutes, Committee of Three, 28 February 1946.

27. Ibid., 20 February 1946. Forrestal spoke up in behalf of Manus and New Guinea; Patterson mentioned the Galapagos.

28. Ibid., 28 February 1946. This is not surprising since, as the reader will recall, someone in the AAF had pointed out the strategic significance of airfields on the southern rim of Asia in early August 1945.

29. Ibid.

30. Quoted in Daniel Yergin, *Shattered Peace: The Origins of the Cold War and the National Security State* (Boston: Houghton Mifflin, 1977), 167.

31. Ibid. On 27 February 1946, Byrnes complimented Kennan on his "splendid analysis," 172. See also Forrestal Diary, vol. 4, 22 February 1946, Forrestal Papers; and Millis and Duffield, 135–40.

32. Yergin, 174–78.

33. R. F. T., memorandum for record, subject: Conference at State Department to Discuss Base Requirements, 12 March 1946, file ABC 686 (6 November 1943), sec. 1G, box 614TS, ABC Decimal File, 1942–1948, OPD, RG 319. On the other hand, the military felt permanent base rights in the Azores need not be sought immediately; for the present, temporary rights to support occupation forces in Europe would satisfy the JCS. Document is now declassified.

34. Minutes of Joint Planning Staff (JPS) 242d meeting, 20 March 1946, sec. 17, file CCS 360 (12-9-42), RG 218. For other evidence of Navy dissatisfaction (Admirals Leahy and Nimitz) with bases south of the equator, see Capt R. L. Dennison, memorandum for Admiral Nimitz, subject: Pacific Island Bases, 11 February 1946, file SWNCC 38 Series, NOA.

35. Joint Chiefs of Staff Decision on JCS 570/58, Overall Examination of U.S. Requirements for Military Bases and Base Rights, 23 March 1946, file CCS 360 (12-9-42), sec. 17, RG 218.

36. For the various drafts of the 1946 modification to JCS 570/40, see JPS 684/17, Overall Examination of U.S. Requirements for Military Bases and Base Rights, 12 April 1946; JPS 684/18, Overall Examination of U.S. Requirements for Military Bases and Base Rights, 27 April 1946, both in file CCS 360 (12-9-42), sec. 18, RG 218. The final draft is JCS 570/62, Overall Examination of U.S. Requirements for Military Rights, 15 May 1946, file CCS 360 (12-9-42), sec. 19, RG 218. JCS 570/62 was submitted to the SWNCC on 4 June 1946, becoming SWNCC 38/35, Overall Examination of U.S. Requirements for Military Rights, 5 June 1946, printed in *Foreign Relations, 1946,* vol. 1, 1174–77.

37. *Foreign Relations, 1946,* vol. 1, 1174–75, SWNCC 38/35, Overall Examination of U.S. Requirements for Military Rights, 5 June 1946. For other examples of military frustration over the confusion between bases and rights, see R. F. T., memorandum for record, subject: Conference at State Department to Discuss Base Requirements, 12 March 1946, file ABC 686 (6 November 1943), sec. 1G, box 614TS, ABC Decimal File, 1942–1948, OPD, RG 319; unsigned memorandum for the Joint Staff Planners, 25 March 1946, file ABC 686 (6 November 1943), sec. 1C, box 612TS, ABC Decimal File, 1942–1948, OPD, RG 319; unsigned memorandum for the assistant secretary of war, subject: Resume of Base Rights of JCS 570/40 Bases, 5 March

1946, file ABC 686 (6 November 1943), sec. 1G, box 614TS, ABC Decimal File, 1942–1948, OPD, RG 319. Documents are now declassified.

38. Minutes of JPS 245th meeting, 17 April 1946 (hereafter JPS 245th meeting, 17 April 1946), sec. 18, file CCS 360 (12-9-42), RG 218.

39. Captain Dennison, memorandum for Op-30 (Op-35 MNO, serial no. 000163P35), 25 March 1946, SWNCC 38 series, NOA.

40. Ibid.

41. SWNCC 38/35, Overall Examination of U.S. Requirements for Military Rights, 5 June 1946, in *Foreign Relations, 1946*, vol. 1, 1174–77.

42. Ibid.

43. JPS 245th meeting, 17 April 1946.

44. Brig Gen F. F. Everest, Army Air Forces (AAF) member of the JPS, memorandum for Gardner, Lincoln, and Campbell, subject: Review of JCS 570/40, 28 June 1946, file ABC 686 (6 November 1943), sec. 1C, box 612TS, ABC Decimal File, 1942–1948, OPD, RG 319. Document is now declassified.

45. Minutes of Air Staff meeting, 17 May 1946, file Minutes of Air Staff Meetings, box 621, Spaatz Papers, Library of Congress (LOC) (hereafter Spaatz Papers).

46. O.S.P., memorandum for Colonel Wood, 3 August 1946; extract of minutes of JPS meeting, 3 July 1946; both in file ABC 686 (6 November 43), sec. 1C, box 612TS, ABC Decimal File, 1942–1948, OPD, RG 319, NA. Documents are now declassified.

47. Ibid., Col John H. Ives, memorandum for General Everest, n.d.

48. Statement by General Spaatz before the US Senate Military Affairs Committee, 15 November 1945, file Addresses and Articles by General Spaatz, box 268, Spaatz Papers.

49. Gen Carl A. Spaatz, "Air Power in the Atomic Age," *Collier's*, 8 December 1945, 11–12 and 83–84.

50. Ibid.; presentation to members of the US Senate Appropriations Committee, Pentagon, 30 April 1946, file Chief of Staff General Correspondence, 1 April–28 May 46, box 250, Spaatz Papers; *New York Herald Tribune*, 27 October 1946, clipping reporting speech by General Spaatz in file Addresses and Articles by General Spaatz, box 268, Spaatz Papers.

51. Spaatz, "Air Power in the Atomic Age," 12.

52. Minutes, Committee of Three, 22 May 1946.

53. General Spaatz to Twohey (news analyst), 31 October 1946, file Chief of Staff General Correspondence, 31 October 1946, box 250, Spaatz Papers.

54. Adm M. B. Gardner, memorandum for Generals Everest and Lincoln, subject: Review of JCS 570/40, 2 July 1946; extract of JPS meeting of 3 July 1946, both in file ABC 686 (6 November 1943), sec. 1C, box 612TS, ABC Decimal File, 1942–1948, OPD, RG 319. The Army and AAF interpreted the Navy's opposition as a "Navy party line" designed "to minimize the importance of the northern approaches especially from the point of view of air operations by VHBs [very heavy bombers]." Documents are now declassified.

55. Col T. C. Musgrave Jr., memorandum for General Spaatz, 8 January 1947, file Navy 2, box 262, Spaatz Papers.

56. Vice Adm Forrest P. Sherman, address to the Senate Armed Services Committee, 23 January 1947 (hereafter Sherman address), file A16-3 Warfare Operations, box 110, series 5, Records of the Strategic Plans Division, NOA.

57. Enclosure no. 2, Troop Deployment for U.S. Peacetime Overseas Bases, War Department Plan for U.S. Peacetime Overseas Bases, 14 February 1946, file AG 322TS (4 Feburary 1946), box 16, Records of the Assistant Secretary of War for Air, RG 407 (Records of the Adjutant General's Office), NA; War Department Plan for Overseas Bases (Post Occupation Period), 1 May 1947, file 68-AAF Bases and Fields (Foreign), box 187R, Decimal File 1947, 68-800, RG 107 (Records of the Secretary of War), NA. Documents are now declassified.

58. Bases along the northeast corridor (Greenland, Iceland, northeast Canada, Newfoundland, and the Azores) do not show a corresponding increase (in fact, the figures drop from 62,000 to 14,000) because the United States had not been able to obtain the necessary rights. Enclosure no. 2, Troop Deployment for U.S. Peacetime Overseas Bases, War Department Plan for U.S. Peacetime Overseas Bases, 14 February 1946, file AG 322TS (4 Feburary 1946), box 16, Records of the Assistant Secretary of War for Air, RG 407 (Records of the Adjutant General's Office), NA; War Department Plan for Overseas Bases (Post Occupation Period), 1 May 1947, file 68-AAF Bases and Fields (Foreign), box 187R, Decimal File 1947, 68-800, RG 107 (Records of the Secretary of War), NA. Documents are now declassified.

59. Enclosure no. 2, Troop Deployment for U.S. Peacetime Overseas Bases, War Department Plan for U.S. Peacetime Overseas Bases, 14 February 1946, file AG 322TS (4 Feburary 1946), box 16, Records of the Assistant Secretary of War for Air, RG 407 (Records of the Adjutant General's Office), NA; War Department Plan for Overseas Bases (Post Occupation Period), 1 May 1947, file 68-AAF Bases and Fields (Foreign), box 187R, Decimal File 1947, 68-800, RG 107 (Records of the Secretary of War), NA. Documents are now declassified.

60. Maj Gen Guy V. Henry, US Army, chairman of the Joint Canadian-US Military Cooperation Committee, memorandum for assistant chief of staff, OPD, Western Hemisphere section, subject: ATC [Air Transport Command] Route between Iceland and Alaska, 10 June 1946, file 360.4, Airways and Routes, box 631, DF Classified 1946–1947, AAF AAG, RG 18 (Records of the AAF), NA; Harry R. Borowski, *A Hollow Threat: Strategic Air Power and Containment Before Korea* (Westport, Conn., and London: Greenwood Press, 1982), 78–79. Document is now declassified.

61. Borowski, 79.

62. Ibid., 79–81.

63. Spaatz, "Air Power in the Atomic Age," 12.

64. Borowski, 81–86.

65. Ibid., 87.

66. Maj Gen Clements McMullen to chief of staff, USAF, subject: Cornwallis Air Strip, 12 November 1947, file Command Strategic, box 257, Spaatz Papers.

67. Ibid., Spaatz to commanding general, Strategic Air Command (SAC), 15 April 1948.

68. Lt Gen Ira C. Eaker, "The Army Air Forces: Its Status, Plans and Policies," address delivered at the National War College, Washington, D.C., 5 June 1947, file 168.6008-3, Vandenberg, August 1947–June 1951, Papers of Lt Gen Ennis C. Whitehead, USAF Historical Research Agency (AFHRA), Maxwell AFB, Ala.; statement of Gen Carl Spaatz before the President's Air Policy Commission, 17 November 1947, 2343, President's Air Policy Commission Records, Harry S. Truman Library (hereafter Truman Papers), Independence, Mo.

69. Forrestal, memorandum for the president, 6 January 1948, folder Secretary of Defense Report Data, box 156, Subject File, President's Secretary's Files, Truman Papers.

70. Spaatz, "Air Power in the Atomic Age," 12.

71. JWPC 416/1 (Revised), Military Position of the United States in the Light of Russian Policy, 8 January 1946, 15, sec. 3, file CCS 092 USSR (3-27-45), RG 218, 48–51.

72. Presentation to members of the US Senate Appropriations Committee, Pentagon, 30 April 1946, file Chief of Staff General Correspondence, 1 April–28 May 46, box 250, Spaatz Papers.

73. Yergin, 233–35. General Eisenhower was an exception.

74. Ibid., 279–80.

75. Ibid., 280–82.

76. Ibid., 283.

77. Ibid., 294.

78. Ibid., 295.

79. The State Department anticipated that the Soviet Union would request the right to establish a base on Bornholm Island. In the briefing book prepared for the Potsdam Conference, the State Department, although preferring continued Danish sovereignty over Bornholm, nonetheless recommended the United States not oppose Soviet demands for the base since the Russians might interpret US opposition as unjustified interference in a purely Soviet-Danish matter and because restraint would tend to strengthen the US case for base rights in Greenland. See "The Berlin Conference Agenda Proposed by the Department of State," vol. 3, Territorial Studies, Europe, Summary of Bornholm Question: Soviet Occupation of Bornholm, 3 July 1945, box 1, President's Naval Aide: Office Files (Security File), Truman Papers; and *New Times*, 1 April 1946, 21.

80. Yergin, 118, 123, and 126.

81. Minutes, Committee of Three, 16 October 1945.

82. Walter Brown Diary, 1 October 1945, folder 602, file Conferences 2-1 Potsdam, Papers of James F. Byrnes, Special Collections, Robert Muldrow Cooper Library, Clemson University, Clemson, S.C.

83. Minutes, Committee of Three, 16 October 1945.

84. James L. Gormly, "Keeping the Door Open in Saudi Arabia: The United States and the Dhahran Airfield, 1945–1946," *Diplomatic History* 4, no. 2 (spring 1980): 198.

85. The following documents, all in RG 218, are some of the key Pincher studies: JWPC 432/5, Staff Studies of Certain Military Operations Deriving

from Concept of Operations for Pincher, 10 June 1946, sec. 2, file CCS 381 USSR (3-2-46); JWPC 432/7, Tentative Over All Strategic Concept and Estimate of Initial Operations, Short Title: Pincher, 18 June 1946, sec. 2, file CCS 381 USSR (3-2-46); JWPC 475/1, Strategic Study of the Area between the Alps and the Himalayas, Short Title: Caldron, 2 November 1946, sec. 3, file CCS 381 USSR (3-2-46); JIS 267/1/F (rev.), Intelligence Estimate of Specific Areas in Southern Europe, the Middle and Near East, and Northern Africa (Soviet Objectives and Capabilities), 14 January 1947, sec. 4, file CCS 381 USSR (3-2-46); JWPC 474/1, Strategic Study of Western and Northern Europe, 13 May 1947, sec. 20, file CCS 092 USSR (3-27-45); JWPC 476/1, The Soviet Threat in the Far East and the Means Required to Oppose It, Short Title: Moonrise, 16 June 1947, sec. 5, file CCS 381 USSR (3-2-46); JWPC 473/1, Strategic Study of the Northeastern Approaches to the North American Continent, Short Title: Deerland, 30 September 1947, sec. 7, file CCS 381 USSR (3-2-46). Documents initiating the preparation of a war plan are: JWPC 496, Global Planning Estimate, 16 July 1947, sec. 6, file CCS 381 USSR (3-2-46); and PM 573, 29 August 1947, file CCS 381 USSR (3-2-46). The first product of the JCS efforts to create a war plan was JSPG 496/1, Broiler, 8 November 1947, sec. 8, file CCS 381 USSR (3-2-46).

86. JWPC 475/1, Strategic Study of the Area between the Alps and the Himalayas, 2 November 1946, sec. 3, file CCS 381 USSR (3-2-46), RG 218, 12–13 and 15–16; JWPC 474/1, Strategic Study of Western and Northern Europe, 13 May 1947, sec. 20, file CCS 092 USSR (3-27-45), RG 218, 5; JSPG 496/1, Broiler, 8 November 1947, sec. 8, file CCS 381 USSR (3-2-46), RG 218, 18–19.

87. JWPC 432/7, Tentative Overall Strategic Concept and Estimate of Initial Operations, Short Title: Pincher, 18 June 1946, sec. 2, file CCS 381 USSR (3-2-46), RG 218, 6 and 10; JWPC 475/1, Strategic Study of the Area between the Alps and the Himalayas, 2 November 1946, sec. 3, file CCS 381 USSR (3-2-46), RG 218, 13; JIS 267/1/F (rev.), Intelligence Estimate of Specific Areas in Southern Europe, the Middle and Near East, and Northern Africa (Soviet Objectives and Capabilities), 14 January 1947, sec. 4, file CCS 381 USSR (3-2-46), RG 218, 1; and JSPG 496/1, Broiler, 8 November 1947, sec. 8, file CCS 381 USSR (3-2-46), RG 218, 19.

88. JWPC 432/5, Staff Studies of Certain Military Operations Deriving from Concept of Operations for Pincher, 10 June 1946, sec. 2, file CCS 381 USSR (3-2-46), RG 218, 5; JWPC 432/7, Tentative Overall Strategic Concept and Estimate of Initial Operations, Short Title: Pincher, 18 June 1946, sec. 2, file CCS 381 USSR (3-2-46), RG 218, 10; and JIS 267/1/F (rev.), Intelligence Estimate of Specific Areas in Southern Europe, the Middle and Near East, and Northern Africa (Soviet Objectives and Capabilities), 14 January 1947, sec. 4, file CCS 381 USSR (3-2-46), RG 218, 6.

89. JWPC 432/5, Staff Studies of Certain Military Operations Deriving from Concept of Operations for Pincher, 10 June 1946, sec. 2, file CCS 381 USSR (3-2-46), RG 218, 8; JWPC 432/7, Tentative Overall Strategic Concept and Estimate of Initial Operations, Short Title: Pincher, 18 June 1946, sec. 2, file CCS 381 USSR (3-2-46), RG 218, 10, 12, and 15; JWPC 474/1,

Strategic Study of Western and Northern Europe, 13 May 1947, sec. 20, file CCS 092 USSR (3-27-45), RG 218, 2, 36, and 46; and JSPG 496/1, Broiler, 8 November 1947, sec. 8, file CCS 381 USSR (3-2-46), RG 218, 25.

90. JWPC 432/7, Tentative Overall Strategic Concept and Estimate of Initial Operations, Short Title: Pincher, 18 June 1946, sec. 2, file CCS 381 USSR (3-2-46), RG 218, 20.

91. Ibid., JWPC 496, Global Planning Estimate, 16 July 1947, sec. 6, 2–3. For similar versions of the strategic concept, see JWPC 475/1, Strategic Study of the Area between the Alps and the Himalayas, 2 November 1946, sec. 3; and JSPG 496/1, Broiler, 8 November 1947, sec. 8, RG 218, 7.

92. Sherman address.

93. JWPC 416/1 (rev.), Military Position of the United States in the Light of Russian Policy, 8 January 1946, sec. 3, file CCS 092 USSR (3-2-45), RG 218; and JWPC 432/5, Staff Studies of Certain Military Operations Deriving from Concept of Operations for Pincher, 10 June 1946, sec. 2, file CCS 381 USSR (3-2-46), RG 218, 24–26.

94. JSPG 496/1, Broiler, 8 November 1947, sec. 8, RG 218, 9 and 45.

95. Ibid., JWPC 432/5, Staff Studies of Certain Military Operations Deriving from Concept of Operations for Pincher, 10 June 1946, sec. 2, 20.

96. JWPC 474/1, Strategic Study of Western and Northern Europe, 13 May 1947, sec. 20, file CCS 092 USSR (3-27-45), RG 218, 30.

97. Charles H. Hildreth, *Short History and Chronology of the USAF in the United Kingdom* (Historical Division, Office of Information, Third Air Force, United States Air Forces in Europe, May 1967), 2 and 10; Brig Gen F. F. Everest, memorandum for General Spaatz, subject: Briefing Material for European Trip, 21 June 1946, box 250, Spaatz Papers.

98. JWPC 474/1, Strategic Study of Western and Northern Europe, 13 May 1947, sec. 20, file CCS 092 USSR (3-27-45), RG 218, 30.

99. JWPC 432/5, Staff Studies of Certain Military Operations Deriving from Concept of Operations for Pincher, 10 June 1946, sec. 2, file CCS 381 USSR (3-2-46), RG 218, 20.

100. JWPC 474/1, Strategic Study of Western and Northern Europe, 13 May 1947, sec. 20, file CCS 092 USSR (3-27-45), RG 218, 30.

101. Chart titled Bombing Radii of Action from Potential Bases, in JWPC 432/7, Tentative Over All Strategic Concept and Estimate of Initial Operations, Short Title: Pincher, 18 June 1946, sec. 2, file CCS 381 USSR (3-2-46), RG 218; and same cite, chart titled Petroleum and Mining Target Coverage in JSPG/4, Joint Outline War Plan, 11 February 1946, sec. 10.

102. JWPC 496, Global Planning Estimate, 16 July 1947, sec. 6, file CCS 381 USSR (3-2-46), RG 218, 6. See also JWPC 474/1, Strategic Study of Western and Northern Europe, 13 May 1947, sec. 20, file CCS 092 USSR (3-27-45), RG 218, 30.

103. See chart titled Bombing Radii of Action from Potential Bases, in JWPC 432/7, Tentative Over All Strategic Concept and Estimate of Initial Operations, Short Title: Pincher, 18 June 1946, sec. 2, file CCS 381 USSR (3-2-46), RG 218.

104. JWPC 416/1 (rev.), Military Position of the United States in the Light of Russian Policy, 8 January 1946, sec. 3, file CCS 092 USSR (3-27-45), RG 218. See also JWPC 475/1, Strategic Study of the Area between the Alps and the Himalayas, 2 November 1946, sec. 3, file CCS 381 USSR (3-2-46), RG 218; JWPC 432/5, Staff Studies of Certain Military Operations Deriving from Concept of Operations for Pincher, 10 June 1946, sec. 2, RG 218; and JWPC 432/7, Tentative Over All Strategic Concept and Estimate of Initial Operations, Short Title: Pincher, 18 June 1946, RG 218; Sherman address; JWPC 474/1, Strategic Study of Western and Northern Europe, 13 May 1947, sec. 20, file CCS 092 USSR (3-27-45), RG 218; and JSPG 496/1, Broiler, 8 November 1947, sec. 8, file CCS 381 USSR (3-2-46), RG 218.

105. JWPC 475/1, Strategic Study of the Area between the Alps and the Himalayas, 2 November 1946, sec. 3, RG 218, 136.

106. JCS 1656, U.S. Security Interests in the Disposition of Tripolitania, 15 April 1946, sec. 6, file CCS 092 USSR (3-27-45), RG 218; and JWPC 475/1, Strategic Study of the Area between the Alps and the Himalayas, 2 November 1946, sec. 3, file CCS 381 USSR (3-2-46), RG 218, 15.

107. JWPC 475/1, Strategic Study of the Area between the Alps and the Himalayas, 2 November 1946, sec. 3, file CCS 381 USSR (3-2-46), RG 218, 15.

108. Ibid., JSPG 496/1, Broiler, 8 November 1947, sec. 8, 20; JIS 267/1/F (rev.), Intelligence Estimate of Specific Areas in Southern Europe, the Middle and Near East, and Northern Africa (Soviet Objectives and Capabilities), 14 January 1947, sec. 4, RG 218, 2.

109. Forrestal, memorandum for the president, 6 January 1948, folder Secretary of Defense Report Data, box 156, Subject File, President's Secretary's Files, Truman Papers.

110. This was never a clear-cut process. The military never came to view an area—except perhaps the Pacific south of the equator—as without strategic value. North Atlantic bases, for example, always remained important for defensive, if not offensive, reasons.

111. JPS 684/29, Overall Examination of U.S. Requirements for Military Bases and Base Rights, 13 February 1947, sec. 29, file CCS 360 (12-9-42), RG 218.

112. Ibid., PM-485, 4 March 1947.

113. Ibid., PM-534, 27 May 1947.

114. Ibid., for successive drafts of the 1947 base plan, see JPS 684/29, Over All Examination of U.S. Requirements for Military Bases and Base Rights, 13 February 1947; JPS 684/30, Over All Examination of U.S. Requirements for Military Bases and Base Rights, 18 April 1947, file ABC 686 (6 November 1943), sec. 1K, box 616TS, ABC Decimal File, 1942–1948, OPD, RG 319; and JPS 684/31, Over All Examination of U.S. Requirements for Military Bases and Base Rights, 24 June 1946, sec. 29, file CCS 360 (12-9-42), RG 218. The final draft is JCS 570/83, Over All Examination of U.S. Requirements for Military Bases and Base Rights, 12 August 1947, file ABC 686 (6 November 1943), sec. 1K, box 616TS, ABC Decimal File, 1942–1948, OPD, RG 319. JCS 570/83 was submitted to the SWNCC on 6 September 1947, becoming SWNCC 38/46,

printed in *Foreign Relations of the United States, 1947*, vol. 1, *General, The United Nations* (hereafter *Foreign Relations, 1947*, vol. 1) (Washington D.C.: GPO, 1972), 766–70. Documents are now declassified.

115. JCS 570/83, annex to appendix B (Tabulation of Base Data), Over All Examination of U.S. Requirements for Military Bases and Base Rights, 12 August 1947, file ABC 686 (6 November 1943), sec. 1K, box 616TS, ABC Decimal File, 1942–1948, OPD, RG 319. The JCS simplified the 1947 plan by dropping the "secondary" and "minor" categories contained in JCS 570/40. Documents are now declassified.

116. Ibid., 667.

117. Ibid., 668 and 672.

118. Ibid., 670–71. Both JCS 570/40 and JCS 570/62 (the mid-1946 modification to JCS 570/40) had used the confusing terms "essential" and "required."

119. Ibid., 665.

120. Ibid., 679.

121. Ibid., 665.

122. The War Department's OPD admitted base requirements should be determined by "national needs" rather than dollar availability, but also pointed out that "an inflexible plan which does not admit realities of fund limitations . . . can only lead to a dispersion of effort rather than an economy of means. The specific danger is that the provision of American standards of living for forces deployed at relatively unimportant bases will drain off vital resources needed at high priority bases thus delaying the full development of technical and operating facilities beyond the danger point." Unsigned memorandum on revision of JPS 684/29, 28 February 1947, file ABC 686 (6 November 1943), sec. 1J, box 616TS, ABC Decimal File, 1942–1948, OPD, RG 319. Even the AAF, usually the least inclined among the services to bow to fiscal constraints, conceded that "the recent era of unlimited funds for military purposes is definitely over and, therefore, we must realistically attempt attainment of cohesive planning with respect to our base developments." Brig Gen W. L. Ritchie, AAF member of the Joint Staff Planners, memorandum for Glover, Lincoln, and Carter, 23 May 1947, enclosure to PM-534, Over All Examination of U.S. Requirements for Military Bases and Base Rights, 27 May 1947, sec. 29, file CCS 360 (12-9-42), RG 218.

123. JPS 684/30, annex B to appendix C (Size of Forces and Availability of Funds for Overseas Bases), Over All Examination of U.S. Requirements for Military Bases and Base Rights, 18 April 1947, file ABC 686 (6 November 1943), sec. 1K, box 616TS, ABC Decimal File, 1942–1948, OPD, RG 319. The actual federal budgets for fiscal years 1948–1950 were $32.95 billion, $39.47 billion, and $39.54 billion, respectively—twice the base planners' estimates. Actual military appropriations during the same years were $11.98, $12.19, and $9.91 billion. See series Y, 457–65, Outlays of the Federal Government: 1789–1970, *Historical Statistics of the United States: Colonial Times to 1970*, Bicentennial Edition, part 2 (Washington, D.C.: GPO, 1975), 1114. Document is now declassified.

124. JPS 684/30, Over All Examination of U. S. Requirements for Military Bases and Base Rights, 18 April 1947, file ABC 686 (6 November 1943), sec. 1K, box 616TS, ABC Decimal File, 1942–1948, OPD, RG 319. Document is now declassified.

125. Ibid.

126. Ibid.

127. Col Walter B. Bryte Jr., memorandum for Col R. B. Warren and Capt R. L. Dennison, n.d., unlabeled file, series 4, Political–Military Affairs Division Records, NOA.

128. Ibid.

129. Ibid.

130. Office of European Affairs, memorandum to Mr. Secretary, subject: U.S. Military Bases in Countries Dealt with by the Office of European Affairs, 16 January 1947, untitled folder marked "Lot no. 5," box 17, Reference Subject Files 1940–1947, Records of the Office of European Affairs, RG 59 (General Records of the Department of State), NA.

131. Unsigned memorandum on revision of JPS 684/29, 28 February 1947, file ABC 686 (6 November 1943), sec. 1J, box 616TS, ABC Decimal File, 1942–1948, OPD, RG 319. Document is now declassified.

132. Col J. E. Bastion Jr., memorandum for John D. Hickerson, subject: Over All Examination of U.S. Requirements for Military Base Rights, 10 March 1947, file P & O 686TS, sec. 4, cases 43–56, box 138TS, OPD, Decimal File, 1946–1948, RG 319; R. B. W. [R. B. Warren], memorandum for record, subject: Conference on Overall Base Planning, 13 March 1947, file ABC 686 (6 November 1943), sec. 1K, box 616TS, ABC Decimal File, 1942–1948, OPD, RG 319. This position is startling, given Sherman's testimony before Congress less than two months before that "the principal initial counter offensive efforts against Russia itself would consist of a strategic air offensive from bases in the British Isles and in the vicinity of Suez, and perhaps from India." Documents are now declassified.

133. John D. Hickerson, memorandum to Col J. E. Bastion Jr., 27 June 1947, file P & O 686TS, sec. 4, cases 43–56, box 138TS, OPD, Decimal File, 1946–1948, RG 319. Document is now declassified.

134. SWNCC 38/46, Over All Examination of U.S. Requirements for Military Bases and Base Rights, 9 September 1947, in *Foreign Relations, 1947*, vol. 1, 766.

135. JPS 684/30, tab to annex to appendix B (Divergent Views on Certain Bases), Over All Examination of U.S. Requirements for Military Bases and Base Rights, 18 April 1947; Lt Colonel Hutchin, memorandum for General Lincoln, 7 May 1947; Lt Colonel Hutchin, memorandum for General Lincoln, 15 May 1947, all in file ABC 686 (6 November 1943), sec. 1K, box 616TS, ABC Decimal File, 1942–1948, OPD, RG 319. Documents are now declassified.

136. Ibid. Col R. B. Warren, memorandum for Captain McLean and Lt Colonel Carlisle, subject: Revision of Overall Base Plan, 24 March 1947; tab to annex to appendix B (Divergent Views on Certain Bases), Over All Examination of U.S. Requirements for Military Bases and Base Rights, 18 April 1947; Lt

Colonel Hutchin, memorandum for General Lincoln, 7 May 1947; G. A. Lincoln, memorandum for Rear Adm C. D. Glover, Brig General Kissner, Captain Carter, subject: JPS 684/30, Over All Examination of U.S. Requirements for Military Bases and Base Rights, 13 May 1947; and Lt Colonel Hutchin, memorandum for General Lincoln, 15 May 1947.

137. JPS 684/30, tab to annex to appendix B (Divergent Views on Certain Bases), Over All Examination of U.S. Requirements for Military Bases and Base Rights, 18 April 1947, file ABC 686 (6 November 1943), sec. 1K, box 616TS, ABC Decimal File, 1942–1948, OPD, RG 319.

138. Ibid., G. A. Lincoln, memorandum for Admiral Glover, General Kissner, Captain Carter, subject: JPS 684/30, Over All Examination of U.S. Requirements for Military Bases and Base Rights, 13 May 1947.

139. Ibid., Admiral Glover, memorandum for Generals Lincoln and Kissner, subject: Recommended Changes to JPS 684/30, 24 April 1947; in same, Lt Colonel Hutchin, memorandum for General Lincoln, 7 May 1947; and Brig Gen William L. Ritchie, memorandum for Glover, Lincoln, and Carter, enclosure to PM-534, Over All Examination of U.S. Requirements for Military Bases and Base Rights, 27 May 1947, sec. 29, file CCS 360 (12-9-42), RG 218.

140. As we have seen, debate over the Azores, Ryukyus, Mariana-Bonin Islands, Hawaiian Islands, Panama and the Caribbean was probably more concerned with interservice politics than strategy.

141. By late 1947, the members of the Joint Staff Planners were Admiral Glover (Gardner's replacement), Navy Captain J. B. Carter, Army Brigadier General Schuyler (Lincoln's replacement), and Brigadier Generals A. W. Kissner and W. L. Ritchie, AAF.

142. PM-573, 29 August 1947, sec. 6, file CCS 381 USSR (3-2-46), RG 218. The plan submitted to the JCS in March 1948 was JCS 1844/1, Short Range Emergency Plan (Grabber), 17 March 1948, sec. 12, in the above file.

143. Ibid. Admiral Glover, memorandum for Maj Gen A. M. Gruenther, subject: Emergency War Plan (Brief), 13 March 1948.

144. Quoted in Russell F. Weigley, *The American Way of War: A History of United States Military Strategy and Policy* (New York: Macmillan Publishing Co., Inc., 1973), 375.

145. Paul Y. Hammond, *Organizing for Defense: The American Military Establishment in the Twentieth Century* (Princeton, N.J.: Princeton University Press, 1961), 237.

146. JCS 1844/4, Brief of Short Range Emergency War Plan, 19 May 1948, sec. 13, file CCS 381 USSR (3-2-46), RG 218.

147. Ibid., 32.

148. Ibid., 39. Bases in northwest India had been dropped from the war plans, perhaps because of the civil war taking place on the Indian subcontinent. Targets in the Soviet Far East were to be attacked from Okinawa in the Ryukyu Islands; these operations would be part of the strategic defensive intended for the Far East.

149. General Vandenberg, memorandum for Secretary of the Air Force Symington, subject: Air Transport Route North Africa, 31 October 1947, file

360.4, Airways and Routes, box 631, DF Classified 1946–1947, AAF AAG, RG 18. Document is now declassified.

150. Ibid., James M. Landis, chairman, Civil Aeronautics Board to the secretary of defense (Forrestal), 3 November 1947; and same cite, Secretary of the Air Force Symington to Landis, 1 December 1947.

151. Col Walter G. Bryte, memorandum for the record, subject: State Department Action Looking toward Reestablishment of North African Air Route, 11 December 1947, folder 135, box 64, Records of the ACC (Air Coordinating Committee), RG 340 (Records of the Secretary of the Air Force), NA.

152. James Forrestal, memorandum for the president, 6 January 1948, file Secretary of Defense Report Data, box 156, Subject File, President's Secretary's Files, Truman Papers.

153. Forrestal Diary, vol. 9, 7 January 1948, Forrestal Papers.

154. Memorandum by the JCS, Views of the Joint Chiefs of Staff on Over All Examination of United States Requirements for Military Bases and Base Rights, 21 August 1948, in *Foreign Relations of the United States, 1948*, vol. 1, part 2, *General: The United Nations* (Washington, D.C.: GPO, 1976), 603–4. These southern rim sites included: Casablanca, Algiers, Tripoli, Cairo- Suez area, Dhahran, Karachi, Oran (Algeria), Tunis-Bizerte (Tunisia), Massaua (Eritrea), Bahrein Island (Persian Gulf), Aden, Hadhramaut (Yemen), Oman, Trucial Oman, Socotra Island (Gulf of Aden), Foggia (Italy), and Kunming (China).

155. Study prepared by the JCS, Views of the Joint Chiefs of Staff on Military Rights in Foreign Territories, undated enclosure to the secretary of defense (Louis A. Johnson) to the secretary of state, 19 May 1949, in *Foreign Relations of the United States, 1949*, vol. 1, *National Security Affairs: Foreign Economic Policy* (Washington, D.C.: GPO, 1976), 304 and 300–11.

156. National Security Council Paper 45/1, "Airfield Construction in the U. K. (United Kingdom) and the Cairo-Suez Area," 15 April 1949, National Security Council Papers, Modern Military Records Branch, NA.

THIS PAGE INTENTIONALLY LEFT BLANK

Chapter 5

Conclusion

The scarring experience of relentless depression and unchecked aggression leading ultimately to world war profoundly affected American policy makers in the 1940s. While the war brought relief to the economy, many feared the depression would resume with the end of the fighting. The war, savagely fought across great distances with terrifying weapons, dashed traditional conceptions of national security. For these reasons, proposals for organizing postwar national and international affairs focused on ensuring prosperity and guaranteeing peace. The American military establishment's plans for a postwar overseas base system were part of the government's effort to address these goals.

Both President Roosevelt and Vice President Henry Wallace seemed able to glimpse the macrocosm of postwar peace and prosperity in strips of concrete airplane runways. Wallace saw their significance early on, recording in his diary in August 1942 that the disposition of air bases held by the Army "in some ways . . . is one of the most important of all the peace problems."[1] That same month he told Adolf Berle that "some mechanism should be worked out whereby these airports could be used in such a way as to increase the commercial traffic of the world" because "anything that helps the world in a big way is going to help the United States."[2] Along with the expansion of commerce, Wallace also wanted overseas airfields to be used as bases of operations for a truly international police force.[3] Roosevelt had a similar vision, and his request late in 1942 for the JCS to prepare a plan for worldwide facilities for a postwar international police force initiated the military's involvement in postwar base planning.[4]

Overseas bases were just one facet of military planning from 1942 to 1948 and an even smaller part of the government's overall postwar program. As developed in this book, however, the subject of overseas bases has been a focal point for examining issues of significance in the field of national security studies.

Among these are the nature of strategic military planning, the consequences of institutional or interservice rivalry, the intricacies of American civil-military relationships, and, ultimately, the character of US foreign policy in the early years of the Cold War.

Strategic military planning is a difficult undertaking, complicated by many variables, including national policy, weapons technology, enemy intentions and capabilities, national resources, and popular opinion. Since World War II, the dramatic acceleration in the speed and destructiveness of modern weapons combined with the proliferating interests of powerful nations in an interdependent, yet socially convulsive world have made the strategic planning task especially formidable— so filled with uncertainty that it may well be beyond the power of those charged with carrying it out to do so rationally. The officers who planned the postwar base system struggled with what were for them (and increasingly for their successors) apparently insoluble intellectual problems.

It is still fashionable to talk about the "military mind," and, carefully defined, the term may have some validity. However, no distinctively military mind was at work in postwar base planning. Most of the military planners, it is true, were career officers including a high percentage of service academy graduates. Yet, some of the most influential planners did not fit this pattern. Most of the officers in the ATC's Plans Division, for example, were civilians temporarily in uniform, having been civil airline executives before the war. One of their number, Capt Oliver J. Lissitzyn enjoyed a status in base planning out of proportion to his relatively junior rank. Following Roosevelt's visit to Alaska in mid-1944, Lissitzyn wrote the joint Army-Navy report directed by the president on postwar civil and military air routes and base facilities in Alaska. Then, in mid-1945, Lissitzyn served on the ad hoc study group formed in the Air Staff to prepare the AAF's reassessment of postwar base needs for use in the military's revision of JCS 570/2. Another officer playing an extremely important role in base planning but also not cut from the career mold was Lt Cmdr Charles B. Gary. A US Naval Academy graduate, he had left the service in the late 1920s, only to be recalled when the war began.[5] Assigned to the Navy's F-14 postwar planning section, Gary wrote much of the so-called "Determination of Requirements," the document providing the geopolitical rationale for the postwar Navy.[6]

Even among the career officers, from whom a monolithic viewpoint might be expected, there were pointed disagreements (over base locations, for example) that cannot be ascribed to the pettiness of interservice rivalry, yet entailed fundamentally different conceptions about the proper extension of American military power. The clash between Admiral Willson and General Embick of the JSSC over Iceland in the summer of 1945 stands out in this regard.[7] This is not to say that more separated the military base planners than bound them together. They possessed common attitudes centered on the "ideology of national preparedness." Civilians throughout the government also shared this worldview, which was not derived from any uniquely military mind, but from the experiences of the 1930s and World War II.

The global conflict taking place as the postwar base planners went about their business introduced enormous complexity into strategic planning. The war was creating a new, though not clearly defined world order, radically altering the United States's role. Additionally, breathtaking advances in weapons technology promised to change how future wars would be fought. In the face of these developments, the planners were often unsure of the direction of national policy and puzzled by the difficulty of designing plans that could encompass rapid, though not precisely predictable, technological change. "The first and most fundamental question to be asked of any prospective war or other military action, writes one noted military historian, is: 'What is it about?'"[8] For military planners during 1942–47, there was no certain answer to this question because US postwar foreign policy lacked precise definition. Their base plans were faithful reflections of the unsettled condition of national policy. Roosevelt's concept of the Four Policemen maintaining world peace through the UN organization left a clear imprint on postwar base plans completed between late 1942 and mid-1945. JCS 570/2 and other plans prepared in this period contemplated the regional application of American force, whereby the United States would police the Western Hemisphere and the Pacific to the Far East, with Europe policed by

Great Britain and the Soviet Union. Yet, the Four Policemen idea was never elaborated in detail. No one knew exactly how the new UN body would operate, and there were doubts that the Grand Alliance would hold together after the war. Consequently, these early plans exhibited tension between strict regionalism and the perceived need to prepare for a wider role, a role reflected in the amorphous strategy of being ready to take on all comers.

From Roosevelt's death to the Truman administration's articulation of containment in 1947, US policy remained uncertain.[9] The Grand Alliance began to dissolve, and American leaders, while seeking to maintain at least the appearance of cooperation with the Soviet Union, steadily moved toward hard and fast confrontation. The joint chiefs' plan, JCS 570/40, worked out during the summer and fall of 1945, reflected the ambiguities in national policy during this period. Regionalism still predominated (no European bases were identified), but a noticeable shift in emphasis occurred from bases in the Pacific to locations in the far north and the northeastern Atlantic. During 1946–47 US national policy and contingency war planning began to crystallize, but base planning, as evidenced by JCS 570/83, did not immediately follow suit. The lag demonstrated that knowing the answer to the question, What is it about? while perhaps necessary for effective strategic planning did not, by itself, guarantee it.

Along with the vicissitudes of national policy, the planners grappled with the challenge presented by swiftly advancing technology: How best to structure plans serving the here and now using weapons then available, while taking into account new weapons sure to appear in arsenals of the not too distant future. The problem, inherent in modern strategic planning, was the source of much confusion. In late 1945, General Spaatz claimed that transpolar warfare using long-range aircraft and missiles might take place *today*. Spaatz was exaggerating the immediate threat. Neither the United States nor the Soviet Union could attack each other effectively across the North Pole between 1945 and 1948. There were no intercontinental missiles, contemporary aircraft lacked sufficient range, and for the time being, the frozen far northern climate proved ill suited to air operations. Yet, in about five years, transpolar warfare would be a real possibility. This development was for all but the most shortsighted, fast approaching with absolute certainty. Spaatz saw little reason to distinguish between the *present* and the *future*; therefore, the AAF campaigned vigorously for far northern bases.

The emphasis on Arctic outposts tended, for a time, to obscure the most pressing requirement—bases along Russia's southern rim in the Middle East and northwest India. Without these bases, the strategic concept operative in war planning (an air offensive using atomic bombs against Soviet industrial centers) could not be fulfilled. The B-29, the only operational very heavy bomber, had a combat radius of only 2,000 nautical miles (NM) and could not reach all the key targets in the Soviet Union from bases in the United Kingdom alone. The B-36, which first flew on 8 August 1946, had a combat radius of 3,700 NM, and could reach those targets without relying on bases close to the Soviet Union. However, the B-36 would not enter the inventory until the second half of 1948 and would not become fully operational until 1951–52. In the here and now of 1946–47, planners had to rely on the B-29 flying from bases in the United Kingdom and along Russia's southern rim.[10] The dilemma of the technological "bird in-the hand" as opposed to the "two in the bush" (or a bigger bird, in this instance) clouded the strategic planning process in the early postwar years.

Strategic military planning is popularly conceived as a board game or map exercise where finite numbers of this or that, the shortest distance between two points, or orders from the sovereign are the hard-and-fast determinants of the strategy required. All of the above, of course, are elements of strategic planning. In the context of post–World War II planning, they are represented by the number of atomic bombs, polar projections, and Roosevelt's Four Policemen.[11] Strategic military planning, however, is not a mechanical exercise. It takes place in a complex political environment, where military planners are political actors, not wooden soldiers. The officers who planned the postwar base network formulated their recommendations with an eye to bureaucratic, domestic, and international politics.

The bureaucratic politics resulting from generations of friction between the military services heavily influenced postwar base planning, but not in the transparent, self-serving way portrayed by some analysts of postwar national security policy. The consequences of interservice rivalry were subtle. The military services have been frequently charged with using institutional yardsticks to measure their defense requirements. The crudest expression of this phenomenon, in the context of base planning, would have been for the military to recommend a large number of bases to justify more personnel, ships, and planes. Some argue (and others have accepted the interpretation) that the military followed precisely this practice in its postwar planning.[12] Such self-serving institutionalism did not appear in base planning during 1942–48. From top to bottom, military planners were aware that the military establishment faced sharp reductions after the war. Even though Forrestal told his admirals early in 1945 that "I don't think we ought to try to interpret what we think Congress will do, we ought to tell them what we want them to do," the men who drew up base plans in the JCS and the individual service staffs had more realistic expectations. The long lists of base locations they identified are misleading; in most instances, the military was not seeking to develop a base but, as General Lincoln put it, "the right to land and get off."

Interservice rivalry affected postwar base planning by causing lengthy delays in preparing the plans and by diminishing their strategic soundness. The officers planning the postwar base system generally agreed on the location and number of bases or base rights required, but they were frequently at odds over the priority (either in terms of acquisition of rights or of development) for specific bases. At stake was the assignment of service roles and missions—consequently, shares of the defense budget. Differences in this area partly explained the nearly six-month delay (May to October 1945) in producing JCS 570/40 even though the JCS were under heavy pressure from the civilian secretaries, the State Department, the ACC, and the Mead Committee. The JCS argued for two months (September–October) about the priority assigned to North Atlantic bases alone. Whether a quicker response from the military as the war was ending in Europe and the Pacific would have resulted in the combined civil and military air system that had been the vision of some seems doubtful; the opposition to granting military base privileges to the United States was too strong in many countries for this to happen. Nevertheless, interservice rivalry held back an early attempt to create such a network. Preparation of the next major base plan (JCS 570/83, February–September 1947) also stalled because of discord between the services. Again, the stumbling block was priority of development. Additionally, by 1947 war planning was centering on a preeminent role for airpower in a conflict with the Soviet Union, the only really viable option open to the decimated American military establishment. Here the interservice struggle over roles and missions was at its peak, delaying completion of the war plan until mid-1948. Even though the base planners knew bases in Great Britain and along Russia's southern rim would be critical to the outcome of any war, including them in JCS 570/83 would only have created further division. Thus, interservice rivalry caused not only the base plan's delay, but was partly responsible for its strategic deficiency.

Interservice bickering over base planning assumes increased importance when viewed in the larger context of American civil and military relationships. In the opinion of the secretaries of state, war, and Navy, the military had enjoyed far too much independence in the postwar base policy area. While Roosevelt had reminded everyone in the letter transmitting JCS 570/2 to the State Department in early 1944 that the whole question of postwar bases would be subject to his final approval (he made only minor changes), the fact was that the military had prepared the plan without consulting civilians in the Departments of State, War, and Navy. Irritated because the joint chiefs' special relationship with the president had left them out of decision making on many key wartime national security matters, the civilian secretaries reasserted their traditional policy-making role by interposing the Committee of Three and the SWNCC between the president and the military late in 1944. The story of the effort by civilian defense officials to gain the upper hand has significance—not because it represents a triumph of civilian control over the military (this strong and enduring principle of the American political system was never much, if at all, threatened during these years), but because it reveals perceptions civilian and military leaders had of their own and each other's roles in creating national security policy.

Vannevar Bush, director of the wartime Office of Scientific Research and Development, summed up the prevailing civilian perspective in a letter to Robert Patterson, secretary of war, in 1946. "The JCS organization," wrote Bush, "should certainly not have authority in any field involving civilian phases for it to some extent bypasses the civilian secretaries. . . . Military men should handle military problems. As a converse, problems relating military and civilian affairs should be handled by civilians with military advice."[13] Taken at face value the military probably would not have quarreled with this delineation of their role. In 1943, members of the JSSC had seen themselves as examining postwar bases "primarily from the military point of view." That same year, the Navy's General Board and the Air Staff's Plans Division claimed to have analyzed postwar bases separately from all political or economic considerations. In 1945, General Arnold told Generals Spaatz and Eaker that "the JCS in carrying out their mission should consider purely military matters. These matters cannot and should not be decided by the civilian secretaries."[14] The questionable premise, of course, was whether at the strategic planning level anything like a "purely military matter" existed. Some staff officers recognized and admitted this openly. Arnold may have understood it also, but it is impossible to penetrate the rhetoric to determine precisely what the military or the civilians meant by the words that they used to describe their roles. One suspects few had thought through the question very deeply. It is more instructive to see how they acted.

The reality was that the civilians, even after resuming their traditional policy-making role via the Committee of Three and the SWNCC, did not initially seek as much control over the content of postwar base planning as their assertion of its political importance seemed to demand. The 1945 plan (JCS 570/40) went forward to the State Department late in the year without discernible influence from the civilian secretaries. For example, Forrestal's views on Iceland had not altered the views Admiral King expressed during the JCS's deliberations in September and October. Rather than exerting influence over the political content of base plans, civilian officials expended most of their effort through the end of 1945 trying to get the military going on postwar base questions (e.g., to revise JCS 570/2) and to present statements of maximum and minimum requirements on specific locations to the State Department.

Beginning in 1946, the civilians showed much more interest in what was actually in the base plans. They forced the military to cut back on overall requirements and suggested dropping rights to bases in the Pacific, south of the equator, and substituting rights to bases in the Middle East or India.

The military, for its part and despite occasional protestations to the contrary, independently assessed the political aspects of defense and foreign policy formulation; the nature of overseas base selection permitted no alternative. The extent of the military's involvement in policy making disturbed civilian officials because it approached the threshold of decision making about the use of force, traditionally a civilian prerogative. Some high-ranking officers were also expressing doubts about the military's role. In 1947, Lt Gen Lauris Norstad, the Air Force's top planner, told Forrestal that continued extensive military participation in diplomatic decisions was "not in the interests of the military establishment which in due course would come to be attacked as exercising too powerful an influence upon our foreign policies."[15] The real problem, however, may not have been increasing military activity in shaping national security policy, but the persistence of the belief that the military and civilians are discrete elements in the foreign and defense policy process, each group adding something uniquely its own to it. The perpetuation of this distinction is pregnant with the potential for conjuring up scapegoats, whether civilian or military, when policies sour.

Base planning was a manifestation of the United States's efforts to define a place in the postwar world. Contrasted with the nation's prewar role, what emerged from the war constituted an enormous expansion of perceived American responsibilities and interests. Some have called this "globalism." The large scale of the military's postwar base plans and the visionary schemes for creating an integrated worldwide system of civil and military air facilities, enhancing American physical and economic security, seem solid evidence for such a conclusion. To the extent that it characterized the nation's postwar role, however, base planning bore little resemblance to the world policeman stance assumed by the United States in ensuing decades.

The regional orientation of the postwar base system persisted well into 1945. Even before the war's end, there was some shifting toward a more global posture. The "globalism" of plans JCS 570/40 in 1945 and JCS 570/83 in 1947 reflected the increasing possibility of war with the Soviet Union rather than a conviction that American force should be applied willy-nilly around the world to keep the peace. The military sought bases (usually *rights* to bases) in Iceland, Greenland, the United Kingdom, the Azores, the Middle East, India, and Japan to fight the Russians, *not* to police Europe or East Asia. The identification of local or regional conflicts with the Soviet threat was a later development. Bracing itself against the inevitable postwar drawdown, the last thing the military wanted was to take "that lid off." On the other hand, bases in the Philippines, Pacific islands, Caribbean, and other parts of Latin America were unabashedly designed to protect the full scope of American interests.

Economic growth, through the expansion of American commercial aviation activities abroad, stood high in the panoply of national interests. Policy makers, mindful of the specter of renewed depression hoped to link military and civil air routes and facilities in a worldwide network that would promote physical and economic security in the postwar world. In places where both military and commercial purposes coincided, some of this vision was realized. In mid-1948 in Alaska, for example, a Scripps-Howard reporter described Brig Gen Frederick V. H. Kimble, the Aleutian sector commander, as "little more than a CAA [Civil Aeronautics Authority] official. It takes all his time, planes and men to maintain his range stations and keep Northwest Airliners off the peaks."[16] The relationship was less symbiotic after the war on the other side of the world. Commercial companies, coveting the European market, saw little to gain from operating the east-west routes, much desired by the military, across North and Central Africa. Helping out the military in Iceland was one thing; operating an airfield in Tunisia or Libya, entirely another.

In the other camp, some defense officials proved unwilling to cooperate. Early in 1946, Secretary of War Patterson, reacted strongly to complaints from embittered soldiers claiming they were being held overseas to maintain air facilities until civil airline employees could arrive. "United States commercial airlines," he noted during an around the world visit to US forces, "if they want to conduct operations, [they] will have to get busy fast. It would be indefensible to string out ATC operations merely to assist commercial airlines in taking over."[17] Patterson soon ordered the AAF to shut down by May 1946, if possible, those ATC operations in Europe, the Mediterranean, Egypt, Iran, and India not directly supporting military missions.[18] When Patterson explained his position to Byrnes and Forrestal at a Committee of Three meeting at the end of February, the secretaries of state and Navy objected, arguing that it was in the national interest to keep the routes going for the civil airlines; Patterson remained adamant about ending military participation.[19]

Certainly there was some cooperation between the government and the private sector; the opportunity to enhance both security and prosperity through a joint civil-military air system was an attractive lure. To the extent that the two joined forces, the outward thrust of the United States during the postwar period was just that much more pervasive and powerful. Still, the interests of the two often diverged, with military requirements taking precedence over economic needs.

Whatever the purpose for overseas air facilities, when military rights had to be acquired from other nations, Americans frequently ran into trouble, and, in some cases even after prolonged negotiations, base rights were not granted. The United States successfully negotiated postwar base agreements (notably before the end of the war) with the Philippines and Brazil and acquired the Pacific islands under a UN trusteeship but was thwarted in an attempt to obtain bases in the Republic of Panama (outside of the Canal Zone). In December 1947, the Panamanian National Assembly unanimously rejected the agreement that the government had signed with the United States.[20]

Negotiations with Portugal for sites in the Azores dragged on throughout the period, and American efforts to secure rights to bases in Greenland and Iceland had mixed results. In June 1946, Patterson suggested to Byrnes that the United States purchase Greenland from Denmark;[21] in September, the JCS formally asked the secretary of state to make the offer.[22] Byrnes approached the Danish foreign minister at a UN meeting in New York in December 1946 with the proposal, which eventually was rejected by the Danes.[23] There was considerable opposition in Iceland to a continuing American military presence on that island. After lengthy negotiations late in 1946, the United States and Iceland agreed to an arrangement whereby the American Overseas Airline Company would be permitted to maintain Meeks Field (renamed Keflavik Airport) as an international airport for a minimum of five years.[24] In this way, the United States secured landing rights for its military aircraft in Iceland. Negotiations went on around the world; sometimes the United States acquired rights, sometimes it did not. Enveloped in the aura of a special sense of mission and virtue, Americans were often blind to the national sensibilities of others. This kind of myopia afflicted (with a few exceptions) both civilians and the military; attempts to acquire postwar base rights suffered accordingly.

In terms of actual numbers of overseas military installations, the American base network shrank significantly from the World War II total of over 3,000 facilities. By July 1949, the Navy operated only 25 overseas bases, closing over 325 since the end of the war.[25] One year later, the Navy possessed but 13 active overseas bases.[26] The Air Force in mid-1949 had 95 overseas installations of all kinds (not all were airfields); one year later, that total had been reduced by 10.[27] These figures have limited value; meaningful comparisons among the prewar, war, and postwar periods probably cannot be drawn. However, when considered along with the difficulties the United States encountered in acquiring postwar rights and the debilitating nature of the rapid demobilization of the military establishment, the picture of the base system they all add up to is something less than imperial.

The elaborate postwar designs conceived early in World War II, for the most part, never materialized. The Grand Alliance did not survive, altering the hopes many had for the course of US foreign policy. Moreover, civil and military aviation interests did not always coincide, preventing completion of the overseas air system that some believed would help assure peace and prosperity. The military services continued to quarrel among themselves for the place of preferment in the defense establishment, resulting in delays and strategic deficiencies in postwar base plans. Finally, prospective foreign hosts for American military bases failed to immediately fall in step alongside the United States on the path it had begun to follow in world affairs.

Notes

1. Diary entry, 13 August 1942, in John M. Blum, ed., *The Price of Vision: The Diary of Henry A. Wallace, 1942–1946* (Boston: Houghton Mifflin Co., 1973), 106.

2. Ibid., diary entry, 23 August 1942, 110.

3. Ibid., diary entry, 28 June 1943, 217–18.

4. Ibid., Roosevelt told Wallace that he kept a world map on the wall to "keep his memory fresh with regard to the airlines of the future."

5. Charles B. Gary, letter to Elliott V. Converse III, author, 30 January 1978.

6. Ibid. The author sent Gary a copy of the "Determination." He confirmed his authorship of it, and said he "could have written the same thing as a civilian holed up in a garret."

7. One analyst of General Embick's ideas argues that by late 1945 the general had reluctantly abandoned continentalism in favor of a global concept of military strategy entailing involvement in Europe, defense of British interests, and opposition to Soviet expansion. See Mark A. Stoler, "From Continentalism to Globalism: General Stanley D. Embick, the Joint Strategic Survey Committee, and the Military View of American National Policy during the Second World War," *Diplomatic History* 6, no. 3 (summer 1982): 303–21.

8. Philip A. Crowl, *The Strategist's Short Catechism: Six Questions without Answers,* Harmon Memorial Lectures in Military History, no. 20 (Colorado Springs, Colo.: USAF Academy, 1978), 4.

9. John Lewis Gaddis finds an American strategy of "patience but firmness" toward the Soviet Union emerging after Kennan's "Long Telegram" had circulated throughout the government early in 1946. See his *Strategies of Containment: A Critical Appraisal of Postwar American National Security Policy* (New York: Oxford University Press, 1982), 21–23.

10. Marcelle Size Knaack, *Encyclopedia of U. S. Air Force Aircraft and Missile Systems,* vol. 2, *Post–World War II Bombers, 1945–1973* (Washington,

D.C.: USAF, Office of Air Force History, 1988), 25. General Spaatz undoubtedly had the B-36 in mind when talking about transpolar warfare in 1945.

11. There were only nine weapons in the American atomic stockpile in mid-1946, 13 in mid-1947, and 50 in mid-1948. See David Alan Rosenberg, "The Origins of Overkill: Nuclear Weapons and American Strategy, 1945–1960," *International Security,* spring 1983, 14; and his "American Atomic Strategy and the Hydrogen Bomb Decision," *Journal of American History* 66, no. 1 (June 1979): 65–68.

12. Perry McCoy Smith, *The Air Force Plans for Peace, 1943–1945* (Baltimore: Johns Hopkins University Press, 1970), 75; and Daniel Yergin, *Shattered Peace: The Origins of the Cold War and the National Security State* (Boston: Houghton Mifflin Company, 1977), 202.

13. Vannevar Bush to Robert Patterson, 17 April 1946, file General Correspondence, 1945–47, box 18, Papers of Robert P. Patterson (hereafter Patterson Papers), Library of Congress (LOC), Washington, D.C.

14. General Arnold, memorandum for General Spaatz and General Eaker, 29 November 1945, file Joint Chiefs of Staff, box 43, Papers of Henry Harley Arnold (hereafter Arnold Papers), LOC.

15. Forrestal Diary, 16 September 1947, vol. 8, Papers of James V. Forrestal, Seeley G. Mudd Library, Princeton University, N.J.

16. Annex to JCS 1295/8, Military Development of Alaska, 26 April 1948 (p. 95), sec. 4, file CCS 660.2 Alaska (3-23-45), RG 218 (Records of the United States Joint Chiefs of Staff), NA.

17. Diary entry, 20 January 1946, "Diary of Trip Around the World, 30 December 1945–25 January 1946," vol. 6, Letters of Robert P. Patterson, Patterson Papers.

18. Lt Gen Ira C. Eaker, memorandum for Maj Gen Harold "Hal" George, subject: ATC Personnel Overseas, 30 January 1946; General Eaker memorandum for the secretary of war, 1 February 1946; and Patterson memorandum for the commanding general, AAF, subject: ATC Routes, 7 February 1946, all in General Eaker Personal and Reading File, 1945–1947, box 8, Records of the Assistant Secretary of War for Air, RG 18 (Records of the Army Air Forces), NA; Maj Gen H. H. Aurand to secretary of war, 7 February 1946, file General Correspondence, box 18; and Patterson to Aurand, 27 February 1947, box 27; both in Patterson Papers.

19. Minutes, Committee of Three, 1944–1947, 28 February 1946, Diplomatic Branch Reference File, NA.

20. For an official Army chronicle of the Panamanian negotiations, see "Top Secret Army Blue Book, Caribbean Defense Command Negotiations Between the Republic of Panama and the United States of America for a Defense Site Agreement," 20 February 1948, file 686, case 1, box 136TS, Plans and Operations Division (P & O) Decimal File, 1946–1948, RG 319 (Records of the Army Staff), NA. Document is declassified.

21. Ibid., letter, Patterson to Byrnes, 19 June 1946, file P & O 686TS (cases 1-22), box 138TS. Document is declassified.

22. Ibid., letter, Joint Chiefs to State Department, 13 September 1946, file P & O 686TS (cases 61-). Document is declassified.

23. NOE: H. F. Cunningham: JT, n.d., Top Secret memorandum, box 6 (Memoranda for General Marshall), Reference Subject Files, 1940–1947, Records of the Office of European Affairs, RG 59 (General Records of the Department of State), NA. Document is declassified.

24. *History of the Army Air Forces in Iceland*, USAF Historical Division, Research Studies Institute, July 1956, file K1110.1235-1, 1941–1947, USAF Historical Research Agency, Maxwell AFB, Ala.

25. *Annual Report of the Chief of Naval Operations to the Secretary of the Navy, Fiscal Year 1949* (Washington, D.C.: Government Printing Office [GPO], 1950), 26.

26. *Semiannual Report of the Secretary of the Navy* (1 January–30 June 1950), in Department of Defense, *Semiannual Report of the Secretary of Defense* (Washington, D.C.: GPO, 1950), 118.

27. Ibid., *Semiannual Report of the Secretary of the Air Force* (1 July–31 December 1949), 211; and *Semiannual Report of the Secretary of the Air Force* (1 January–30 June 1950), 168.

THIS PAGE INTENTIONALLY LEFT BLANK

SELECTED BIBLIOGRAPHY

Archives and Manuscript Collections

US Air Force Historical Research Agency (AFHRA)

Materials from AFHRA are identified in the notes by decimal index number.

Air Transport Command (300.---).
Assistant Chief of Air Staff [AC/AS], Plans (145.---).
Assistant Chief of the Air Staff, Intelligence (142.---).
Papers of Ennis C. Whitehead (168.6008).
Postwar Division, AC/AS, Plans (145.86).

Harry S. Truman Library, Independence, Missouri

Papers of Harry S. Truman.
Papers of Samuel I. Rosenman.
President's Air Policy Commission Records.

The Library of Congress, Washington, D.C.

Papers of Carl Spaatz.
Papers of Henry Harley Arnold.
Papers of Robert P. Patterson.
Papers of William D. Leahy.

MacArthur Memorial Archives, Norfolk, Virginia

Record Group (RG) 4. Records of General Headquarters, United States Army Forces Pacific (USAFPAC), 1942–1945.
RG 5. Records of General Headquarters, Supreme Commander for the Allied Powers (SCAP), 1945–1951.
RG 9. Collection of Messages (Radiograms), 1945–1951.

The National Archives, Washington, D.C./College Park, Maryland

Minutes of Meetings of the Committee of Three, 1944–1947.

National Security Council Papers.

RG 18. Records of the Army Air Forces: Records, AAF Air Adjutant General.

RG 59. General Records of the Department of State: Records of the Office of European Affairs.

RG 80. General Records of the Department of the Navy: Records of Secretary of the Navy James Forrestal, 1940–1947; Records of the Under Secretary of the Navy, 1940–1944.

RG 107. Records of the Office of the Secretary of War: Records of the Office of the Assistant Secretary of War for Air.

RG 165. Records of the War Department General and Special Staffs: Records of the Office of the Chief of Staff; Records of the Operations Division.

RG 218. Records of the United States Joint Chiefs of Staff.

RG 319. Records of the Army Staff.

RG 340. Records of the Office of the Secretary of the Air Force: Records of the Air Coordinating Committee.

RG 341. Records of Headquarters, United States Air Force, 1942–1956.

RG 353. Records of Interdepartmental and Intradepartmental Committees—State Department: State-War-Navy Coordinating Committee/State-Army-Navy-Air Force (SWNCC/SANACC) Records.

RG 407. Records of the Adjutant General's Office, 1917–1958.

Operational Archives Branch, Naval Historical Center, Washington, D.C.

Interview of Rear Adm Charles J. Moore, USN, retired, by John T. Mason Jr., 26 July 1966.

Papers of Chester W. Nimitz.

Papers of Ernest J. King.

Papers of Richard E. Byrd.

Papers of William D. Leahy.

Records, Chief of Naval Operations.

———. COMINCH (Commander in Chief, US Fleet).

———. Political Military Affairs Division.

———. Strategic Plans Division.

———. SWNCC 38 Series.

———. SWNCC 59 Series.

Robert Muldrow Cooper Library, Clemson University, Clemson, South Carolina

Papers of James F. Byrnes.

Seeley G. Mudd Manuscript Library, Princeton University, New Jersey

Diary of Henry L. Stimson (microfilm copy).

Papers of Bernard M. Baruch.

Papers and Diary of James V. Forrestal.

Papers of John Foster Dulles.

Private Sources

Interviews of Vice Adm E. R. McLean Jr., USN, retired, by the author, 26 April and 24 August 1977.

Letter from Charles B. Gary to the author, 30 January 1978.

Other Unpublished Sources

Davis, Vincent. "Politics and Postwar Defense Policy: The Origins of the Postwar U.S. Navy, 1943–1946 and After." PhD diss., Princeton University, 1961.

Hildreth, Charles H. "Short History and Chronology of the USAF in the United Kingdom, 1942–1967." Third Air Force Historical Office, 1967.

Miller, John Andrew. "Air Diplomacy: The Chicago Civil Aviation Conference of 1944 in Anglo-American Wartime Relations and Postwar Planning." PhD diss., Yale University, 1971.

Public Documents

Truman, Harry S. *Public Papers of the Presidents of the United States: Harry S. Truman, 1945.* Washington, D.C.: GPO, 1961.

US House. Subcommittee on Pacific Bases of the Committee on Naval Affairs, *Study of Pacific Bases*, 79th Cong., 1st sess., 1945, H.R. 154, Report no. 104.

US Senate. *Special Committee to Investigate the National Defense Program*, 79th Cong., 1st sess., 6 July 1945, Senate Report no. 110, pt. 2, *Investigations Overseas.*

US Department of Defense. *Semi-Annual Report of the Secretary of the Air Force, 1 July–31 December 1949*, in *Semi-Annual Report of the Secretary of Defense.* Washington, D.C.: Government Printing Office (GPO), 1950.

———. *Semi-Annual Report of the Secretary of the Air Force, 30 June 1950*, in *Semi-Annual Report of the Secretary of Defense.* Washington, D.C.: GPO, 1950.

———. *Annual Report of the Chief of Naval Operations to the Secretary of the Navy, Fiscal Year 1949.* Washington, D.C.: GPO, 1950.

———. *Semi-Annual Report of the Secretary of the Navy, 1 January–30 June 1950*, in *Semi-Annual Report of the Secretary of Defense.* Washington, D.C.: GPO, 1950.

US Department of State. *Foreign Relations of the United States, Conference of Berlin (Potsdam), 1945.* Vol. 1. Washington, D.C.: GPO, 1960.

———. *Foreign Relations of the United States, 1945.* Vol. 4, *Europe.* Washington, D.C.: GPO, 1968.

———. *Foreign Relations of the United States, 1945.* Vol. 5, *Europe.* Washington, D.C.: GPO, 1967.

———. *Foreign Relations of the United States, 1945.* Vol. 6, *The British Commonwealth, The Far East.* Washington, D.C.: GPO, 1969.

———. *Foreign Relations of the United States, 1946.* Vol. 1, *General: The United Nations.* Washington, D.C.: GPO, 1972.

———. *Foreign Relations of the United States, 1947.* Vol. 1, *General: The United Nations.* Washington, D.C.: GPO, 1973.

————. *Foreign Relations of the United States, 1948.* Vol. 1, pt. 2, *General: The United Nations.* Washington, D.C.: GPO, 1976.

————. *Foreign Relations of the United States, 1949.* Vol. 1, *National, Security Affairs: Foreign Economic Policy.* Washington, D.C.: GPO, 1976.

Newspapers

New York Times, 1945–1947.
Washington Post, 6 September 1945.

Books

Acheson, Dean. *Present at the Creation: My Years in the State Department.* New York: Signet, New American Library, 1970.

Albion, Robert Greenhalgh, and Robert Howe Connery. *Forrestal and the Navy.* New York: Columbia University Press, 1962.

Allison, Graham T. *Essence of Decision: Explaining the Cuban Missile Crisis.* Boston: Little, Brown and Company, 1971.

Arnold, Henry Harley. *Global Mission.* New York: Harper and Brothers, 1949.

Baruch, Bernard M. *Baruch: The Public Years.* New York: Holt, Rinehart, and Winston, 1960.

Berle, Beatrice B., and Travis B. Jacobs, eds. *Navigating the Rapids, 1918–1971: From the Papers of Adolf A. Berle.* New York: Harcourt Brace Jovanovich, Inc., 1973.

Blum, John Morton, ed. *The Price of Vision: The Diary of Henry A. Wallace, 1942–1946.* Boston: Houghton Mifflin Company, 1973.

————. *V Was for Victory: Politics and American Culture during World War II.* New York: Harcourt Brace Jovanovich, Inc., 1976.

Borowski, Harry R. *A Hollow Threat: Strategic Air Power and Containment before Korea.* Westport, Conn.: Greenwood Press, 1982.

Buell, Thomas B. *The Quiet Warrior: A Biography of Admiral Raymond A. Spruance.* Boston: Little, Brown and Company, 1974.

Building the Navy's Bases in World War II. Vol. 2. Washington, D.C.: US Bureau of Yards and Docks, 1947.

Burns, James MacGregor. *Roosevelt: The Soldier of Freedom.* New York: Harcourt Brace Jovanovich, Inc., 1970.

Bush, Vannevar. *Pieces of the Action.* New York: William Morrow and Company, Inc., 1970.

Byrnes, James F. *All in One Lifetime.* New York: Harper and Brothers, 1958.

———. *Speaking Frankly.* New York: Harper and Brothers, 1947.

Campbell, Thomas M. *Masquerade Peace: America's UN Policy, 1944–1945.* Tallahassee: Florida State University Press, 1973.

Campbell, Thomas M., and George C. Herring, eds. *The Diaries of Edward R. Stettinius, Jr., 1943–1946.* New York: New Viewpoints, Franklin Watts, Inc., 1975.

Churchill, Winston S. *The Second World War: Triumph and Tragedy.* Boston: Houghton Mifflin Company, 1953.

Cline, Ray S. *Washington Command Post: The Operations Division.* Washington, D.C.: Office of the Chief of Military History, Department of the Army, 1968.

Conn, Stetson, Rose C. Engelman, and Byron Fairchild. *Guarding the United States and Its Outposts.* Washington, D.C.: Office of the Chief of Military History, Department of the Army, 1964.

———. *The Framework of Hemisphere Defense.* Washington, D.C.: Office of the Chief of Military History, Department of the Army, 1960.

Crowl, Philip A. *The Strategist's Short Catechism: Six Questions Without Answers.* Harmon Memorial Lectures in Military History. No. 20. US Air Force Academy, Colo., 1978.

Davies, R. E. G. *A History of the World's Airlines.* London: Oxford University Press, 1964.

———. *Airlines of the United States Since 1914.* London: Putnam and Company Limited, 1972.

Davis, Vincent G. *Postwar Defense Policy and the United States Navy, 1943–1946.* Chapel Hill: University of North Carolina Press, 1962, 1966.

Divine, Robert A. *Roosevelt and World War II.* Baltimore: Johns Hopkins University Press, 1969.

———. *Second Chance: The Triumph of Internationalism in America During World War II.* New York: Atheneum, 1967.

Donovan, Robert J. *Conflict and Crisis: The Presidency of Harry S. Truman, 1945–1948.* New York: W. W. Norton and Company, Inc., 1977.

Feis, Herbert. *Between War and Peace: The Potsdam Conference.* Princeton, N.J.: Princeton University Press, 1960.

———. *From Trust to Terror: The Onset of the Cold War, 1945–1950.* New York: W. W. Norton and Company, Inc., 1970.

Ferrell, Robert H., ed. *Off the Record: The Private Papers of Harry S. Truman.* New York: Harper and Row, 1980.

Gaddis, John Lewis. *Strategies of Containment: A Critical Appraisal of Postwar American National Security Policy.* New York: Oxford University Press, 1982.

———. *The United States and the Origins of the Cold War, 1941–1947.* New York: Columbia University Press, 1972.

Gardner, Lloyd C. *Architects of Illusion: Men and Ideas in American Foreign Policy, 1941–1949.* Chicago: Quadrangle Books, 1970.

Hammond, Paul Y. *Organizing for Defense: The American Military Establishment in the Twentieth Century.* Princeton: Princeton University Press, 1961.

Haynes, Richard F. *The Awesome Power: Harry S. Truman as Commander in Chief.* Baton Rouge: Louisiana State University Press, 1973.

Hull, Cordell. *The Memoirs of Cordell Hull.* 2 vols. New York: MacMillan Company, 1948.

Huntington, Samuel P. *The Soldier and the State: The Theory and Politics of Civil-Military Relations.* New York: Vintage Books, 1957.

Kennan, George F. *Memoirs 1925–1950.* New York: Bantam Books, 1969.

King, Ernest J., and Walter Muir Whitehill. *Fleet Admiral King: A Naval Record*. New York: W. W. Norton and Company, Inc., 1952.

Knaack, Marcelle Size. *Encyclopedia of U. S. Air Force Aircraft and Missile Systems*. Vol. II. *Post–World War II Bombers, 1945–1973*. Washington, D.C.: USAF, Office of Air Force History, 1988.

Kolko, Gabriel. *The Politics of War: The World and United States Foreign Policy, 1943–1945*. New York: Random House, Inc., 1968.

Kolko, Joyce, and Gabriel Kolko. *The Limits of Power: The World and United States Foreign Policy, 1945–1954*. New York: Harper and Row, Publishers, Inc., 1972.

LaFeber, Walter. *America, Russia and the Cold War, 1945–1980*. 4th ed. New York: John Wiley and Sons, 1980.

Leahy, William D. *I Was There*. New York. Whittlesey House, 1950.

Leighton, Richard M., and Robert W. Coakley. *Global Logistics and Strategy, 1943–1945*. Washington, D.C.: Office of the Chief of Military History, Department of the Army, 1968.

Louis, Wm. Roger. *Imperialism at Bay: The United States and the Decolonization of the British Empire, 1941–1945*. New York: Oxford University Press, 1978.

Maddox, Robert James. *The New Left and the Origins of the Cold War*. Princeton, N.J.: Princeton University Press, 1973.

Matloff, Maurice. *Strategic Planning for Coalition Warfare, 1943–1944*. Washington, D.C.: Office of the Chief of Military History, Department of the Army, 1959.

McCann, Frank D., Jr. *The Brazilian-American Alliance, 1937–1945*. Princeton, N.J.: Princeton University Press, 1973.

Mee, Charles L., Jr. *Meeting at Potsdam*. New York: Dell Publishing Co., Inc., 1975.

Miller, Merle. *Plain Speaking: An Oral Biography of Harry S. Truman*. New York: Berkley Publishing Corporation, 1974.

Millett, Allan R. *The American Political System and Civilian Control of the Military: A Historical Perspective*. Mershon Center Position Papers in the Policy Sciences. Number

Four. Columbus: Mershon Center of the Ohio State University, 1979.

Millis, Walter, ed. *The Forrestal Diaries.* New York: Viking Press, 1951.

Moran, Lord. *Churchill: The Struggle for Survival, 1940–1945.* Boston: Houghton Mifflin Company, 1966.

Motter, T. H. Vail. *The Persian Corridor and Aid to Russia.* Washington, D.C.: Office of the Chief of Military History, Department of the Army, 1952.

Notter, Harley A. *Postwar Foreign Policy Preparation, 1939–1945.* Washington, D.C.: Department of State, 1949.

Paterson, Thomas G. *On Every Front: The Making of the Cold War.* New York: W. W. Norton and Company, Inc., 1979.

———. *Soviet-American Confrontation: Postwar Reconstruction and the Origins of the Cold War.* Baltimore: Johns Hopkins University Press, 1973.

Polenberg, Richard. *War and Society: The United States, 1941–1945.* New York: J. B. Lippincott Company, 1972.

Potter, E. B. *Nimitz.* Annapolis, Md.: Naval Institute Press, 1976.

Range, Willard D. *Franklin D. Roosevelt's World Order.* Athens, Ga.: University of Georgia Press, 1959.

Rogow, Arnold A. *James Forrestal: A Study of Personality, Politics, and Policy.* New York: MacMillan Company, 1963.

Schnabel, James F. *The History of the Joint Chiefs of Staff: The Joint Chiefs of Staff and National Policy, 1945–1947.* Washington, D.C.: Historical Division, Joint Chiefs of Staff, 1979.

Sherry, Michael S. *Preparing for the Next War: American Plans for Post-War Defense, 1941–1945.* New Haven: Yale University Press, 1977.

Sherwin, Martin J. *A World Destroyed: The Atomic Bomb and the Grand Alliance.* New York: Alfred A. Knopf, 1975.

Smith, Gaddis. *American Diplomacy During the Second World War, 1941–1945.* New York: John Wiley and Sons, 1965.

Smith, Henry Ladd. *Airways Abroad: The Story of American World Air Routes.* Madison: University of Wisconsin Press, 1950.

Smith, Perry McCoy. *The Air Force Plans for Peace, 1943–1945.* Baltimore: Johns Hopkins University Press, 1970.

Solberg, Carl. *Conquest of the Skies: A History of Commercial Aviation in America.* Boston: Little, Brown and Company, 1979.

Sparrow, John C. *History of Personnel Demobilization in the United States Army.* Washington, D.C.: Office of the Chief of Military History, Department of the Army, 1952.

Spykman, Nicholas John. *America's Strategy in World Politics: The United States and the Balance of Power.* New York: Harcourt Brace and Company, 1942.

———. *The Geography of the Peace.* New York: Harcourt Brace and Company, 1944.

Stettinius, Edward R., Jr. *Roosevelt and the Russians: The Yalta Conference.* New York: Crowell-Collier, MacMillan, 1949.

Stimson, Henry L., and McGeorge Bundy. *On Active Service in Peace and War.* New York: Harper and Brothers, 1947.

Truman, Harry S. *Memoirs: Year of Decisions.* New York: Signet, New American Library, 1955.

Tucker, Robert W. *The Radical Left and American Foreign Policy.* Baltimore: Johns Hopkins University Press, 1971.

Van Zandt, J. Parker. *The Geography of World Air Transport.* Washington, D.C.: Brookings Institution, 1944.

Weigley, Russell F. *The American Way of War: A History of United States Military Strategy and Policy.* New York: MacMillan Publishing Co., Inc., 1973.

Weller, George. *Bases Overseas: An American Trusteeship in Power.* New York: Harcourt Brace and Company, 1944.

Who's Who in America. 39th ed., 1976–1977. Chicago: Marquis' Who's Who, 1976.

Who's Who in Aviation: A Directory of Living Men and Women Who Have Contributed to the Growth of Aviation in the United States, 1942–1943. New York: Ziff-Davis, 1942.

Williams, William Appleman. *The Tragedy of American Diplomacy.* 2d rev. and enl. ed. New York: Dell Publishing Company, Inc., 1972.

Yergin, Daniel. *Shattered Peace: The Origins of the Cold War and the National Security State.* Boston: Houghton Mifflin Co., 1977.

Articles

Adler, Les K., and Thomas G. Paterson. "Red Fascism: The Merger of Nazi Germany and Soviet Russia in the American Image of Totalitarianism, 1930's–1950's." *American Historical Review* 75 (April 1970): 1046–64.

"Bornholm Soap Bubble, The." *New Times* (April 1946): 21.

Brownell, George A. "The Air Coordinating Committee: A Problem in Federal Staff Work." *The Journal of Air Law and Commerce* 14 (autumn 1947): 405–35.

Gaddis, John Lewis. "The Emerging Post-Revisionist Synthesis on the Origins of the Cold War." *Diplomatic History* 7, no. 3 (summer 1983): 171–90.

Gormly, James L. "Keeping the Door Open in Saudi Arabia: The United States and the Dhahran Airfield, 1945–46." *Diplomatic History* 4, no. 2 (spring 1980): 189–205.

Huntington, Samuel P. "Transnational Organizations in World Politics." *World Politics* 25, no. 3 (April 1973): 333–68.

Maier, Charles S. "Revisionism and the Interpretation of Cold War Origins." *Perspectives in American History* 4 (1970): 313–47.

Richardson, J. L. "Cold War Revisionism: A Critique." *World Politics* 24 (1972): 579–612.

Rosenberg, David Alan. "American Atomic Strategy and the Hydrogen Bomb Decision." *Journal of American History* 66, no. 1 (June 1979): 62–87.

―――. "The Origins of Overkill: Nuclear Weapons and American Strategy, 1945–1960." *International Security* (spring 1983): 3–71.

Schaffer, Ronald. "General Stanley D. Embick: Military Dissenter." *Military Affairs* 33 (October 1973): 89–95.

Schlesinger, Arthur M., Jr. "Origins of the Cold War." *Foreign Affairs* 46, (October 1967): 22–52.

Sellen, Robert W. "Origins of the Cold War: An Historiographical Survey." *West Georgia College Studies in the Social Sciences* 9 (June 1970): 57–98.

Skop, Arthur Lloyd. "The Primacy of Domestic Politics: Eckart Kehr and the Intellectual Development of Charles A. Beard." *History and Theory* 12 (1974): 119–31.

Spaatz, Carl. "Air Power in the Atomic Age." *Collier's* 116 (8 December 1945): 11ff.

Stoler, Mark A. "From Continentalism to Globalism General Stanley D. Embick, the Joint Strategic Survey Committee, and the Military View of American National Policy during the Second World War." *Diplomatic History* 6, no. 3 (summer 1982): 303–21.

Index

228

Circling the Earth
United States Plans for a Postwar Overseas Military Base System, 1942–1948

Air University Press Team

Chief Editor
George Porter

Copy Editor
Mary J. Moore

Cover Art and Book Design
Daniel M. Armstrong

*Composition and
Prepress Production*
Vivian D. O'Neal

Quality Review
Tammi Long

Print Preparation
Joan Hickey

Distribution
Diane Clark

www.ingramcontent.com/pod-product-compliance
Lightning Source LLC
Chambersburg PA
CBHW081358270326
41930CB00015B/3337